BERLITZ TRAVEL GUIDES

BERLITZ®

EUROPEAN
PHRASE BOOK

By the staff of Berlitz Guides

Library of Congress Catalog Card Number: 73-20997

16th printing 1988

Printed in Switzerland

Berlitz Guides
Avenue d'Ouchy 61
1000 Lausanne 6, Switzerland

Contents

Preface

You're about to visit several countries in Europe and we've attempted to provide you with a useful phrase book featuring key phrases in 14 different European languages.

Our book is simple to use, since the language sections are divided into topics, from arrival to eating out, from shopping to emergencies. Each expression appears with a code to pronunciation next to it. Simply read this imitated pronunciation as if it were English, stressing the syllables that are printed in bold type. It is based on Standard British pronunciation, though we have tried to take into account General American pronunciation as well.

This European Phrase Book is made up of key extracts from 14 complete phrase books published by Berlitz. If you plan to spend a longer period of time in one country or language area, you'd be well advised to obtain a complete 192-page single language phrase book. It contains detailed travel information and tips, as well as useful phrases.

The phrases featured in each language of this book are also available in cassette form to help you prepare for your trip. The cassette is also available with a full-length phrase book at booksellers and record shops as a "Cassettepak".

Bon Voyage!

DANISH

Guide to Pronunciation

Letter	Approximate pronunciation	Symbol	Example	
Consonants				
b, c, f, h, l, m, n, v	as in English			
d	1) when at the end of the word, or between two vowels, like **th** in **this**	dh	**med**	mehdh
	2) otherwise, as in English	d	**dale**	darler
g	1) at the beginning of a word or syllable, as in **go**	g	**glas**	glahss
	2) when at the end of a word after a long vowel or before unstressed **e**, like **chs** in Scottish lo**ch**, but weaker and voiced	ğ	**kage**	karğer
	3) usually mute after **i**, **y**, and sometimes mute after **a**, **e**, **o**		**sige**	seeer
j, hj	like **y** in yet	y	**ja**	yah

k, p, t	1) when at the beginning of a word, as in kite, pill and to	ķ	**kaffe**	**kah**fer
		p	**pude**	**poo**dher
		t	**tale**	**tar**ler
	2) otherwise like **g, b, d** in go, bit and **do**	g	**lække**	**leh**ger
		b	**stoppe**	**sdo**ber
		d	**sætte**	**seh**der
l	always as in leaf, never as in bell	l	**vel**	vehl
r	pronounced in the back of the throat, as in French	r	**rose**	**roa**ser
s	always as in see	s/ss	**skål**	sgawl
			haster	**hahss**derr
sj	like **sh** in sheet	sh	**sjælden**	**sheh**lern
w	for Danes this is the same as **v**			
z	like **s** in so	s	**zone**	**soa**ner

Vowels

Vowels are generally long in stressed syllables when followed by *at most* one consonant. If followed by two consonants (or more), or in unstressed syllables, they are generally short.

a	1) when long, like **a** in car; it can also be pronounced like **a** in bad, but longer	ar*	**bade**	**bar**dher
	2) when short, like long **a**, or more like **a** in cart	ah	**hat**	hahd
	3) you will also hear, as alternatives to the above, a more or less "flat" pronunciation of **a**, which can be like **a** in hat, or tend towards **e** in let; it can be long or short	ai	**tale**	**tai**ler
		æ	**tak**	tæg
e	1) when long, the same quality as **a** in plate, but longer, and a pure vowel, not a diphthong	ay	**mere**	**may**rer
	2) when short, somewhere between the **a** in plate and the **i** in hit	ay	**fedt**	fayd
	3) when short, also like **e** in met	eh	**let**	lehd
	4) when unstressed, like **a** in about	er*	**gammel**	**gah**merl
i	1) when long, like **ee** in bee	ee	**bide**	**bee**dher
	2) when short, like **ee** in meet	ee	**liter**	**lee**derr

o	1) when long, like **aw** in s**aw**, but with the tongue higher in the mouth; quite like **u** in p**u**t	oa	**skole**	**s**g**oa**ler
	2) when short, more or less the same quality of sound	oa	**bonde**	**boa**ner
	3) when short, also like **o** in l**o**t	o	**godt**	g**o**d
u	1) when long, like **oo** in p**oo**l	oo	**pude**	p**oo**dher
	2) when short, like **oo** in l**oo**t	oo	**nu**	n**oo**
y	put your tongue in the position for the **ee** of b**ee**, but round your lips as for the **oo** of p**oo**l; the vowel you pronounce like this should be more or less correct	ew	**byde** **lytte**	b**ew**dher l**ew**der
æ	1) when long, like the first part of the word **air**	ai	**bære**	b**ai**rer
	2) when short, like **e** in g**e**t, but next to **r** it sounds more like the **a** of h**a**t	eh æ	**ægte** **værre**	**eh**gder v**æ**rer
å	1) when long, like **aw** in s**aw**	aw	**åben**	**aw**bern
	2) when short, like **o** in **o**n	o	**ånd**	**o**n
ø	like **ur** in f**ur**, but with the lips rounded; can be long or short	ur*	**frøken** **øl**	f**r**ur**ger**n u**r**l

Diphthongs

av	like **ow** in n**ow**	ow	**hav**	h**ow**
ej	like **igh** in s**igh**	igh	**nej**	n**igh**
ev	like **e** in g**e**t followed by a short **u** as in p**u**t	ehoo	**evne**	**ehoo**ner
ou	like **o** in g**o**t followed by a short **u** as in p**u**t	ooo	**lov**	l**ooo**
øi	like **oi** in **oi**l	oi	**øje**	**oi**er
øv	like **ur** in h**ur**t followed by a short **u** as in p**u**t	uroo*	**søvnig**	s**u**r**oo**nee

---

* The **r** should not be pronounced when reading this transcription.

N.B. 1) Many Danish speakers put a glottal stop in or after long vowels (like the Cockney pronunciation of **t** in **wa'er**). Although it has a certain distinctive role, you will be understood perfectly well if you do not use it, so we have not shown it in our transcriptions;
2) **dd** and **gg** between vowels are pronounced like **d** in **d**o and **g** in **g**o;
3) the letter **d** is not pronounced in **nd** and **ld** at the end of a word or syllable (*mand* = **mahn**, *guld* = **gool**) or before unstressed **e** or before **t** or **s** in the same syllable (*plads* = **plahs**).

Some basic expressions

Yes.	**Ja.**	yar
No.	**Nej.**	nay
Please.	**Vær så venlig.**	vair saw **vehn**lee
Thank you.	**Tak.**	tahk
Thank you very much.	**Mange tak.**	**mahng**er tahk
That's all right.	**Å, jeg be'r.**	aw yay bayr

Greetings

Good morning.	**Godmorgen.**	goadh**morern**
Good afternoon.	**Goddag.**	goadh**dai**
Good evening.	**Godaften.**	goadh**ahf**dern
Good night.	**Godnat.**	goadh**nahd**
Good-bye.	**Farvel.**	fahr**vehl**
See you later.	**På gensyn.**	paw **gehn**sewn
This is Mr....	**Det er hr...**	day air hehr
This is Mrs....	**Det er fru...**	day air froo
This is Miss...	**Det er frøken...**	day air **frur**gern
I'm very pleased to meet you.	**Det glæder mig at træffe Dem.**	day **glaid**herr migh aht **treh**fer dehm
How are you?	**Hvordan har De det?**	**vor**dahn harr dee day
Very well, thank you. And you?	**Fint, tak. Og De?**	fint tahk. o dee
Fine.	**Fint.**	fint
Excuse me.	**Undskyld.**	**oons**gewl

Questions

Where?	**Hvor?**	vor
Where is...?	**Hvor er...?**	vor air
Where are...?	**Hvor er...?**	vor air
When?	**Hvornår?**	vor**nawr**
What?	**Hvad?**	vah(dh)
How?	**Hvordan?**	vor**dahn**
How much?	**Hvor meget?**	vor **migh**erd

How many?	**Hvor mange?**	vor **mahng**er
Who?	**Hvem?**	vehm
Why?	**Hvorfor?**	vor**for**
Which?	**Hvilken/Hvilket?**	**vil**gern/**vil**gerd
What do you call this?	**Hvad hedder dette?**	vahdh **heh**derr **deh**der
What do you call that?	**Hvad hedder det?**	vahdh **heh**derr day
What does this mean?	**Hvad betyder dette?**	vahdh ber**tew**derr **deh**der
What does that mean?	**Hvad betyder det?**	vahdh ber**tew**derr day

Do you speak...?

Do you speak English?	**Taler De engelsk?**	**tai**lerr dee **ehng**erlsg
Do you speak German?	**Taler De tysk?**	**tai**lerr dee tewsg
Do you speak French?	**Taler De fransk?**	**tai**lerr dee frahnsg
Do you speak Spanish?	**Taler De spansk?**	**tai**lerr dee spahnsg
Do you speak Italian?	**Taler De italiensk?**	**tai**lerr dee eetahlee**aynsg**
Could you speak more slowly, please?	**Vil De tale langsommere?**	vil dee **tai**ler **lahng**somerrer
Please point to the phrase in the book.	**Vær så venlig at pege på sætningen i bogen.**	vair saw **vehn**lee ahd **pigh**er paw **sehd**ningern ee **baw**(g)ern
Just a minute. I'll see if I can find it in this book.	**Et øjeblik. Jeg vil se, om jeg kan finde det i denne bog.**	ehd **oi**erblig. yay vil say om yay kahn **fin**ner day ee **deh**ner baw(g)
I understand.	**Jeg forstår.**	yay for**sdawr**
I don't understand.	**Jeg forstår ikke.**	yay for**sdawr** igger

Can...?

| Can I have...? | **Kan jeg få...?** | kahn yay faw |
| Can we have...? | **Kan vi få...?** | kahn vee faw |

DANISH

Can you show me...?	Kan De vise mig...?	kahn dee **vee**sser migh
Can you tell me...?	Kan De sige mig...?	kahn dee **see**yer migh
Can you help me, please?	Vil De være så venlig at hjælpe mig?	vil dee **vai**rer saw **vehn**lee ahd **yehl**per migh

Wanting

I'd like...	Jeg vil gerne have...	yay vil **gehr**ner **hai**(wer)
We'd like...	Vi vil gerne have...	vee vil **gehr**ner **hai**(wer)
Please give me...	Vær så venlig at give mig...	vair saw **vehn**lee ahd **gee** migh
Give it to me please.	Vær så venlig at give mig det.	vair saw **vehn**lee ahd **gee** migh day
Please bring me...	Vær så venlig at hente...til mig.	vair saw **vehn**lee ahd **hehn**der...til migh
Bring it to me, please.	Vær så venlig at hente det til mig.	vair saw **vehn**lee ahd **hehn**der day til migh
I'm hungry.	Jeg er sulten.	yay air **sool**tern
I'm thirsty.	Jeg er tørstig.	yay air **turrss**tee
I'm tired.	Jeg er træt.	yay air trehd
I'm lost.	Jeg er faret vild.	yay air **far**rerd veel
It's important.	Det er vigtigt.	day air **vig**dee(t)
It's urgent.	Det haster.	day **hahss**derr
Hurry up!	Skynd Dem!	sgurn dehm

It is/There is...

It is/It's...	Det er...	day air
Is it...?	Er det...?	air day
It isn't...	Det er ikke...	day air **ig**ger
There is/There are...	Der er...	dair air
Is there/Are there...?	Er der...?	air dair
There isn't/There aren't...	Der er ikke...	dair air **ig**ger
There isn't any/There aren't any.	Der er ingen.	dair air **ing**ern

A few common words

big/small	**stor/lille**	sdoar/**lill**er
quick/slow	**hurtig/langsom**	**hoor**dee/**lahng**som
early/late	**tidlig/sen**	**teedh**lee/sayn
cheap/expensive	**billig/dyr**	**bill**ee/dewr
near/far	**nær/fjern**	nair/**fyehrn**
hot/cold	**varm/kold**	vahrm/kol
full/empty	**fuld/tom**	fool/tom
easy/difficult	**let/vanskelig**	lehd/**vahnss**gerlee
heavy/light	**tung/let**	toong/lehd
open/shut	**åben/lukket**	**aw**bern/**loo**gerd
right/wrong	**rigtig/forkert**	**rig**dee/for**kayrd**
old/new	**gammel/ny**	**gah**merl/new
old/young	**gammel/ung**	**gah**merl/oong
beautiful/ugly	**smuk/grim**	smoog/grim
good/bad	**god/dårlig**	goadh/**dawr**lee
better/worse	**bedre/værre**	**behdh**rer/**veh**rer

Some prepositions and a few more useful words

at	**ved**	vaydh
on	**på**	paw
in	**i**	ee
to	**til**	til
from	**fra**	frar
inside	**indeni**	**inn**ernee
outside	**udenfor**	**oo**dhernfor
up	**op**	ob
down	**ned**	naydh
before	**før**	furr
after	**efter**	**ehf**derr
with	**med**	maydh
without	**uden**	**oo**dhern
through	**gennem**	**geh**nerm
towards	**imod**	eem**oadh**
until	**indtil**	intil
during	**i løbet af**	ee **lu**rberd ahf
and	**og**	o
or	**eller**	**eh**lerr
not	**ikke**	**ig**ger
nothing	**intet**	**in**derd
none	**ingen**	**ing**ern
very	**meget**	**migh**erd
also	**også**	**os**ser
soon	**snart**	snahrd
perhaps	**måske**	moss**gay**
here	**her**	hair

there	**der**	dair
now	**nu**	noo
then	**så**	saw

Arrival

Your passport, please.	**Deres pas!**	**deh**rerss pahss
Here it is.	**Værs'go.**	**vehr**sgoa
Have you anything to declare?	**Har De noget at for-tolde?**	harr dee **noa**gerd ahd fort**o**ller
No, nothing at all.	**Nej, intet.**	nigh **in**derd
Porter!	**Drager!**	**drah**gerr
Can you help me with my luggage, please?	**Vil De hjælpe mig med min bagage?**	vil dee **yehl**per migh maydh meen bah**gai**sher
That's my suitcase.	**Det er min kuffert.**	day air meen **koo**ferrd
Where's the bus to the centre of town, please?	**Hvor holder bussen til centrum?**	vor **hol**lerr **boo**ssern til **sehn**troam
This way, please.	**Denne vej.**	**deh**ner vigh

Changing money

| Can you change a traveller's cheque, please? | **Kan De indløse en rejsecheck?** | kahn dee **in**lursser ayn **righ**sserchehg |
| Where's the nearest bank, please? | **Hvor er den nærmeste bank?** | vor air dehn **nair**mersder bahnk |

Car rental

I'd like a car.	**Jeg vil gerne leje en vogn.**	yay vil **gehr**ner **ligh**er ayn **voa**(g)ern
For how long?	**Hvor længe?**	vor **lehng**er
A day/Four days/ A week/Two weeks.	**En dag/Fire dage/ En uge/to uger.**	ayn dai/**feer**er **dai**(g)er/ ayn **oo**(g)er/toa **oo**(g)err

Taxi

| Where can I get a taxi? | **Hvor kan jeg få en taxa?** | vor kahn yay faw ayn **tah**gsah |
| What's the fare to ...? | **Hvad koster det til ...?** | vahdh **koss**derr day til |

Take me to this address, please.	**Kør mig til denne adresse.**	kurr migh til **deh**ner ah**dreh**sser
I'm in a hurry.	**Jeg har travlt.**	yay harr trowlt
Could you drive more slowly, please?	**Vil De være venlig at køre lidt langsommere?**	vil dee **vair**er **vehn**lee ahd **kurr**er let **lahng**somerrer

Hotel and other accommodation

My name is...	**Mit navn er...**	mid nown air
Have you a reservation?	**Har De reserveret?**	harr di raysehr**vair**erd
Yes, here's the confirmation.	**Ja, her er bekræftelsen.**	yar hair air ber**krehf**derl-sern
I'd like...	**Jeg vil gerne have...**	yay vil **gehr**ner **hai**(wer)
I'd like a single room/a double room.	**Jeg vil gerne have et enkeltværelse/et dobbeltværelse.**	yay vil **gehr**ner **hai**(wer) ayd **ehng**gerldvairaylser/ ayd **do**berldvairaylser
a room with a bath/ with a shower	**et værelse med bad/med brusebad**	ayd **vair**aylser maydh bardh/maydh **broos**ser-bardh

How much?

What's the price per night/per week/per month?	**Hvor meget koster det pr. nat/pr. uge/ pr. måned?**	vor **migh**erd **koss**derr day pehr nahd/pehr **oo**(g)er/ pehr **maw**nerdh
May I see the room?	**Må jeg se værelset?**	maw yay say **vair**aylserd
I'm sorry, I don't like it.	**Jeg synes ikke om det.**	yay **sew**nerss **ig**ger om day
Yes, that's fine. I'll take it.	**Ja, det er godt. Det tager jeg.**	yar day air god day **tar**(g)err yay
What's my room number, please?	**Hvilket nummer har mit værelse?**	**vil**kerd **noo**merr harr mid **vair**aylser
Number 123.	**Nummer 123.**	**noo**merr 123

Service, please

| Who is it? | **Hvem er det?** | vehm air day |
| Just a minute. | **Et øjeblik.** | ayd **oier**blig |

DANISH

| Come in! The door's open. | Kom ind! Døren er åben. | kom in **dur**rern air **aw**bern |
| May we have breakfast in our room? | Kan vi få morgenmad på værelset? | kahn vee faw **mor**(g)ernmahdh paw **vair**aylserd |

Breakfast

I'll have...	Jeg vil gerne have...	yay vil **gehr**ner hai(wer)
I'll have some fruit juice.	Jeg vil gerne have noget frugtsaft.	yay vil **gehr**ner hai(wer) noa(g)erd **froogd**sahfd
a boiled egg	et kogt æg	ayd kogd ehg
a fried egg	et spejlæg	ayd **sbigh**lehg
some bacon/some ham	noget bacon/noget skinke	**noa**(g)erd **bay**kern/ **noa**(g)erd **sging**gerr
some toast	noget ristet brød	**noa**(g)erd **ris**derd brurd
a pot of tea	en kande te	ayn **kah**ner tay
a cup of tea	en kop te	ayn kob tay
some coffee	noget kaffe	**noa**(g)erd **kah**fer
some chocolate	noget chokolade	**noa**(g)erd shoagoa**lard**her
more butter	mere smør	**may**rer smurr
some hot water	noget varmt vand	**noa**(g)erd **vahrmd** vahn

Difficulties

The central heating doesn't work.	Centralvarmen virker ikke.	sehn**trarl**vahrmen **veer**gerr **ig**ger
the light/the socket the tap/the toilet	lyset/stikkontaken vandhanen/toilettet	**lew**sserd/**sdig**gondahgdern **vahn**harnern/toile**hd**erd
There's no hot water.	Der er ikke noget varmt vand.	dair air **ig**ger **noa**(g)erd **vahrmd** vahn
May I see the manager, please?	Jeg vil gerne tale med direktøren.	yay vil **gehr**ner **tai**ler maydh direhg**tur**rern

Telephone—Mail

There's a call for you.	Der er telefon til Dem.	dair air taylay**foan** til dehm
Hold the line, please.	Et øjeblik.	ayd **oier**blig
Operator, I've been cut off.	Frøken, jeg er blevet afbrudt.	**frur**gern yay air **blay**verd **ow**brood

Did anyone telephone me?	**Er der blevet ringet til mig?**	air dair **blay**verd **ring**erd til migh
Is there any mail for me?	**Er der post til mig?**	air dair possd til migh
Are there any messages for me?	**Er der en besked til mig?**	air dair ayn ber**sgaydh** til migh

Checking out

May I have my bill, please?	**Må jeg bede om regningen?**	maw yay **bay**dher om **righ**ningern
We're in a great hurry.	**Vi skal skynde os.**	vee sgahl **sgur**ner oss
It's been a very enjoyable stay.	**Det har været et meget behageligt ophold.**	day harr **vai**rerd ayd **migh**erd berhargerligd **ob**hol

Eating out

Good evening, sir/ Good evening, madam.	**Godaften hr./ Godaften frue.**	goadh**ahf**dern hehr/ goadh**ahf**dern **froo**er
Good evening. I'd like a table for two, please.	**Godaften. Jeg vil gerne have et bord til to.**	goadh**ahf**dern. yay vil **gehr**ner **hai**(wer) ayd bord til toa
Do you have a fixed-price menu?	**Har De en "dagens middag"?**	harr dee ayn **dai**(g)ernss **mid**dar(g)
May I see the à la carte menu?	**Må jeg se spisekortet?**	maw yay say **sbee**serkor-derd
May we have an ashtray, please?	**Må vi få et askebæger?**	maw vee faw ayd **ahss**gerbeh(g)err
some bread	**noget brød**	**noa**(g)erd brurdh
a fork	**en gaffel**	ayn **gahf**erl
a knife	**en kniv**	ayn kneeoo
a spoon	**en ske**	ayn sgay
a plate	**en tallerken**	ayn tah**lehr**gern
a glass	**et glas**	ayd glahss
a napkin	**en serviet**	ayn sehr**viehd**
another chair	**en stol til**	ayn sdoal til
Where's the gentlemen's toilet (men's room)?	**Hvor er herretoilettet?**	vor air **heh**rertoaahlehderd
Where's the ladies' toilet (ladies' room)?	**Hvor er dametoilettet?**	vor air **dar**mertoaahlehderd

DANISH

Appetizers

I'd like some . . .	**Jeg vil gerne have . . .**	yay vil **gehr**ner **hai**(wer)
I'd like some assorted appetizers.	**Jeg vil gerne have forskellig hors d'oeuvre.**	yay vil **gehr**ner **hai**(wer) fossgehlee or**durvr**
orange juice	**noget orangesaft**	**noa**gert oa**rahng**shersahft
ham	**skinke**	s**ging**ger
melon	**melon**	may**loan**
pâté	**postej**	poss**digh**
smoked salmon	**røget laks**	rur(g)ert lahgs
shrimps (shrimp)	**rejer**	**righ**er

Soup

Have you any . . . ?	**Har De . . . ?**	harr dee
Have you any chicken soup?	**Har De hønsekødssuppe?**	harr dee **hurnss**(g)er-gurds**sooper**
vegetable soup	**grønsagssuppe**	**grurn**sar(gs)soaber
onion soup	**løgsuppe**	**lurg**soaber

Fish

I'd like some . . .	**Jeg vil gerne have . . .**	yay vil **gehr**ner **hai**(wer)
I'd like some fish.	**Jeg vil gerne have fisk.**	yay vil **gehr**ner **hai**(wer) fisg
sole	**søtunge**	**sur**doanger
trout	**ørred**	**urr**erd
lobster	**hummer**	**hoa**merr
crayfish	**krebs**	**kreh**bss
prawns	**store rejer**	**stoa**rer **righ**err
I'd like it . . .	**Jeg vil gerne have den . . .**	yay vil **gehr**ner **hai**(wer) dehn
I'd like it steamed.	**Jeg vil gerne have den dampkogt.**	yay vil **gehr**ner **hai**(wer) dehn **dahmp**kogd
grilled	**grilleret**	gri**lay**rerd
boiled	**kogt**	kogd
baked	**stegt i ovnen**	**sdehgd** ee **oaoo**nern
fried	**stegt**	**sdehgd**

Meat—Poultry—Game

I'd like some . . .	Jeg vil gerne have . . .	yay vil **gehr**ner **hai**(wer)
I'd like some beef.	Jeg vil gerne have oksekød.	yay vil **gehr**ner **hai**(wer) **og**serkurd
a beef steak	en engelsk bøf	ayn **ehng**erlsk burf
some roast beef	roastbeef	**ross**dbif
a veal cutlet	en kalvekotelet	ayn **kahl**verkoaterlehd
mutton	fårekød	**fawr**erkurdh
lamb	lammekød	**lah**morkurdh
a pork chop	en svinekotelet	ayn **svee**nerkoaterlehd
roast pork	flæskesteg	**flehss**gersdigh
hare	hare	**harr**er
chicken	kylling	**kew**ling
roast chicken	stegt kylling	**sdehgd kew**ling
duck	and	ahn
How do you like your meat?	Hvordan vil De gerne have Deres kød tilberedt?	vor**dahn** vil dee **gehr**ner **hai**(wer) **day**rerss kurdh **til**berrayd
rare	rødt	rurd
medium	medium	**may**deeom
well done	gennemstegt	**geh**nermsdehgd

DANISH

Vegetables

What vegetables have you got?	Hvilke grønsager har De?	**vil**ger **grurn**sar(g)err harr dee
I'd like some . . .	Jeg vil gerne have . . .	yay vil **gehr**ner **hai**(wer)
I'd like some asparagus.	Jeg vil gerne have asparges.	yay vil **gehr**ner **hai**(wer) ahss**rah**rerss
green beans	grønne bønner	**grur**ner **bur**nerr
mushrooms	champignoner	**shahng**pinyongnerr
carrots	gulerødder	**gool**errurderr
onions	løg	lurg
red cabbage	rødkål	**rurdh**kawl
spinach	spinat	sbi**naid**
rice	ris	reess
peas	ærter	**air**terr
tomatoes	tomater	toa**mai**derr
green salad	grøn salat	grurn sah**laid**
potatoes	kartofler	**kahr**toflerr

Desserts

Nothing more, thanks.	**Tak, ikke mere.**	tahk igger mayrer
Just a small portion, please.	**Kun en lille portion.**	koon ayn liller porsyoan
Have you any ice-cream?	**Har De is?**	harr dee eess
fruit salad	**frugtsalat**	froagdsahlaid
fresh fruit	**frisk frugt**	frisg froogd
cheese	**ost**	oossd

Drink

What would you like to drink?	**Hvad ønsker De at drikke?**	vahdh urnskerr dee ahd drigger
I'll have a beer, please.	**Jeg vil gerne have en øl.**	yay vil gehrner hai(wer) ayn url
I'll have a whisky, please.	**Jeg vil gerne have en whisky.**	yay vil gehrner hai(wer) ayn wisskee

Wine

I'd like a bottle of wine.	**Jeg vil gerne have en flaske vin.**	yay vil gehrner hai(wer) ayn flahssger veen
red wine	**rødvin**	rurdhveen
rosé wine	**rosé-vin**	roasayveen
white wine	**hvidvin**	vidhveen
Cheers!	**Skål!**	skawl

The bill (check)

May I have the bill (check) please?	**Jeg vil gerne have regningen.**	yay vil gehrner hai(wer) righningern
Is service included?	**Er det med be-tjening?**	air day mehdh ber-tyayning
Everything's included.	**Alt er iberegnet.**	ahlt air eeberrighnert
Thank you, that was a very good meal.	**Mange tak, det smagte fortræffeligt.**	mahnger tahk day smargder fortrehferligd

Travelling

Where's the railway station, please?	**Hvor er banegården?**	vor air bainergawr(d)ern

Where's the ticket office, please?	**Hvor er billet-kontoret?**	vor air bi**lehd**kontoarerd
I'd like a ticket to ...	**Jeg vil gerne have en billet til ...**	yay vil **gehr**ner **hai**(wer) ayn bi**lehd** til
First or second class?	**Første eller anden klasse?**	**furr**ster **ehl**err **ahn**dern **klah**sser
First class, please.	**Første klasse.**	**furr**ster **klah**sser
Single or return (one way or round-trip)?	**Enkelt eller retur?**	**ehng**gerld **ehl**err rer**toor**
Do I have to change trains?	**Skal jeg skifte tog?**	sgahl yigh **sgif**der taw(g)
What platform does the train leave from?	**Fra hvilken perron afgår toget?**	frar **vil**gern peh**rong** ow-gawr **taw**gerd
Where's the nearest underground (subway) station?	**Hvor er den nærmeste under-grundsstation?**	vor air dehn **nair**mersder oanerrgroansss**dah**shoan
Where's the bus station, please?	**Hvor er rutebil-stationen?**	vor air **roo**derbeelsdah-shoanern
When's the first bus to ... ?	**Hvornår kører den første bus til ... ?**	vor**nawr** kurrerr dehn **furs**der booss til
the last bus	**den sidste bus**	dehn **see(d)**sder booss
the next bus	**den næste bus**	dehn **neh**sder booss
Please let me off at the next stop.	**Jeg vil gerne af ved næste stoppested.**	yay vil **gehr**ner ahv vaydh **neh**sder s**dob**bersdehdh

Relaxing

What's on at the cinema (movies)?	**Hvad går der i bio-grafen?**	vahdh gawr dair ee bioa-**grar**fern
What's on at the theatre?	**Hvad går der på teatret?**	vahdh gawr dair paw tay**ai**drerd
What time does the film begin? And the play?	**Hvornår begynder filmen? Og stykket?**	vor**nawr** ber**gew**nerr **fil**mern? o s**tew**gerd
Are there any tickets for tonight?	**Er der flere billetter til i aften?**	air dair **flay**rer bi**lehd**err til ee **ahf**dern
Where can we go dancing?	**Hvor kan vi gå ud og danse?**	vor kahn vee gaw oodh o **dahn**ser
Would you like to dance?	**Vil De danse?**	vil dee **dahn**ser

DANISH

Introductions

How do you do?	Goddag.	goadhdai
How are you?	Hvordan har De det?	vordahn harr dee day
Very well, thank you. And you?	Godt, tak. Og De?	god tahk. o dee
May I introduce Miss Philips?	Må jeg præsentere Dem for frøken Philips?	maw yigh praiserntayrer dehm for frurgern Philips
My name is...	Mit navn er...	mid nown air
I'm very pleased to meet you.	Det glæder mig at træffe Dem.	day glaidherr migh ahd trehfer dehm
How long have you been here?	Hvor længe har De været her?	vor lahnger harr dee vairerd hair
It was nice meeting you.	Det har glædet mig at træffe Dem.	day harr glaidherd migh ahd trehfer dehm

Dating

Would you like a cigarette?	Må jeg byde Dem en cigaret?	maw yay bewdher dehm ayn sigahrehd
May I get you a drink?	Må jeg byde Dem en drink?	maw yay bewdher dehm ayn drink
Do you have a light, please?	Undskyld, kan De give mig ild?	oonsgewl kahn dee geever migh il
Are you waiting for someone?	Venter De på nogen?	vehnderr dee paw noagern
Are you free this evening?	Er De ledig i aften?	air dee laydhee ee ahfdern
Where shall we meet?	Hvor skal vi mødes?	vor sgahl vee murdherss
What time shall I meet you?	Hvornår skal vi mødes?	vornawr sgahl vee murdherss
May I take you home?	Må jeg følge Dem hjem?	maw yay furlger dehm yehm
Thank you, it's been a wonderful evening.	Tusind tak, det har været en vidunderlig aften.	toossin tahg day harr vairerd ayn vidhoanerrlee ahfdern
What's your telephone number?	Hvad er Deres telefonnummer?	vahdh air dayrerss taylerfoannoomerr
Do you live alone?	Bor De alene?	boar dee ahlayner

| What time is your last train? | Hvornår går Deres sidste tog? | vornawr gawr dayrerss seessder tawg |
| Good-night . . . | Godnat . . . | goadhnahd |

Banks

Where's the nearest bank, please?	Hvor er den nærmeste bank?	vor air dehn nairmersder bahnk
Where can I cash some traveller's cheques?	Hvor kan jeg ind-løse rejsechecks?	vor kahn yay inlursser righssershehks
What time does the bank open/What time does it close?	Hvornår åbner banken/Hvornår luk-ker den?	vornawr awbnerr bahnggern/vornawr loagerr dehn
I'm expecting some money from home. Has it arrived?	Jeg venter nogle penge hjemmefra. Er de kommet?	yay vehnderr no(g)ler pehnger yehmerfrar. air dee kommerd
Can you give me some small change, please?	Vil De give mig nogle småpenge?	vill dee gee(ver) migh no(g)ler smawpehnger

Shops, stores and services

Where is the nearest chemist's (pharmacy)?	Hvor er det nærmeste apotek?	vor air day nairmersder ahpoatayg
the nearest hair-dresser's	den nærmeste frisør	dehn nairmersder frisurr
the photo shop	fotoforretningen	foatoaforehdningern
the jeweller's	guldsmeden	goolsmaydhern
the department store	stormagasinet	sdoarmahgahsseenerd
the police station	politistationen	poleeteestahshoanern
the garage	parkeringshuset	pahrkayringsshoosserd
How do I get there?	Hvordan kommer jeg derhen?	vordahn kommerr yay dehrhehn
Is it within walking distance?	Kan man nemt gå derhen?	kahn mahn nehmd gaw dehrhehn

Service

Can you help me, please?	Vil De hjælpe mig?	vil dee yehlber migh
Can you show me this? And that, too.	Vil De vise mig den her? Og den der.	vil dee veeser migh dehn hair? o dehn dair
It's too expensive/too big/too small.	Den er for dyr/for stor/for lille.	dehn air for dewr/for stoar/for liller

DANISH

Can you show me some more?	**Kan De vise mig nogle flere?**	kahn dee **vee**sser migh **no(g)**ler **flay**rer
something better something cheaper	**noget bedre noget billigere**	noa(g)erd **beh**dhrer noa(g)erd **billig**gerrer
How much is this? And that?	**Hvor meget koster den her? Og den der?**	vor **migh**erd **koss**derr dehn hair? o dehn dair
It's not quite what I want.	**Det er ikke helt det, jeg gerne vil have.**	day air **igg**er hayld day yay **gehr**ner vil **hai**(wer)
I like it.	**Den kan jeg lide.**	dehn kahn yay **lee**(dher)

Chemist's (Pharmacy)

| I'd like something for a cold/for a cough/for travel sickness. | **Jeg vil gerne have noget mod forkølelse/mod hoste/ mod køresyge.** | yay vil **gehr**ner **hai**(wer) noa(g)erd moadh for**kur**lerlser/moadh **hoass**der/ moadh **kurr**ersew(g)er |
| Can you recommend something for hay-fever/for sunburn? | **Kan De anbefale noget mod høfeber/mod solforbrænding?** | kahn dee **ahn**berfailer noa(g)erd moadh **hur**fayberr/moadh **soal**forbrehning |

Toiletry

May I have some razor blades?	**Må jeg få nogle barberblade?**	maw yay faw **no(g)**ler bahr**bayr**blaidher
some shaving cream some toothpaste	**noget barbercreme noget tandpasta**	noagerd bahr**bay**kraym noagerd **tahn**pahsdah
I'd like some soap.	**Jeg vil gerne have noget håndsæbe.**	yay vil **gehr**ner **hai**(wer) noa(g)erd **hon**saiber
some suntan oil	**noget sololie**	noa(g)erd **soal**oalyer

At the barber's

I'd like a haircut, please.	**Jeg vil gerne klippes.**	yay vil **gehr**ner **klibb**erss
Short/Leave it long.	**Kort/Lad det være langt.**	kord/lahdh day **vai**rer lahngd
A razor cut, please.	**Skåret med barberblad.**	**sgaw**rerd maydh bahr**bayr**blahdh

DANISH

At the hairdresser's

I'd like a shampoo and set, please.	**Jeg vil gerne have en vask og vandondulation.**	yay vil **gehr**ner **hai**(wer) ayn vahsg o **vahn**ondoolahshoan
I'd like a bleach.	**Jeg vil gerne have en blegning.**	yay vil **gehr**ner **hai**(wer) ayn **bligh**ning
a permanent	**en permanent**	ayn pehr**mah**nehnd
a colour rinse	**en skylning**	ayn **sgewl**ning
a manicure	**en manicure**	ayn mahni**kewr**

Photography

I'd like a film for this camera.	**Jeg vil gerne have en film til dette apparat.**	yay vil **gehr**ner **hai**(wer) ayn film til **deh**der ahbah**rard**
This camera doesn't work.	**Dette apparat virker ikke.**	**deh**der ahbah**rard** **veer**ger **ig**ger

At the post office

Where's the nearest post office, please?	**Hvor er det nærmeste posthus?**	vor air day **nair**mersder **possd**hooss
I'd like to send this by express (special delivery)/by air mail.	**Jeg vil gerne sende dette ekspres/som luftpost.**	yay vil **gehr**ner **seh**ner **deh**der ehks**brehss**/som **loofd**possd

Service stations

Where is the nearest service station, please?	**Hvor er den nærmeste servicestation?**	vor air dehn **nair**mersder **surr**visssdahshoan
Fill her up, please.	**Vil De fylde den op?**	vil dee **few**ler dehn ob
Check the oil, please.	**Vil De kontrollere oliestanden?**	vil dee kontroa**lay**rer **oal**yersdahnern
Would you check the tyres?	**Vil De kontrollere dækkene?**	vil dee kontroa**lay**rer **deh**gerner

Street directions

Can you show me on the map where I am?	**Vil De vise mig på kortet, hvor jeg er?**	vil dee **vee**ser migh paw **kor**terd vor yay air
You're on the wrong road.	**De er ikke på den rigtige vej.**	dee air **ig**ger paw dehn **rayg**di(g)er vigh

DANISH

DANISH

Go back to ...	**Kør tilbage til ...**	kurr tilbai(g)er til
Go straight ahead.	**Kør ligeud.**	kurr lee(g)eroodh
It's on the left/on the right.	**Det er til venstre/til højre.**	day air til **vehn**strer/til **hol**rer

Accidents

May I use your telephone?	**Må jeg låne Deres telefon?**	maw yay **law**ner **day**rerss tayler**foan**
Call a doctor quickly.	**Tilkald straks en læge.**	tilkahl sdrahgs ayn **lai**ger
Call an ambulance.	**Tilkald en ambulance.**	tilkahl ayn ahmboo**lahng**ser
Please call the police.	**Tilkald politiet.**	tilkahl polee**tee**erd

Numbers

zero	nul	nool
one	en	ayn
two	to	toa
three	tre	tray
four	fire	**feer**er
five	fem	fehm
six	seks	sehgs
seven	syv	**sew**oo
eight	otte	**odder**
nine	ni	nee
ten	ti	tee
eleven	elleve	**ehl**ver
twelve	tolv	tol
thirteen	tretten	**treh**tern
fourteen	fjorten	**fyor**tern
fifteen	femten	**fehm**tern
sixteen	seksten	**sehgs**tern
seventeen	sytten	**sew**tern
eighteen	atten	**ah**tern
nineteen	nitten	**nit**tern
twenty	tyve	**tew**ver
twenty-one	en og tyve	ayn o **tew**ver
thirty	tredive	**trehd**ver
forty	fyrre	**fewr**er
fifty	halvtreds	hahl**trayss**
sixty	tres	trayss
seventy	halvfjerds	hahl**fyehrss**
eighty	firs	feerss
ninety	halvfems	hahl**fehm**ss

one hundred	**hundrede**	hoonrerdher
one thousand	**tusind**	toossin
ten thousand	**ti tusind**	tee toossin

Days

It's Sunday.	**Det er søndag.**	day air surndai
Monday	**mandag**	mahndai
Tuesday	**tirsdag**	teerssdai
Wednesday	**onsdag**	oanssdai
Thursday	**torsdag**	torssdai
Friday	**fredag**	fraydai
Saturday	**lørdag**	lurrdai
yesterday	**i går**	ee gawr
today	**i dag**	ee dai
tomorrow	**i morgen**	ee mor(g)ern
morning/afternoon	**formiddag/ eftermiddag**	formiddai/ehfderrmiddai
evening/night	**aften/nat**	ahfdern/nahd

Months

January	**januar**	yahnooarr
February	**februar**	faybrooarr
March	**marts**	mahrdss
April	**april**	ahpreel
May	**maj**	migh
June	**juni**	yoonee
July	**juli**	yoolee
August	**august**	owgoossd
September	**september**	sehbtehmberr
October	**oktober**	ogtoaberr
November	**november**	noavehmberr
December	**december**	daysehmberr
Merry Christmas!	**Glædelig jul! Godt nytår!**	glaidherlee yool! goad newdawr
Happy New Year!		

DANISH

DUTCH

Guide to Pronunciation

Letter	Approximate pronunciation	Symbol	Example	

Consonants

c, f, h, k, l, m, n, p, q, t, v, x, y, z	as in English			
	as in English, but when at the end of a word, like **p** in c**u**p	b p	**ben** **heb**	behn hehp
ch	1) generally like **ch** in Scottish lo**ch**	kh	**nacht**	nahkht
	2) in words of French origin like **sh** in **sh**ut	sh	**cheque**	shehk
chtj	like Dutch **ch** followed by Dutch **j**	khy	**nichtje**	nikʰyer
d	as in English, but, when at the end of a word, like **t** in hi**t**	d t	**doe** **bed**	doo beht
g	1) generally like **ch** in Scottish lo**ch**, but often slightly softer and voiced	ǧ	**goed**	ǧoot
	2) in a few words of French origin, like **s** in plea**s**ure	zh	**genie**	zhernee
	3) like **ch** in Scottish lo**ch** when at the end of a word	kh	**deeg**	daykh

j	like **y** in **yes**	y	**ja**	**y**ar
nj	like **ñ** in Spanish se**ñ**or or like **ni** in on**i**on	ñ	ora**nj**e	oarah**ñ**er
r	always trilled, either in the front or the back of the mouth	r	**warm**	va**hr**m
s	always like **s** in **s**it	s/ss	**roos**	**r**oas**s**
sj, stj	like **sh** in **sh**ut	sh	mei**sj**e	may**sh**er
sch	like **s** followed by a Dutch **ch**	skh	**sch**rijven	**skh**rayver(n)
th	like **t**	t	**th**ee	**t**ay
tj	like **ty** in hi**t y**ou	ty	ka**tj**e	kah**ty**er
w	something like **v**, but with the bottom lip raised a little higher	v	**w**ater	**v**arterr

Vowels

In Dutch a vowel is *short* when followed by two consonants, or by one consonant at the end of a word. It is *long* when it is at the end of a word, or before a consonant followed by a vowel, or when written double.

a	1) when short, between **a** in c**a**t and **u** in c**u**t, or like **o** in American c**o**llege	ah	**kat**	**k**aht
	2) when long, like **a** in c**a**rt	ar*	**vader**	**v**arderr
e	1) when short, like **e** in b**e**d	eh	**bed**	**b**eht
	2) when long, like **a** in l**a**te, but a pure vowel	ay	**zee**	**z**ay
	3) in unstressed syllables, like **a** in **a**bove	er*	**zitten**	**z**ittern
eu	(long) like **eu** in French f**eu**; approximately like **u** in f**u**r, said with rounded lips	ur*	**deur**	**d**urr
i	1) when short, like **i** in b**i**t	i	**kind**	**k**int
	2) when long (also spelt *ie*), like **ee** in b**ee**	ee	**bier**	**b**eer
	3) sometimes, in unstressed syllables, like **a** in **a**bove	er*	**monnik**	**m**onnerk
ij	sometimes, in unstressed syllables, like **a** in **a**bove	er*	**lelijk**	**l**aylerk
o	1) when short, like a very short version of **aw** in l**aw**n	o	**pot**	**p**ot
	2) when long, something like **oa** in r**oa**d, but a pure vowel and with more rounded lips	oa	**boot**	**b**oat

---

* The r should not be pronounced when reading this transcription.

oe	(long) like **oo** in m**oo**n and well rounded	oo	**hoe**	hoo
u	1) when short, something like **u** in h**u**rt, but with rounded lips	er*	**bus**	berss
	2) when long, like **u** in French s**u**r or **ü** in German f**ü**r; say **ee**, and without moving your tongue, round your lips.	ew	**nu**	new

Diphthongs

ai	like **igh** in s**igh**	igh	**ai**	igh
ei, ij	between **a** in l**a**te and **igh** in s**igh**	ay	**reis**	rayss
au, ou	Dutch short **o** followed by a weak, short **u**-sound; can sound very much like **ow** in n**ow**	ow	**koud**	kowt

The following diphthongs have a long vowel as their first element:

aai	like **a** in c**a**t followed by a short **ee** sound	aree*	**draai**	draree
eeuw	like **a** in l**a**te followed by a short **oo** sound	ayoo	**leeuw**	layoo
ieuw	like **ee** in fr**ee**, followed by a short **oo** sound	eeoo	**nieuw**	neeoo
ooi	like **o** in wr**o**te followed by a short **ee** sound	oaee	**nooit**	noaeet
oei	like **oo** in s**oo**n, followed by a short **ee** sound	ooee	**roeit**	rooeet
ui	like **u** in f**u**r, followed by a short Dutch **u** sound, as described in **u** number 2)	urew*	**huis**	hurewss
uw	like the sound described in **u** number 2), followed by a weak **oo** sound	ewoo	**duw**	dewoo

---

* The **r** should not be pronounced when reading this transcription.

N.B.
1) When two consonants are next to each other, one will often influence the other even if it is not in the same word, e.g., *ziens* is pronounced **zeenss**, but in the expression *tot ziens*, it is pronounced **seenss** under the influence of the **t** before it.
2) In the **-en** ending of verbs and plural nouns, the **n** is generally dropped in everyday speech.

DUTCH

DUTCH

Some basic expressions

Yes.	**Ja.**	yar
No.	**Nee.**	nay
Please.	**Alstublieft.**	ahlsstew**bleeft**
Thank you.	**Dank U.**	dahngk ew
Thank you very much.	**Hartelijk dank.**	**hahr**terlerk dahngk
That's all right.	**Niets te danken.**	neets ter **dahngk**ern

Greetings

Good morning.	**Goedemorgen.**	g̊ooder**morg̊**ern
Good afternoon.	**Goedemiddag.**	g̊ooder**midd**ahkh
Good evening.	**Goedenavond.**	g̊ooden**ar**vernt
Good night.	**Goedenacht.**	g̊ooder**nahkht**
Good-bye.	**Tot ziens.**	tot seenss
See you later.	**Tot straks.**	tot strahks
This is Mr. . . .	**Dit is Mijnheer . . .**	dit iss mer**nayr**
This is Mrs. . . .	**Dit is Mevrouw . . .**	dit iss mer**vrow**
This is Miss . . .	**Dit is Juffrouw . . .**	dit iss **yer**frow
I'm very pleased to meet you.	**Aangenaam kennis te maken.**	**arn**g̊ernarm **keh**nerss ter **mar**kern
How are you?	**Hoe gaat het?**	hoo **g̊ar**tert
Very well, thank you.	**Heel goed, dank U.**	hayl g̊oot dahngk ew
And you?	**En U?**	ehn ew
Fine.	**Uitstekend.**	urewt**stay**kernt
Excuse me.	**Neemt U me niet kwalijk.**	naymt ew mer neet **kvar**lerk

Questions

Where?	**Waar?**	varr
Where is . . . ?	**Waar is . . . ?**	varr iss
Where are . . . ?	**Waar zijn . . . ?**	varr zayn
When?	**Wanneer?**	vahn**nayr**
What?	**Wat?**	vaht
How?	**Hoe?**	hoo
How much?	**Hoeveel?**	hoo**vayl**
How many?	**Hoeveel?**	hoo**vayl**

Who?	**Wie?**	vee
Why?	**Waarom?**	var**rom**
Which?	**Welk/Welke?**	vehlk/**vehl**ker
What do you call this?	**Hoe noemt U dit?**	hoo noomt ew dit
What do you call that?	**Hoe noemt U dat?**	hoo noomt ew daht
What does this mean?	**Wat betekent dit?**	vaht ber**tay**kernt dit
What does that mean?	**Wat betekent dat?**	vaht ber**tay**kernt daht

Do you speak . . . ?

Do you speak English?	**Spreekt U Engels?**	spraykt ew **ehng**erlss
Do you speak German?	**Spreekt U Duits?**	spraykt ew durewts
Do you speak French?	**Spreekt U Frans?**	spraykt ew frahnss
Do you speak Spanish?	**Spreekt U Spaans?**	spraykt ew sparnss
Do you speak Italian?	**Spreekt U Italiaans?**	spraykt ew itahli**arnss**
Could you speak more slowly, please?	**Kunt U wat langzamer spreken, alstublieft?**	kernt ew vaht **lahng**zarmerr **spray**kern ahlsstew**bleeft**
Please point to the phrase in the book.	**Wijs me de zin aan in het boek, alstublieft.**	vayss mer der zin arn in heht book ahlsstew**bleeft**
Just a minute. I'll see if I can find it in this book.	**Een ogenblik. Ik zal proberen het in dit boek op te zoeken.**	een oag̃ernblik. ik zahl proa**bay**rern heht in dit book op te **zook**ern
I understand.	**Ik begrijp het.**	ik ber**g̃rayp**heht
I don't understand.	**Ik begrijp het niet.**	ik ber**g̃rayp**heht neet

Can . . . ?

| Can I have . . . ? | **Mag ik . . . hebben?** | mahk ik . . . **heh**bern |
| Can we have . . . ? | **Mogen wij . . . hebben?** | moa**g̃**ern vay . . . **heh**bern |

DUTCH

Can you show me...?	Kunt U me... tonen?	kernt ew mer...toanern
Can you tell me...?	Kunt U mij zeggen...?	kernt ew may zehgern
Can you help me, please?	Kunt U mij helpen, alstublieft?	kernt ew may hehlpern ahlsstewbleeft

Wanting

I'd like...	Ik wil graag...	ik vil grarkh
We'd like...	Wij willen graag...	vay villern grarkh
Please give me...	Geeft U me..., alstublieft.	gayft ew mer...ahlssteebleeft
Give it to me, please.	Geeft U het me, alstublieft.	gayft ew heht mer ahlsstewbleeft
Please bring me...	Brengt U me..., alstublieft.	brehngt ew mer...ahlsstewbleeft
Bring it to me, please.	Brengt U het me, alstublieft.	brehngt ew heht mer ahlsstewbleeft
I'm hungry.	Ik heb honger.	ik hehp hongerr
I'm thirsty.	Ik heb dorst.	ik hehp dorst
I'm tired.	Ik ben moe.	ik behn moo
I'm lost.	Ik ben verdwaald.	ik behn verrdvarlt
It's important.	Het is belangrijk.	heht iss berlahngrayk
It's urgent.	Het is dringend.	heht iss dringernt
Hurry up!	Vlug!	vlerkh

It is/There is...

It is/It's...	Het is...	heht iss
Is it...?	Is het...?	iss heht
It isn't...	Het is niet...	heht iss neet
There is/There are...	Er is/Er zijn...	ehr iss/ehr zayn
Is there/Are there...?	Is er/Zijn er...?	iss ehr/zayn ehr
There isn't/There aren't...	Er is geen/Er zijn geen...	ehr iss gayn/ehr zayn gayn
There isn't any/There aren't any.	Er is er geen/Er zijn er geen.	ehr iss ehr gayn/ehr zayn ehr gayn

A few common words

big/small	**groot/klein**	ǧroat/klayn
quick/slow	**snel/langzaam**	snehl/**lahng**zarm
early/late	**vroeg/laat**	vrookh/lart
cheap/expensive	**goedkoop/duur**	ǧoot**koap**/dewr
near/far	**dichtbij/ver**	dikht**bay** vehr
hot/cold	**warm/koud**	vahrm/kowt
full/empty	**vol/leeg**	vol/laykh
easy/difficult	**gemakkelijk/moeilijk**	ǧer**mah**kerlerk/**mooee**lerk
heavy/light	**zwaar/licht**	zvarr/likht
open/shut	**open/dicht**	**oa**pern/dikht
right/wrong	**juist/verkeerd**	yurewst/ver**kayrt**
old/new	**oud/nieuw**	owt/neeoo
old/young	**oud/jong**	owt/yong
beautiful/ugly	**mooi/lelijk**	moaee/**lay**lerk
good/bad	**goed/slecht**	ǧoot/slehkht
better/worse	**beter/slechter**	**bay**ter/**slehkh**terr

Some prepositions and a few more useful words

at	**te**	ter
on	**op**	op
in	**in**	in
to	**naar**	narr
from	**van**	vahn
inside	**binnen**	**bin**nern
outside	**buiten**	**burew**tern
up	**op**	op
down	**neer**	nayr
before	**voor**	voar
after	**na**	nar
with	**met**	meht
without	**zonder**	**zon**derr
through	**door**	doar
towards	**naar**	narr
until	**tot**	tot
during	**tijdens**	**tay**dernss
and	**en**	ehn
or	**of**	off
not	**niet**	neet
nothing	**niets**	neets
none	**geen**	ǧayn
very	**zeer**	zayr
also	**ook**	oak
soon	**spoedig**	**spoo**derkh
perhaps	**misschien**	miss**kheen**

DUTCH

here	**hier**	heer
there	**daar**	darr
now	**nu**	new
then	**dan**	dahn

Arrival

Your passport, please.	**Uw paspoort, alstublieft.**	ewoo **pahss**poart ahlsstew**bleeft**
Here it is.	**Alstublieft.**	ahlsstew**bleeft**
Have you anything to declare?	**Hebt U iets aan te geven?**	hehpt ew eets arn ter **ğa**yvern
No, nothing at all.	**Nee, helemaal niets.**	nay **hay**lermarl neets
Porter!	**Kruier!**	krurewer
Can you help me with my luggage, please?	**Kunt U me met mijn bagage helpen, alstublieft?**	kernt ew mer meht mayn bah**ğar**zher **hehl**pern ahlsstew**bleeft**
That's my suitcase.	**Dat is mijn koffer.**	daht iss mayn **koff**err
Where's the bus to the centre of town, please?	**Waar is de bus naar het centrum, alstublieft?**	varr iss der berss narr heht **sehn**trerm ahlsstew**bleeft**
This way, please.	**Hierlangs, alstublieft.**	**heer**lahngss ahlsstew**bleeft**

Changing money

| Can you change a traveller's cheque, please? | **Kunt U een reischeque wisselen, alstublieft?** | kernt ew ern **rayss**shehk **vis**erlern ahlsstew**bleeft** |
| Where's the nearest bank, please? | **Waar is de dichtst-bijzijnde bank, alstublieft?** | varr iss der **dikhtst**bayzaynder bahngk ahlsstew**bleeft** |

Car rental

I'd like a car.	**Ik wil graag een auto huren.**	ik vil ğrarkh ern **ow**toa **hew**rern
For how long?	**Voor hoe lang?**	voar hoo lahng
A day/Four days/ A week/Two weeks.	**Een dag/Vier dagen/Een week/Twee weken.**	ayn dahkh/veer **dah**ğer(n)/ayn vayk/tvay **vay**kern

DUTCH

Taxi

Where can I get a taxi?	**Waar kan ik een taxi krijgen?**	varr kahn ik ern **tak**see **kray**ġern
What's the fare to...?	**Wat kost het naar...?**	vaht kost heht narr
Take me to this address, please.	**Breng me naar dit adres, alstublieft.**	brehng mer narr dit ah-**drehss** ahlsstew**bleeft**
I'm in a hurry.	**Ik heb haast.**	ik hehp harst
Could you drive more slowly, please?	**Wilt U wat langzamer rijden, alstublieft?**	vilt ew vaht **lahng**zarmerr **ray**dern ahlsstew**bleeft**

Hotel and other accommodation

My name is...	**Mijn naam is...**	mayn narm iss
Have you a reservation?	**Hebt U gereserveerd?**	hehpt ew ġerrayserr**vayrt**
Yes, here's the confirmation.	**Ja, hier is de bevestiging.**	yar heer iss der ber-**vehss**stiġing
I'd like...	**Ik wil graag...**	ik vil ġrarkh
I'd like a single room/a double room.	**Ik wil graag een éénpersoonskamer/een tweepersoonskamer.**	ik vil ġrarkh een **ayn**perrsoansskarmerr/ern **tvay**perrsoansskarmerr
a room with a bath/with a shower	**een kamer met bad/met douche**	ern **kar**merr meht baht/meht **doo**sher

How much?

What's the price per night/per week/per month?	**Hoeveel is het per nacht/per week/per maand?**	hoo**vayl** iss heht pehr nahkht/pehr vayk/pehr marnt
May I see the room?	**Mag ik de kamer zien?**	mahkh ik der **kar**merr zeen
I'm sorry, I don't like it.	**Het spijt me, hij bevalt me niet.**	heht spayt mer hay ber-**vahlt** mer neet
Yes, that's fine. I'll take it.	**Ja, dat is goed. Die neem ik.**	yar daht iss ġoot. dee naym ik
What's my room number, please?	**Wat is mijn kamernummer, alstublieft?**	vaht iss mayn **kar**merrner-merr ahlsstew**bleeft**
Number 123.	**Nummer 123.**	**ner**merr 123.

DUTCH

DUTCH

Service, please

Who is it?	**Wie is daar?**	vee iss darr
Just a minute.	**Een ogenblikje.**	ern oağernblikyer
Come in! The door's open.	**Binnen! De deur is open.**	binern. der durr iss oapern
May we have breakfast in our room?	**Kunnen we in onze kamer ontbijten?**	kernern ver in onzer kar-merr ontbaytern

Breakfast

I'll have ...	**Ik neem ...**	ik naym
I'll have some fruit juice.	**Ik neem vruchtensap.**	ik naym vrerkhternsahp
a boiled egg	**een gekookt ei**	ern ğerkoakt ay
a fried egg	**een gebakken ei**	ern ğerbahkern ay
some bacon/some ham	**spek/ham**	spehk/hahm
some toast	**toast**	toast
a pot of tea	**een kannetje thee**	ern kahnertyer tay
a cup of tea	**een kopje thee**	ern kopyer tay
some coffee	**koffie**	kofee
some chocolate	**chocola**	shoakoalar
more butter	**nog wat boter**	nokh vaht boaterr
some hot water	**wat warm water**	vaht vahrm varterr

Difficulties

The central heating doesn't work.	**De centrale verwarming werkt niet.**	der sehntrarler verrvahrming vehrkt neet
the light/the socket	**het licht/het stopcontact**	heht likht/heht stopkontahkt
the tap/the toilet	**de kraan/het toilet**	der krarn/heht tvahleht
There's no hot water.	**Er is geen warm water.**	ehr iss ğayn vahrm varterr
May I see the manager, please?	**Mag ik de direkteur spreken, alstublieft?**	mahkh ik der deererkturr spraykern ahlsstewbleeft

Telephone—Mail

There's a call for you.	**Er is telefoon voor U.**	ehr iss taylerfoan voar ew
Hold the line, please.	**Blijft U aan het toestel, alstublieft.**	blayft ew arn heht toosterl ahlsstewbleeft

Operator, I've been cut off.	**Juffrouw, mijn gesprek is verbroken.**	yerfrow mayn ğersprehk iss verrbroakern
Did anyone telephone me?	**Heeft er iemand voor mij opgebeld?**	hayft ehr eemahnt voar may opğerbehlt
Is there any mail for me?	**Is er post voor mij?**	iss ehr post voar may
Are there any messages for me?	**Heeft iemand een boodschap voor mij achtergelaten?**	hayft eemahnt ern boatskhahp voar may ahkhterrğerlartern

Checking out

May I have my bill, please?	**Mag ik de rekening, alstublieft?**	mahkh ik der raykerning ahlsstewbleeft
We're in a great hurry.	**Wij hebben erge haast.**	vay hehbern ehrğer harst
It's been a very enjoyable stay.	**Wij hebben het hier erg prettig gehad.**	vay hehbern het heer ehrkh prehterkh ğerhaht

Eating out

Good evening, sir/ Good evening, madam.	**Goedenavond, Mijnheer/Goedenavond Mevrouw.**	ğoodernarvernt mernayr ğoodernarvernt mervrow
Good evening. I'd like a table for two, please.	**Goedenavond. Ik wil graag een tafel voor twee personen.**	ğoodernarvernt. ik vil ğrarkh ern tarferl voar tvay perrsoanern
Do you have a fixed-price menu?	**Hebt U een menu à prix fixe?**	hehpt ew ern mernewah pree feeks
May I see the à la carte menu?	**Mag ik het menu à la carte?**	mahkh ik heht mernew ah lah kahrt
May we have an ashtray, please?	**Kunt U ons een asbak brengen, alstublieft?**	kernt ew onss ern ahssbahk brehngern ahlsstewbleeft
some bread	**wat brood**	vat broat
a fork	**een vork**	ern vork
a knife	**een mes**	ern mehss
a spoon	**een lepel**	ern layperl
a plate	**een bord**	ern bort
a glass	**een glas**	ern ğlahss
a napkin	**een servet**	ern sehrveht
another chair	**nog een stoel**	nokh ern stool

| Where s the gentle-men's toilet (men's room)? | **Waar is het heren-toilet?** | varr iss heht **hayrern-**tvahleht |
| Where's the ladies' toilet (ladies' room)? | **Waar is het dames-toilet?** | varr iss heht **darmerss-**tvahleht |

Appetizers

I'd like some...	**Ik wil graag...**	ik vil ğrarkh
I'd like some assorted appetizers.	**Ik wil graag hors-d'oeuvre varié.**	ik vil ğrarkh or durvr vahreeay
orange juice	**sinaasappelsap**	**see**narsahperlsahp
ham	**ham**	hahm
melon	**meloen**	mer**loon**
pâté	**paté**	pah**tay**
smoked salmon	**gerookte zalm**	ğer**roak**ter zahlm
shrimps (shrimp)	**garnalen**	ğahr**nar**lern

Soup

Have you any...?	**Hebt U...?**	hehpt ew
Have you any chicken soup?	**Hebt U kippesoep?**	hehpt ew **ki**persoop
vegetable soup	**groentesoep**	**ğroon**tersoop
onion soup	**uiensoep**	**urew**ernsoop

Fish

I'd like some...	**Ik wil graag...**	ik vil ğrarkh
I'd like some fish.	**Ik wil graag vis.**	ik vil ğrarkh viss
sole	**zeetong**	**zay**tong
trout	**forel**	foa**rehl**
lobster	**kreeft**	krayft
crayfish	**rivierkreeft**	ree**veer**krayft
prawns	**steurgarnalen**	**sturr**ğahrnarlern
I'd like it...	**Graag...**	ğrarkh
I'd like it steamed.	**Graag gestoomd.**	ğrarkh ğer**stoamt**
grilled	**gegrilleerd**	ğer**ğri**layrt
boiled	**gekookt**	ğer**koakt**
baked	**in de oven ge-bakken**	in der **oa**vern ğer**bahk**ern
fried	**gebakken**	ğer**bahk**ern

Meat—Poultry—Game

I'd like some...	**Ik wil graag ...**	ik vil ģrarkh
I'd like some beef.	**Ik wil graag rundvlees.**	ik vil ģrarkh **rernt**vlayss
a beef steak	**een biefstuk**	ern **beef**sterk
some roast beef	**rosbief**	**ross**beef
a veal cutlet	**een kalfskotelet**	ern **kahlfs**koaterleht
mutton	**schapevlees**	**skhah**pervlayss
lamb	**lamsvlees**	**lahmss**vlayss
a pork chop	**een varkenskotelet**	ayn **vahr**kernsskoaterleht
roast pork	**varkensfricandeau**	**vahr**kernssfreekahndoa
hare	**haas**	harss
chicken	**kip**	kip
roast chicken	**gebraden kip**	ģer**bra**rdern kip
duck	**eend**	aynt
How do you like your meat?	**Hoe wenst U het vlees?**	hoo vehnst ew heht vlayss
rare	**rood**	roat
medium	**lichtgebakken**	**likht**ģerbahkern
well done	**doorgebakken**	**doar**ģerbahkern

Vegetables

What vegetables have you got?	**Wat voor groenten hebt U?**	vaht voar **ģroon**tern hehpt ew
I'd like some...	**Ik wil graag ...**	ik vil ģrarkh
I'd like some asparagus.	**Il wil graag asperges.**	ik vil ģrarkh ahss**pehr**zherss
green beans	**sperziebonen**	**spehr**zeeboanern
mushrooms	**champignons**	shahmpeeñongss
carrots	**worteltjes**	**vor**terltyehss
onions	**uien**	**ure**wern
red cabbage	**rode kool**	**roa**der koal
spinach	**spinazie**	spee**nar**zee
rice	**rijst**	rayst
peas	**doperwtjes**	**dop**ehrtyerss
tomatoes	**tomaten**	toa**mar**tern
green salad	**sla**	slar
potatoes	**aardappelen**	**arr**dahperlern

Desserts

Nothing more, thanks.	**Niets meer, dank U.**	neets mayr dangk ew

DUTCH

Just a small portion, please.	**Een kleine portie, alstublieft.**	ern **klay**ner **por**see ahlsstewbleeft
Have you any ice-cream?	**Hebt U ijs?**	hehpt ew ayss
fruit salad	**vruchtensla**	**vrerkh**ternslar
fresh fruit	**vers fruit**	vehrss frurewt
cheese	**kaas**	karss

Drink

What would you like to drink?	**Wat wilt U drinken?**	vaht vilt ew **dring**kern
I'll have a beer, please.	**Een pils, alstublieft.**	ern pilss ahlsstew**bleeft**
I'll have a whisky, please.	**Een whisky, alstublieft.**	ern **viss**kee ahlsstewbleeft

Wine

I'd like a bottle of wine.	**Ik wil graag een fles wijn.**	ik vil ğrarkh ern flehss vayn
red wine	**rode wijn**	**roa**der vayn
rosé wine	**rosé**	**roa**zay
white wine	**witte wijn**	**vit**er vayn
Cheers!	**Proost!**	proast

The bill (check)

May I have the bill (check) please?	**Mag ik de rekening, alstublieft?**	mahkh ik der **ray**kerning ahlsstewbleeft
Is service included?	**Is de bediening inbegrepen?**	iss der ber**dee**ning inberğraypern
Everything's included.	**Alles inclusief.**	**ah**lerss inklew**zeef**
Thank you, that was a very good meal.	**Dank U, het was een uitstekende maaltijd.**	dangk ew heht vahss ern **urewt**staykernder **mar**ltayt

Travelling

| Where's the railway station, please? | **Waar is het station, alstublieft?** | varr iss heht stah**shon** ahlsstewbleeft |
| Where's the ticket office, please? | **Waar is het loket, alstublieft?** | varr iss heht loa**keht** ahlsstewbleeft |

I'd like a ticket to...	**Ik wil graag een kaartje naar...**	ik vil ģrarkh ern **karr**tyer narr
First or second class?	**Eerste of tweede klas?**	**ayr**ster off **tvay**der klahss
First class, please.	**Eerste klas, alstublieft.**	**ayr**ster klahss ahlsstew**bleeft**
Single or return (one way or round-trip)?	**Enkele reis of retour?**	**ehng**kerler rayss off rer**toor**
Do I have to change trains?	**Moet ik overstappen?**	moot ik **oa**verrstahpern
What platform does the train leave from?	**Van welk perron vertrekt de trein?**	vahn vehlk peh**ron** verr**trehkt** der trayn
Where's the nearest underground (subway) station?	**Waar is het dichtstbijzijnde metrostation?**	varr iss hert **dikhtst**bayzaynder **meh**troastah**shon**
Where's the bus station, please?	**Waar is het busstation, alstublieft?**	varr iss heht **berss**stahshon ahlsstew**bleeft**
When's the first bus to...?	**Om hoe laat vertrekt de eerste bus naar...?**	om hoo lart verr**trehkt** der **ayr**ster berss narr
the last bus	**de laatste bus**	der **lart**ster berss
the next bus	**de volgende bus**	der **vol**ģernder berss
Please let me off at the next stop.	**Wilt U me bij de volgende halte laten uitstappen?**	vilt ew mer bay der **vol**ģernder **hahl**ter **lar**tern **urewt**stahpern

Relaxing

English	Dutch	Pronunciation
What's on at the cinema (movies)?	**Wat wordt er in de bioscoop gegeven?**	vaht vort ehr in der beeo**skoap** ģer**ģay**vern
What's on at the theatre?	**Wat wordt er in de schouwburg gegeven?**	vahr vort ehr in der **skhow**berkh ģer**ģay**vern
What time does the film begin? And the play?	**Om hoe laat begint de film? En het toneelstuk?**	om hoo lart ber**ģint** der film? ehn hert toa**nayl**sterk
Are there any tickets for tonight?	**Zijn er nog plaatsen vrij voor vanavond?**	zayn ehr nokh **plart**sern vray voar vahn**ar**vont
Where can we go dancing?	**Waar kunnen we gaan dansen?**	varr **ker**nern ver ģarn **dahn**sern
Would you like to dance?	**Wilt u dansen?**	vilt ew **dahn**sern

DUTCH

Introductions

How do you do?	**Hoe maakt U het?**	hoo markt ew heht
How are you?	**Hoe gaat het?**	hoo ğart heht
Very well, thank you. And you?	**Uitstekend, dank U. En U?**	urewt**stay**kernt dahngk ew. ehn ew
May I introduce Miss Philips?	**Mag ik U Juffrouw Philips voorstellen?**	mahkh ik ew **yer**frow Philips **voar**stehlern
My name is . . .	**Mijn naam is . . .**	mayn narm iss
I'm very pleased to meet you.	**Prettig kennis met U te maken.**	**preh**terkh **keh**nerss meht ew ter **mar**kern
How long have you been here?	**Hoelang bent U al hier?**	**hoo**lahng behnt ew ahl heer
It was nice meeting you.	**Het was mij een genoegen.**	heht vahss may ayn ğer**noo**ğern

Dating

Would you like a cigarette?	**Wilt u een sigaret?**	vilt ew ayn see**ğar**reht
May I get you a drink?	**Mag ik U iets te drinken aanbieden?**	mahkh ik ew eets ter **dring**kern **arn**beedern
Do you have a light, please?	**Hebt U een vuurtje, alstublieft?**	hehpt ew ern **vewrt**yer ahlsstew**bleeft**
Are you waiting for someone?	**Wacht U op iemand?**	vahkht ew op **ee**mahnt
Are you free this evening?	**Bent U vanavond vrij?**	behnt ew vahn**ar**vont vray
Where shall we meet?	**Waar spreken we af?**	varr **spray**kern ver ahf
What time shall I meet you?	**Hoe laat spreken we af?**	hoo lart **spray**kern ver ahf
May I take you home?	**Mag ik U naar huis brengen?**	mahkh ik ew narr hurewss **brehng**ern
Thank you, it's been a wonderful evening.	**Dank U, het was een heerlijke avond.**	dahngk ew heht vahss ern **hayr**lerker **ar**vernt
What's your telephone number?	**Wat is uw telefoonnummer?**	vaht iss ewoo tayler**foan**nermerr
Do you live alone?	**Woont U alleen?**	voant ew ah**leen**
What time is your last train?	**Om hoe laat gaat uw laatste trein?**	om hoo lart ğart ewoo **lart**ster trayn
Good-bye.	**Tot ziens.**	tot seenss

Banks

Where's the nearest bank, please?	**Waar is de dichtstbijzijnde bank, alstublieft?**	varr iss der **dikht**stbayzaynder bahngk ahlsstewbleeft
Where can I cash some traveller's cheques?	**Waar kan ik reischeques inwisselen?**	varr kahn ik **rayss**shehks inviserlern
What time does the bank open? What time does it close?	**Om hoe laat gaat de bank open? Om hoe laat gaat hij dicht?**	om hoo lart ğart der bahngk **oa**pern? om hoo lart ğart hay dikht
I'm expecting some money from home. Has it arrived?	**Ik verwacht geld van thuis. Is het aangekomen?**	ik verr**vahkht** ğehlt vahn turewss. iss heht **arn**ğerkoamern
Can you give me some small change, please?	**Kunt U me wat kleingeld geven, alstublieft?**	kernt ew mer vaht **klayn**ğehlt **ğay**vern ahlsstew**bleeft**

Shops, stores and services

Where is the nearest chemist's (pharmacy)?	**Waar is de dichtstbijzijnde apotheek?**	varr iss der **dikhtst**bayzaynder arpoa**tayk**
the nearest hairdresser's	**de dichtstbijzijnde kapper**	der **dikhtst**bayzaynder **kah**perr
the photo shop	**de fotowinkel**	der **foa**toavingkerl
the jeweller's	**de juwelier**	der yewver**leer**
the department store	**het warenhuis**	heht **var**trrnhurewss
the police station	**het politiebureau**	heht polee(t)seebewroa
the garage	**de garage**	der ğah**rar**zher
How do I get there?	**Hoe kom ik daar?**	hoo kom ik darr
Is it within walking distance?	**Is het te lopen?**	iss heht ter **loa**pern

Service

Can you help me, please?	**Kunt U mij helpen, alstublieft?**	kernt ew may **hehl**pern ahlsstew**bleeft**
Can you show me this? And that, too.	**Kunt U me dit laten zien? En dat ook.**	kernt ew mer dit **lar**tern zeen ehn dat oak
It's too expensive/ too big/too small.	**Het is te duur/te groot/te klein.**	heht iss ter dewr/ter **ğroat/ter **klayn

Can you show me some more?	**Kunt U me er nog wat laten zien?**	kernt ew mer ehr mokh vaht lartern zeen
something better	**iets beters**	eets **bay**terrss
something cheaper	**iets goedkopers**	eets ğoot**koa**perss
How much is this? And that?	**Hoeveel is dit? En dat?**	hoo**vayl** iss dit? ehn daht
It's not quite what I want.	**Het is niet precies wat ik zoek.**	heht iss neet prer**seess** vaht ik zook
I like it.	**Het bevalt me.**	heht ber**vahlt** mer

Chemist's (Pharmacy)

| I'd like something for a cold/for a cough/for travel sickness. | **Ik wil graag iets tegen een verkoudheid/tegen hoesten/tegen wagenziekte.** | ik vil ğrarkh eets **tay**ğern ern verkow**thayt**/**tay**ğern **hoos**tern/**tay**ğern vargern**zeek**ter |
| Can you recommend something for hay-fever/for sunburn? | **Kunt U mij iets tegen hooikoorts aanbevelen/tegen zonnebrand?** | kernt ew may eets **tay**ğern **hoaee**koarts arnbe**vay**lern/**tay**ğern **zo**nerbrahnt |

Toiletry

May I have some razor blades?	**Mag ik scheer-mesjes?**	mahkh ik **skhayr**meh-sherss
some shaving cream	**scheercrème**	**skhayr**kraim
some toothpaste	**tandpasta**	**tahnt**pahstarr
I'd like some soap.	**Ik wil graag zeep.**	ik vil ğrarkh zayp
some suntan oil	**zonne-olie**	**zo**neroalee

At the barber's

I'd like a haircut, please.	**Knippen, alstublieft.**	**kni**pern ahlsstew**bleeft**
Short/Leave it long.	**Kort/Laat het lang.**	kort/lart heht lahng
A razor cut, please.	**Met het mes, alstublieft.**	meht heht mehss ahlsstew**bleeft**

At the hairdresser's

| I'd like a shampoo and set, please. | **Wassen en water-golven, alstublieft.** | **vah**sern ehn **var**terrğol-vern ahlsstew**bleeft** |

DUTCH

I'd like a bleach.	**Ik wil het laten bleken.**	ik vil heht **lar**tern **blay**kern
a permanent	**een permanent**	ern pehrmar**neht**
a colour rinse	**een kleurspoeling**	ern **klurr**spooling
a manicure	**een manicure**	ern marnee**kew**rer

Photography

| I'd like a film for this camera. | **Ik wil graag een film voor dit toestel.** | ik vil ǵrarkh ern film voar dit **toos**terl |
| This camera doesn't work. | **Deze camera doet het niet.** | **day**zer **kar**merrah doot heht neet |

At the post office

| Where's the nearest post office, please? | **Waar is het dichtstbijzijnde postkantoor, alstublieft?** | varr iss heht **dikhtst**-bayzaynder **post**kahn-toar ahlsstew**bleeft** |
| I'd like to send this by express (special delivery)/by air mail. | **Ik wil dit per express versturen/per luchtpost.** | ik vil pehr ehks**prehss** verste**w**rern/pehr **lerkht**post |

Service stations

Where is the nearest service station, please?	**Waar is het dichtstbijzijnde benzinestation, alstublieft?**	varr iss heht **dikhtst**-bayzaynder behn-**zee**nerstahshon ahlsstew**bleeft**
Fill her up, please.	**Vol, alstublieft.**	vol ahlsstew**bleeft**
Check the oil, please.	**Wilt U de olie controleren, alstublieft?**	vilt ew der **oa**lee kon-troalayrern ahlsstew**bleeft**
Would you check the tyres?	**Wilt U de banden controleren?**	vilt ew der **bahn**dern kon-troa**lay**rern

Street directions

Can you show me on the map where I am?	**Kunt U mij op de kaart aanwijzen waar ik ben?**	kern ew may op der karrt **arn**vayzern varr ik behn
You're on the wrong road.	**U bent verkeerd gereden.**	ew behnt verr**kayrt** ǵer-**ray**dern
Go back to ...	**Rijd terug naar ...**	rayt ter**rerkh** narr

DUTCH

| Go straight ahead. | **Rijd rechtuit.** | rayt **rehkh**turewt |
| It's on the left/on the right. | **Het is aan de linkerkant/aan de rechterkant.** | heht iss arn der **ling**kerkahnt/arn der **rehkh**terkahnt |

Accidents

May I use your telephone?	**Mag ik van uw telefoon gebruik maken?**	mahkh ik vahn ewoo tayler**foan** ğer**brurewk marker**n
Call a doctor quickly.	**Roep vlug een dokter.**	roop vlerkh ern **dok**terr
Call an ambulance.	**Roep een ambulance.**	roop ern ahmbew**lahns**er
Please call the police.	**Roep de politie, alstublieft.**	roop de po**lee**(t)see **ahls**stew**bleeft**

Numbers

zero	**nul**	nurl
one	**een**	ayn
two	**twee**	tvay
three	**drie**	dree
four	**vier**	veer
five	**vijf**	vayf
six	**zes**	zehss
seven	**zeven**	**zay**vern
eight	**acht**	ahkht
nine	**negen**	**nay**ğern
ten	**tien**	teen
eleven	**elf**	ehlf
twelve	**twaalf**	tvarlf
thirteen	**dertien**	**dehr**teen
fourteen	**veertien**	**vayr**teen
fifteen	**vijftien**	**vayf**teen
sixteen	**zestien**	**zehss**teen
seventeen	**zeventien**	**zay**vernteen
eighteen	**achttien**	**ahkh**teen
nineteen	**negentien**	**nay**ğernteen
twenty	**twintig**	**tvin**terkh
twenty-one	**eenentwintig**	**ayn**ernt**vin**terkh
thirty	**dertig**	**dehr**terkh
forty	**veertig**	**vayr**terkh
fifty	**vijftig**	**vayf**terkh
sixty	**zestig**	**zehss**terkh
seventy	**zeventig**	**zay**vernterkh
eighty	**tachtig**	**tahkh**terkh
ninety	**negentig**	**nay**ğernterkh

one hundred	**honderd**	**hon**derrt
one thousand	**duizend**	**durew**zernt
ten thousand	**tienduizend**	**teen**durewzernt

Days

| It's Sunday. | **Het is zondag.** | heht iss **zon**dahkh |

Monday	**maandag**	**marn**dahkh
Tuesday	**dinsdag**	**dinss**dahkh
Wednesday	**woensdag**	**voonss**dahkh
Thursday	**donderdag**	**don**derrdahkh
Friday	**vrijdag**	**vray**dahkh
Saturday	**zaterdag**	**zar**terrdahkh

yesterday	**gisteren**	**ġi**sterrern
today	**vandaag**	vahn**darkh**
tomorrow	**morgen**	**morġ**ern
morning/afternoon	**ochtend/namiddag**	**okh**ternt/narmi**dankh**
evening/night	**avond/nacht**	**ar**vernt/nahkht

Months

January	**januari**	yahne**war**ree
February	**februari**	fehvre**war**ree
March	**maart**	marrt
April	**april**	ah**pril**
May	**mei**	may
June	**juni**	**yew**nee
July	**juli**	**yew**lee
August	**augustus**	ow**ġerss**terss
September	**september**	sehp**tehm**berr
October	**oktober**	ok**toa**berr
November	**november**	noa**vehm**berr
December	**december**	day**sehm**berr

| Merry Christmas! | **Prettig Kerstfeest!** | **preh**terkh **kehrst**fayst! |
| Happy New Year! | **Gelukkig Nieuwjaar!** | er-**lerkerkh neeoo**yarr |

DUTCH

FINNISH

Guide to Pronunciation

Letter	Approximate pronunciation	Symbol	Example	
Consonants				
k, m, n, p, t, v	as in English			
d	as in rea**d**y, but sometimes very weak	d	**taide**	tigh**d**ay
g	only found after **n**; **ng** is pronounced as in si**ng**er	ng	**sangen**	sah**ng**ayn
h	as in **h**ot, whatever its position in the word	h	**Lahti**	lah**h**ti
j	like **y** in **y**ou	y	**ja**	**y**ah
l	as in **l**et	l	**talo**	tah**l**oa
r	always rolled	r	**raha**	**r**ahhah
s	always as in **s**et	s/ss	**sillä** kiitos	sill**æ** kee**t**oass

FINNISH

Vowels

a	like **a** in c**a**r, but shorter	ah	**matala**	**mah**tahlah
e	like **a** in l**a**te	ay	**kolme**	**koal**may
i	like **i** in p**i**n	i	**takki**	**tah**kki
o	like **aw** in l**aw**, but shorter	oa	**olla**	**oal**lah
u	like **u** in p**u**ll	oo	**hupsu**	**hoop**soo
y	like **u** in French s**u**r or **ü** in German **ü**ber; say **ee** as in s**ee** and round your lips while still trying to pronounce **ee**	ew	**yksi**	**ewk**si
ä	like **a** in h**a**t	æ	**äkkiä**	**æk**kiæ
ö	like **ur** in f**ur**, but with the lips rounded and without any r-sound	ur	**tyttö**	**tewt**tur

N.B. The letters **b, c, f, q, š, sh, w, x, z, ž** and **å** are only found in words borrowed from foreign languages, and they are pronounced as in the language of origin.

Diphthongs

In Finnish, diphthongs occur only in the first syllable of a word, except for those ending in **-i**, which can occur anywhere. They should be pronounced as a combination of the two vowel sounds represented by the spelling. The first vowel is pronounced louder in the following diphthongs: **ai, ei, oi, ui, yi, äi, öi, au, eu, ou, ey, äy, öy, iu**; the second vowel is louder in: **ie, uo, yö**.

Double letters

Remember that in Finnish *every* letter is pronounced, therefore a letter written double is pronounced long. Thus, the **kk** in ku**kk**a should be pronounced like the two k-sounds in the words thi**ck c**oat. Similarly, the **aa** in k**aa**tua should be pronounced long (like **a** in English c**a**r). These distinctions are important, not least because ku**k**a has a different meaning from ku**kk**a and **k**atua a different meaning from k**aa**tua.

Stress

A strong stress always falls on the first syllable of a word.

Some basic expressions

Yes.	**Kyllä.**	kewllæ
No.	**Ei.**	ay
Please.	**Olkaa hyvä.**	oalkar hewvæ
Thank you.	**Kiitos.**	keetoass
Thank you very much.	**Kiitoksia paljon.**	keetoaksiah pahlyoan
That's all right.	**Ei kestä.**	ay kaysstæ

Greetings

Good morning.	**Hyvää huomenta.**	hewvææ hoooamayntah
Good afternoon.	**Hyvää päivää.**	hewvææ pæivææ
Good evening.	**Hyvää iltaa.**	hewvææ iltar
Good night.	**Hyvää yötä.**	hewvææ ewurtæ
Good-bye.	**Näkemiin.**	nækaymeen
See you later.	**Pikaisiin näkemiin.**	pikighsseen nækaymeen
This is Mr....	**Tämä on herra ...**	tæmæ oan hayrrah
This is Mrs....	**Tämä on rouva ...**	tæmæ oan roavah
This is Miss ...	**Tämä on neiti ...**	tæmæ oan nayti
I'm very pleased to meet you.	**Hauska tutustua.**	howsskah tootoosstooah
How are you?	**Mitä kuuluu?**	mitæ kooloo
Very well, thank you.	**Erittäin hyvää, kiitos.**	ayrittæin hewvææ keetoass
And you?	**Entä teille?**	ayntæ tayllay
Fine.	**Kiitos hyvää.**	keetoass hewvææ
Excuse me.	**Anteeksi.**	ahntayksi

Questions

Where?	**Missä?**	misssæ
Where is ...?	**Missä on ...?**	misssæ oan
Where are ...?	**Missä ovat ...?**	misssæ oavaht
When?	**Milloin?**	milloyn
What?	**Mikä?**	mikæ
How?	**Kuinka?**	kooingkah
How much?	**Kuinka paljon?**	kooingkah pahlyoan

How many?	Kuinka monta?	kooingkah moantah
Who?	Kuka?	kookah
Why?	Miksi?	miksi
Which?	Mikä?	mikæ
What do you call this?	Miksi tätä kutsutaan?	miksi tætæ kootsootarn
What do you call that?	Miksi tuota kutsutaan?	miksi toooatah kootsootarn
What does this mean?	Mitä tämä tarkoittaa?	mitæ tæmæ tahrkoyttar
What does that mean?	Mitä tuo tarkoittaa?	mitæ toooa tahrkoyttar

Do you speak ... ?

Do you speak English?	Puhutteko englantia?	poohoottaykoa aynglahntiah
Do you speak German?	Puhutteko saksaa?	poohoottaykoa sahksah
Do you speak French?	Puhutteko ranskaa?	poohoottaykoa rahnskar
Do you speak Spanish?	Puhutteko espanjaa?	poohoottaykoa aysspahnyar
Do you speak Italian?	Puhutteko italiaa?	poohoottaykoa italiar
Could you speak more slowly, please?	Voisitteko puhua hitaammin?	voysittaykoa poohooah hitarmmin
Please point to the phrase in the book.	Olkaa hyvä ja näyttäkää lause kirjasta.	oalkar hewvæ yah næewttækææ lowsay kiryahsstah
Just a minute. I'll see if I can find it in this book.	Hetkinen. Katson löydänkö sen tästä kirjasta.	haytkinayn. kahtsoan lurewdængkur sayn tæsstæ kiryahsstah
I understand.	Ymmärrän.	ewmmærræn
I don't understand.	En ymmärrä.	ayn ewmmærræ

Can ... ?

Can I have ... ?	Voinko saada ... ?	voyngkoa sardah
Can we have ... ?	Voimmeko saada ... ?	voymmaykoa sardah
Can you show me ... ?	Voitteko näyttää minulle ... ?	voyttaykoa næewttææ minoollay

| Can you tell me . . . ? | **Voitteko sanoa minulle . . . ?** | **voytt**aykoa **sah**noaah minoollay |
| Can you help me, please? | **Voitteko auttaa minua?** | **voytt**aykoa **owt**tar minooah |

Wanting

I'd like . . .	**Haluaisin . . .**	**hah**looighssin
We'd like . . .	**Haluaisimme . . .**	**hah**looighssimmay
Please give me . . .	**Olkaa hyvä ja antakaa minulle . . .**	**oal**kar **hew**væ yah **ahn**tahkar minoollay
Give it to me, please.	**Antakaa se minulle.**	**ahn**tahkar say minoollay
Please bring me . . .	**Tuokaa minulle . . .**	**tooo**akar minoollay
Bring it to me, please.	**Tuokaa se minulle.**	**tooo**akar say minoollay
I'm hungry.	**Minun on nälkä.**	minoon oan **næl**kæ
I'm thirsty.	**Minun on jano.**	minoon oan **yah**noa
I'm tired.	**Olen väsynyt.**	**oal**ayn **væ**sewnewt
I'm lost.	**Olen eksyksissä.**	**oal**ayn **ayk**sewksisssæ
It's important.	**Se on tärkeää.**	say oan **tær**kayǽæ
It's urgent.	**Sillä on kiire.**	**sill**æ oan **kee**ray
Hurry up!	**Pitäkää kiirettä!**	**pit**ækǽæ **kee**rayttæ

It is/There is . . .

It is/It's . . .	**Se on . . .**	say oan
Is it . . . ?	**Onko se . . . ?**	**oang**koa say
It isn't . . .	**Se ei ole . . .**	say ay **oal**ay
There is/There are . . .	**Siellä on . . .**	**siayll**æ oan
Is there/Are there . . . ?	**Onko siellä . . . ?**	**oang**koa **siayll**æ
There isn't/There aren't . . .	**Siellä ei ole . . .**	**siayll**æ ay **oal**ay
There isn't any/ There aren't any.	**Ei ole yhtään.**	ay **oal**ay **ewht**ǽæn

A few common words

big/small	**suuri/pieni**	**soor**i/**peeay**ni
quick/slow	**nopea/hidas**	**noa**payah/**hid**ahss
early/late	**aikaisin/myöhään**	**igh**kighssin/**mewurh**ǽæn

FINNISH

cheap/expensive	halpa/kallis	hahlpah/kahlliss
near/far	lähellä/kaukana	læhayllæ/kowkahnah
hot/cold	kuuma/kylmä	koomah/kewlmæ
full/empty	täysi/tyhjä	tæewsi/tewhyæ
easy/difficult	helppo/vaikea	haylppoa/vighkayah
heavy/light	painava/kevyt	pighnahvah/kayvewt
open/shut	avoin/suljettu	ahvoyn/soolyayttoo
right/wrong	oikea/väärä	oykayah/vææræ
old/new	vanha/uusi	vahnhah/oosi
old/young	vanha/nuori	vahnhah/noooari
beautiful/ugly	kaunis/ruma	kowniss/roomah
good/bad	hyvä/huono	hewvæ/hoooanoa
better/worse	parempi/huonompi	pahraympi/hoooanoampi

Some prepositions and a few more useful words

at	-lla, -llä	-llah, -llæ
on	päällä	pææællæ
in	-ssa, -ssä	-ssah, -ssæ
to	-lle	-llay
from	-sta, -stä	-stah, -stæ
inside	sisäpuolella	sisæpoooalayllah
outside	ulkopuolella	oolkaopoooalayllah
up	ylös	ewlurss
down	alas	ahlahss
before	ennen	aynnayn
after	jälkeen	yælkayn
with	kanssa	kahnssah
without	ilman	ilmahn
through	läpi	læpi
towards	kohti	koahti
until	asti	ahssti
during	aikana	ighkahnah
and	ja	yah
or	tai	tigh
not	ei	ay
nothing	ei mitään	ay mitææn
none	ei yhtään	ay ewhtææn
very	erittäin	ayrittæin
also	myös	mewurss
soon	pian	piahn
perhaps	ehkä	ayhkæ
here	tässä	tæsssæ
there	tuossa	toooasssah
now	nyt	newt
then	sitten	sittayn

Arrival

Your passport, please.	**Passinne, olkaa hyvä.**	pahsssinnay oalkar hewvæ
Here it is.	**Tässä.**	tæsssæ
Have you anything to declare?	**Onko teillä mitään tullattavaa?**	oangkoa tayllä mitææn toollahttahvar
No, nothing at all.	**Ei, ei mitään.**	ay ay mitææn
Porter!	**Kantaja!**	kahntahyah
Can you help me with my luggage, please?	**Voitteko auttaa minua kantamaan matkatavarani?**	voyttaykoa owttar minooah kahntahmarn mahtkahtahvahrahni
That's my suitcase.	**Tuo on minun matkalaukkuni.**	toooa oan minoon matkahlowkkooni
Where's the bus to the centre of town, please?	**Mistä lähtee bussi keskikaupungille?**	misstæ læhtay boosssi kaysskikowpoonggillay
This way, please.	**Tätä tietä, olkaa hyvä.**	tætæ tiaytæ oalkar hewvæ

Changing money

Can you change a traveller's cheque, please?	**Voitteko vaihtaa matkašekin?**	voyttaykoa vighhtar mahtkahshaykin
Where's the nearest bank, please?	**Missä on lähin pankki?**	misssæ oan læhin pahnkki

Car rental

I'd like a car.	**Haluaisin auton.**	hahlooighsin owtoan
For how long?	**Kuinka pitkäksi aikaa?**	kooingkah pitkæksi ighka
A day/Four days/ A week/Two weeks.	**Päiväksi/Neljäksi päiväksi/Viikoksi/ Kahdeksi viikoksi.**	pæivæksi/naylyæksi pæivæksi/veekoaksi/ kahhdayksi veekoaksi

Taxi

Where can I get a taxi?	**Mistä voin saada taksin?**	misstæ voyn sardah tahksin
What's the fare to . . . ?	**Paljonko se maksaa . . . ?**	pahlyoangkoa say mahksar

Take me to this address, please.	Viekää minut tähän osoitteeseen.	viaykææ minoot tæhæn oasoyttayssayn
I'm in a hurry.	Minulla on kiire.	minoollah oan keeray
Could you drive more slowly, please?	Voisitteko ajaa hitaammin?	voysittaykoa ahyar hitarmmin

Hotel and other accommodation

My name is...	Nimeni on...	nimayni oan
Have you a reservation?	Onko teillä varaus?	oangkoa tayllæ vahrahooss
Yes, here's the confirmation.	Kyllä, tässä on vahvistus.	kewllæ tæsssæ oan vahhvisstooss
I'd like...	Haluaisin...	hahlooighsin
I'd like a single room/a double room.	Haluaisin yhden hengen huoneen/ kahden hengen huoneen.	hahlooighsin ewhdayn hayngayn hoooanayn/ kahhdayn hayngayn hoooanayn
a room with a bath/with a shower	huoneen jossa on kylpy/jossa on suihku	hoooanayn yoasssah oan kewlpew/yoasssah oan sooihkoo

How much?

What's the price per night/per week/per month?	Paljonko hinta on yöltä/viikolta/ kuukaudelta?	pahlyoangkoa hintah oan ewurltæ/veekoaltah/ kookowdayltah
May I see the room?	Saanko nähdä huoneen?	sarngkoa næhdæ hoooanayn
I'm sorry, I don't like it.	Valitan, mutta en pidä siitä.	vahlitahn moottah ayn pidæ seetæ
Yes, that's fine. I'll take it.	Kyllä, se sopii mainiosti. Otan sen.	kewllæ say soapee mighnioassti. oatahn sayn
What's my room number, please?	Mikä on huoneeni numero?	mikæ oan hoooanayni noomayroa
Number 123.	Numero 123.	noomayroa 123

Service, please

Who is it?	Kuka siellä?	kookah siayllæ
Just a minute.	Hetkinen.	haytkinayn
Come in! The door's open.	Sisään! Ovi on auki.	sissææn! oavi oan owki
May we have breakfast in our room?	Voimmeko saada varhaisaamiaisen huoneeseemme?	voymmaykoa sardah vahrhighssarmiighssayn hooanayssaymmay

Breakfast

I'll have ...	Haluaisin ...	hahlooighssin
I'll have some fruit juice.	Haluaisin hedelmämehua.	hahlooighssin haydaylmæmayhooah
a boiled egg	keitetyn munan	kaytaytewn moonahn
a fried egg	paistetun munan	pighsstaytoon moonahn
some bacon/some ham	pekonia/kinkkua	paykoaniah/kinkkooah
some toast	paahtoleipää	parhtoalaypææ
a pot of tea	annoksen teetä	ahnnoaksayn taytæ
a cup of tea	kupin teetä	koopin taytæ
some coffee	kahvia	kahhviah
some chocolate	kaakaota	karkahoatah
more butter	lisää voita	lisæææ voytah
some hot water	kuumaa vettä	koomar vayttæ

Difficulties

The central heating doesn't work.	Keskuslämmitys ei toimi.	kaysskoosslæmmitewss ay toymi
the light/the socket	valo/pistorasia	vahloa/pisstoarahssiah
the tap/the toilet	hana/wc	hahnah/vay say
There's no hot water.	Kuumaa vettä ei tule.	koomar vayttæ ay toolay
May I see the manager, please?	Haluaisin tavata johtajan.	hahlooighssin tahvahtah yoahtahyahn

Telephone—Mail

There's a call for you.	Teille on puhelu.	tayllay oan poohayloo
Hold the line, please.	Hetkinen, olkaa hyvä.	haytkinayn oalkar hewvæ
Operator, I've been cut off.	Keskus, puhelu katkesi.	kaysskooss poohayloo kahtkayssi
Did anyone telephone me?	Onko kukaan soittanut minulle?	oangkoa kookarn soytttahnoot minoollay
Is there any mail for me?	Onko minulle mitään postia?	oangkoa minoollay mitæææn poasstiah
Are there any messages for me?	Onko minulle mitään viestejä?	oangkoa minoollay mitæææn viaysstayyæ

FINNISH

Checking out

May I have my bill, please?	**Saisinko laskuni?**	**sigh**singkoa **lahss**kooni
We're in a great hurry.	**Meillä on kova kiire.**	**mayll**æ oan **koa**vah **kee**ray
It's been a very enjoyable stay.	**Nautimme kovasti oleskelustamme.**	**now**timmay **koa**vahşti **oa**laysskayloosstahmmay

Eating out

Good evening, sir/ Good evening, madam.	**Hyvää iltaa.**	**hew**væ(æ) **il**tar
Good evening. I'd like a table for two, please.	**Hyvää iltaa. Haluaisin pöydän kahdelle.**	**hew**væ(æ) **il**tar. **hah**looighsin **purew**dæn **kahh**dayllay
Do you have a fixed-price menu?	**Onko teillä päivän ateriaa?**	**oang**koa **tayll**æ **pæiv**æn **ah**tayriar
May I see the à la carte menu?	**Saanko à la carte -ruokalistan?**	**sarng**koa ah lah kahrt **roooa**kahlisstahn
May we have an ashtray, please?	**Saisimmeko tuhkakupin?**	**sigh**simmaykoa **toohk**ah-**koo**pin
some bread	**leipää**	**layp**æ(æ)
a fork	**haarukan**	**harr**ookahn
a knife	**veitsen**	**vayt**sayn
a spoon	**lusikan**	**loo**sikahn
a plate	**lautasen**	**low**tahsayn
a glass	**lasin**	**lah**sin
a napkin	**lautasliinan**	**low**tahsleenahn
another chair	**vielä yhden tuolin**	**via**ylay **ewh**dayn **tooo**alin
Where's the gentlemen's toilet (men's room)?	**Missä on miestenhuone?**	**misss**æ oan **miay**staynhoooanay
Where's the ladies' toilet (ladies' room)?	**Missä on naistenhuone?**	**misss**æ oan **nigh**staynhoooanay

Appetizers

I'd like some ...	**Haluaisin ...**	**hah**looighssin
I'd like some assorted appetizers.	**Haluaisin alkupala-valikoiman.**	**hah**looighssin **ahl**koopah-lahvahlikoymahn
orange juice	**appelsiinimehua**	**ah**ppaylseenimayhooah
ham	**kinkkua**	**kink**kooah

FINNISH

melon	**melonia**	**may**loaniah
pâté	**pasteijaa**	**pahs**stayar
smoked salmon	**savustettua lohta**	**sah**voosstayttooah **loah**tah
shrimps (shrimp)	**katkarapuja**	**kaht**kahrahpooyah

Soup

Have you any . . . ?	**Onko teillä . . . ?**	**oang**koa tayl**læ**
Have you any chicken soup?	**Onko teillä kanakeittoa?**	**oang**koa tayl**læ kah**nahkayttoaah
vegetable soup	**vihanneskeittoa**	**vi**hahnnaysskayttoaah
onion soup	**sipulikeittoa**	**si**poolikayttoaah

Fish

I'd like some . . .	**Haluaisin . . .**	**hah**looighssin
I'd like some fish.	**Haluaisin kalaa.**	**hah**looighssin **kah**lar
sole	**merianturaa**	**may**riahntoorah
trout	**taimenta**	**tigh**mayntah
lobster	**hummeria**	**hoom**mayiah
crayfish	**rapuja**	**rah**pooyah
prawns	**isoja katkarapuja**	isoayah **kaht**kahrahpooyah
I'd like it . . .	**Haluaisin sen . . .**	**hah**looighssin sayn
I'd like it steamed.	**Haluaisin sen höyrytettynä.**	**hah**looighssin sayn **hurew**rewtayttewnæ
grilled	**pariloituna**	**pah**riloytoonah
boiled	**keitettynä**	**kay**ttayttewnæ
baked	**uunissa paistettuna**	**oon**isssah **pighss**tayttoonah
fried	**paistettuna**	**pighss**tayttoonah

Meat—Poultry—Game

I'd like some . . .	**Haluaisin . . .**	**hah**looighssin
I'd like some beef.	**Haluaisin naudanlihaa.**	**hah**looighssin **now**dahnlihar
a beef steak	**pihvin**	**pih**vin
some roast beef	**paahtopaistia**	**parh**toapighsstiah
a veal cutlet	**vasikanleikkeen**	**vah**sikahnlaykkayn
mutton	**lammasta**	**lahm**mahsstah
lamb	**karitsanlihaa**	**kah**ritsahnlihar
a pork chop	**porsaankyljyksen**	**por**sarngkewlyewksayn

FINNISH

roast pork	**porsaanpaistia**	porsaanpighsstiah
hare	**jäniksenlihaa**	yæniksaynlihar
chicken	**kanaa**	kahnar
roast chicken	**kanapaistia**	kahnahpighsstiah
duck	**ankkaa**	ahnkkar
How do you like your meat?	**Miten valmistettuna haluatte lihan?**	mitayn vahlmisstayttoonah hahlooahttay lihahn
rare	**vähän paistettuna**	væhæn pighsstayttoonah
medium	**puolikypsänä**	poooalikewpsænæ
well done	**hyvin paistettuna**	hewvin pighsstayttoonah

Vegetables

What vegetables have you got?	**Mitä vihanneksia teillä on?**	mitæ vihahnnayksiah **tayl**lah oan
I'd like some ...	**Haluaisin ...**	hahlooighssin
I'd like some asparagus.	**Haluaisin parsaa.**	hahlooighssin **pahr**sar
green beans	**vihreitä papuja**	vihraytæ **pah**pooyah
mushrooms	**sieniä**	siayniæ
carrots	**porkkanoita**	porkkahnoitah
onions	**sipulia**	sipooliah
red cabbage	**punakaalia**	poonahkarliah
spinach	**pinaattia**	pinarttiah
rice	**riisiä**	reesiæ
peas	**herneitä**	hayrnaytæ
tomatoes	**tomaatteja**	toamarttayyah
green salad	**vihreätä salaattia**	vihrayætæ sahlarttiah
potatoes	**perunoita**	payroonoitah

Desserts

Nothing more, thanks.	**Ei muuta, kiitos.**	ay **moo**tah **kee**toass
Just a small portion, please.	**Vain pieni annos.**	vighn **piay**ni **ahn**noass
Have you any ice-cream?	**Onko teillä jäätelöä?**	oang**koa tayl**læ yææ-tayluræ
fruit salad	**hedelmäsalaattia**	haydaylmæsahlarttiah
fresh fruit	**tuoreita hedelmiä**	toooaraytah haydaylmiæ
cheese	**juustoa**	yoosstoa

Drink

What would you like to drink?	**Mitä haluaisitte juoda?**	mitæ **hah**looighssittay **joo**oadah
I'll have a beer, please.	**Haluaisin oluen.**	**hah**looighssin **oa**looayn
I'll have a whisky, please.	**Haluaisin viskin.**	**hah**looighssin **viss**kin

Wine

I'd like a bottle of wine.	**Haluaisin pullon viiniä.**	**hah**looighssin **pool**loan **vee**niæ
red wine	**punaviiniä**	**poon**ahveeniæ
rosé wine	**rosé-viiniä**	**roa**sayveeniæ
white wine	**valkoviiniä**	**vahl**koaveeniæ
Cheers!	**Kippis!**	**kipp**iss

The bill (check)

May I have the bill (check) please?	**Saisinko laskun?**	**sigh**singkoa **lahss**koon
Is service included?	**Sisältyykö siihen palvelu?**	**si**sæltewkur **see**hayn **pahl**vayloo
Everything's included.	**Kaikki on mukana.**	**kigh**kki oan **moo**kahnah
Thank you, that was a very good meal.	**Kiitoksia, se oli erittäin hyvä ateria.**	**kee**toaksiah say **oa**li **ayritt**æin **hew**væ **ah**tayriah

Travelling

Where's the railway station, please?	**Missä on rautatieasema?**	**miss**sæ oan **row**tahtiay-**ahss**aymah
Where's the ticket office, please?	**Missä on lippumyymälä?**	**miss**sæ oan **li**poo-**mew**mælæ
I'd like a ticket to...	**Haluaisin lipun ...**	**hah**looighssin **li**poon
First or second class?	**Ensimmäinen vai toinen luokka?**	**ayn**simmæinayn vigh **toy**nayn **looo**akkah
First class, please.	**Ensimmäinen.**	**ayn**simmæinayn
Single or return (one way or round-trip)?	**Yhdensuuntainen vai edestakainen?**	**ewh**daynsoontighnayn vigh **ay**daysstahkighnayn

Do I have to change trains?	Täytyykö minun vaih- taa junaa?	tæewtewkur minoon vighhtar yoonar
What platform does the train leave from?	Miltä laiturilta juna lähtee?	miltæ lightooriltah yoonah læhtay
Where's the nearest underground (subway) station?	Missä on lähin maanalaisen asema?	misssæ oan læhin marnhahlighssayn ahsaymah
Where's the bus station, please?	Missä on linja- autoasema?	misssæ oan linyah owtoa- ahssaymah
When's the first bus to . . . ?	Milloin lähtee en- simmäinen bussi . . . ?	milloyn læhtay aynsim- mæinayn boosssi
the last bus the next bus	viimeinen bussi seuraava bussi	veemaynayn boosssi sayoorarvah boosssi
Please let me off at the next stop.	Päästäisittekö minut pois seuraavalla pysäkillä?	pææsstæissittaykur minoot poyss sayoor- rarvahllah pewsækillæ

Relaxing

What's on at the cinema (movies)?	Mitä elokuvissa esitetään?	mitæ ayloakoovisssah aysitaytææn
What's on at the theatre?	Mitä teatterissa esitetään?	mitæ tayahttayrisssah aysitaytææn
What time does the film begin? And the play?	Mihin aikaan elokuva alkaa? Entä näytelmä?	mihin ighkarn ayloakoovah ahlkarr? ayntæ næewtaylmæ
Are there any tickets for tonight?	Onko täksi illaksi vielä lippuja?	oangkoa tæksi illaksi viaylæ lippooyah
Where can we go dancing?	Mihin voimme mennä tanssimaan?	mihin voymmay maynnæ tahnsssimarn
Would you like to dance?	Haluaisitteko tanssia?	hahlooighssittaykoa tahnsssiah

Introductions

How do you do?	Hyvää päivää.	hewvææ pæivææ
How are you?	Mitä kuuluu?	mitæ kooloo
Very well, thank you. And you?	Kiitos, erittäin hyvää. Entä teille?	keetoass ayrrittæin hewvææ. ayntæ tayllay
May I introduce Miss Philips?	Saanko esitellä neiti Philipsin?	sarngkoa aysitayllæ nayti filipsin

My name is . . .	**Minun nimeni on . . .**	minoon nimayni oan
I'm very pleased to meet you.	**Hauska tavata.**	howsskah tahvahtah
How long have you been here?	**Kauanko olette ollut täällä?**	kowahngkoa oalayttay oalloot tæællæ
It was nice meeting you.	**Oli hauska tavata.**	oali howsskah tahvahtah

Dating

Would you like a cigarette?	**Haluaisitteko savukkeen?**	hahlooighssittaykoa savookkayn
May I get you a drink?	**Saanko tarjota teille lasillisen?**	sarngkoa tahryoatah tayllay lahsillissayn
Do you have a light, please?	**Onko teillä tulta?**	oangkoa tayllæ tooltah
Are you waiting for someone?	**Odotatteko jotakuta?**	oadoatahttaykoa yoatahkootah
Are you free this evening?	**Oletteko vapaa tänä iltana?**	oalayttaykoa vahpar tænæ iltahnah
Where shall we meet?	**Missä tapaamme?**	misssæ tahparmmay
What time shall I meet you?	**Mihin aikaan tapaan teidät?**	mihin ighkarn tahparn taydæt
May I take you home?	**Saanko saattaa teidät kotiin?**	sarngkoa sarttar taydæt koateen
Thank you, it's been a wonderful evening.	**Kiitos, oli ihana ilta.**	keetoass oali ihahnah iltah
What's your telephone number?	**Mikä on puhelinnumeronne?**	mikæ oan poohaylinnoomayroannay
Do you live alone?	**Asutteko yksin?**	ahsoottaykoa ewksin
What time is your last train?	**Mihin aikaan viimeinen junanne lähtee?**	mihin ighkarn veemaynayn yoonahnnay læhtay
Good-night . . .	**Hyvää yötä . . .**	hewvææ ewurtæ

Banks

| Where's the nearest bank, please? | **Missä on lähin pankki?** | misssæ oan læhin pahnkki |
| Where can I cash some traveller's cheques? | **Missä voin vaihtaa matkašekkejä?** | misssæ voyn vighhtar mahtkahshaykkayyæ |

FINNISH

What time does the bank open? What time does it close?	Mihin aikaan pankki avataan? Mihin aikaan se suljetaan?	mihin ighkarn pahnkki ahvahtarn? mihin ighkarn say soolyaytarn
I'm expecting some money from home. Has it arrived?	Odotan rahaa kotoa. Onkohan se jo tullut?	oadoatahn rahhar koatoaah. oangkoahahn say yoa toolloot
Can you give me some small change, please?	Voitteko antaa minulle hiukan vaihtorahaa?	voyttaykoa ahntar minoollay hiookahn vighhtoarahhar

Shops, stores and services

Where is the nearest chemist's (pharmacy)?	Missä on lähin apteekki?	misssæ oan læhin ahptaykki
the nearest hairdresser's	lähin kampaamo	læhin kahmparmoa
the photo shop	valokuvausliike	vahloakoovahoossleekay
the jeweller's	kultaseppä	kooltassayppæ
the department store	tavaratalo	tahvahrahtahloa
the police station	poliisiasema	poaleessiahssaymah
the garage	pysäköintitalo	pewsækurintitahloa
How do I get there?	Miten sinne pääsee?	mitayn sinnay pææsay
Is it within walking distance?	Onko se kävelymatkan päässä?	oangkoa say kævaylewmahtkahn pææsssæ

Service

Can you help me, please?	Voitteko auttaa minua?	voyttaykoa owttaa minooah
Can you show me this? And that, too.	Voitteko näyttää minulle tätä? Ja myös tuota.	voyttaykoa næewttææ minoollay tætæ? yah mewurss toooatah
It's too expensive/ too big/too small.	Se on liian kallis/ liian suuri/liian pieni.	say oan leeahn kahllis/ leeahn soori/leeahn piayni
Can you show me some more?	Voitteko näyttää minulle vielä joitakin muita?	voyttaykoa næewtiææ minoollay viaylæ yoytahkin mooitah
something better	jotakin parempaa	yoatahkin pahraympar
something cheaper	jotakin halvempaa	yoatahkin hahlvaympar

How much is this? And that?	Paljonko tämä maksaa? Entä tuo?	pahlyoangkoa tæmæ mahksar? ayntæ toooa
It's not quite what I want.	Se ei ole aivan sitä mitä haluan.	say ay oalay ighvahn sitæ mitæ hahlooahn
I like it.	Pidän siitä.	pidæn seetæ

Chemist's (Pharmacy)

| I'd like something for a cold/for a cough/for travel sickness. | Haluaisin jotakin vilustumiseen/yskään/matkapahoinvointiin. | hahlooighssin yoatahkin viloosstoomissayn/ewsskææn/mahtkahpahhoynvoynteen |
| Can you recommend something for hayfever/for sunburn? | Voitteko suositella jotakin heinänuhaan/auringonpolttamaan? | voyttaykoa soooasitayllah yoatahkin haynænooharn/owringoanpoalttahmarn |

Toiletry

May I have some razor blades?	Saisinko parranajokoneenteriä?	sighsingkoa pahrrahnahyoakoanayntayriæ
some shaving cream some toothpaste	partavaahdoketta hammastahnaa	pahrtahvarhdoakayttah hahmmahsstahhnar
I'd like some soap. some suntan oil	Haluaisin saippuaa. aurinköljyä	hahlooighssin sighppooar owringkoaurlyewæ

At the barber's

I'd like a haircut, please.	Haluaisin hiustenleikkuun.	hahlooighssin hioosstaynlaykkoon
Short/Leave it long.	Lyhyiksi/Jättäkää ne pitkiksi.	lewhewiksi/yættækææ nay pitkiksi
A razor cut, please.	Veitsileikkuu, olkaa hyvä.	vaytsilaykkoo oalkar hewvæ

At the hairdresser's

I'd like a shampoo and set, please.	Haluaisin pesun ja kampauksen.	hahlooighssin paysoon yah kahmpahooksayn
I'd like a bleach.	Haluaisin vaalennuksen.	hahlooighssin varlaynnooksayn
a permanent a colour rinse a manicure	permanentin värihuuhtelun käsienhoidon	payrmahnayntin værihoohtayloon kæsiaynhoydoan

Photography

| I'd like a film for this camera. | Haluaisin filmin tähän kameraan. | hahlooighssin filmin tæhæn kahmayrarn |
| This camera doesn't work. | Tämä kamera ei toimi. | tæmæ kahmayrah ay toymi |

At the post office

| Where's the nearest post office, please? | Missä on lähin postitoimisto? | misssæ oan læhin poasstitoymisstoa |
| I'd like to send this by express (special delivery)/by air mail. | Haluaisin lähettää tämän pikakirjeenä/lentopostitse. | hahlooighssin læhayttææ tæmæn pikahkiryaynæ/layntoapoasstitsay |

Service stations

Where is the nearest service station, please?	Missä on lähin huoltoasema?	misssæ oan læhin hoooaltoaahssaymah
Fill her up, please.	Tankki täyteen, olkaa hyvä.	tahnkki tæewtayn oalkar hewvæ
Check the oil, please.	Tarkistakaa öljy.	tahrkisstahkar urlyew
Would you check the tyres?	Tarkistaisitteko renkaat?	tahrkisstighssittaykoa rayngkart

Street directions

Can you show me on the map where I am?	Voitteko näyttää minulle kartalta missä olen?	voyttaykoa næewttææ minoollay kahrtahltah misssæ oalayn
You're on the wrong road.	Olette väärällä tiellä.	oalayttay væærællæ teeayllæ
Go back to ...	Menkää takaisin ...	mayngkææ tahkighssin
Go straight ahead.	Ajakaa suoraan eteenpäin.	ahyahkar soooaraan aytaynpæin
It's on the left/on the right.	Se on vasemmalla/oikealla.	say oan vahsaymmahllah/oykayahllah

Accidents

| May I use your telephone? | Saanko käyttää puhelintanne? | sarngkoa kæewttææ poohaylintahnnay |
| Call a doctor quickly. | Kutsukaa nopeasti lääkäri. | kootsookar noapayahssti læækæri |

| Call an ambulance. | **Kutsukaa am-bulanssi.** | kootsookar ahm-boolahnsssi |
| Please call the police. | **Olkaa hyvä ja kut-sukaa poliisi.** | oalkar hewvæ yah kootsookar poaleessi |

Numbers

zero	**nolla**	noallah
one	**yksi**	ewksi
two	**kaksi**	kahksi
three	**kolme**	koalmay
four	**neljä**	naylyæ
five	**viisi**	veesi
six	**kuusi**	koosi
seven	**seitsemän**	saytsaymæn
eight	**kahdeksan**	kahhdayksahn
nine	**yhdeksän**	ewhdayksæn
ten	**kymmenen**	kewmmaynayn
eleven	**yksitoista**	ewksitoysstah
twelve	**kaksitoista**	kahksitoysstah
thirteen	**kolmetoista**	koalmaytoysstah
fourteen	**neljätoista**	naylyætoysstah
fifteen	**viisitoista**	veesitoysstah
sixteen	**kuusitoista**	koositoysstah
seventeen	**seitsemäntoista**	saytsaymæntoysstah
eighteen	**kahdeksantoista**	kahhdayksahntoysstah
nineteen	**yhdeksäntoista**	ewhdayksæntoysstah
twenty	**kaksikymmentä**	kahksikewmmayntæ
twenty-one	**kaksikymmentäyksi**	kahksikewmmayntæewksi
thirty	**kolmekymmentä**	koalmaykewmmayntæ
forty	**neljäkymmentä**	naylyækewmmayntæ
fifty	**viisikymmentä**	veesikewmmayntæ
sixty	**kuusikymmentä**	koosikewmmayntæ
seventy	**seitsemänkymmentä**	saytsaymængkewmmayntæ
eighty	**kahdeksankymmentä**	kahhdayksahngkewmmayntæ
ninety	**yhdeksänkymmentä**	ewhdayksængkewmmayntæ
one hundred	**sata**	sahtah
one thousand	**tuhat**	toohat
ten thousand	**kymmenentuhatta**	kewmmaynayntoohahttah

Days

It's Sunday.	**On sunnuntai.**	oan soonnoontigh
Monday	**maanantai**	marnahntigh
Tuesday	**tiistai**	teesstigh
Wednesday	**keskiviikko**	kaysskiveekkoa

FINNISH

Thursday	torstai	toarsstigh
Friday	perjantai	payryayntigh
Saturday	lauantai	lowahntigh
yesterday	eilen	aylayn
today	tänään	tænææn
tomorrow	huomenna	hoooamaynnah
morning/afternoon	aamupäivä/iltapäivä	armoopæivæ/iltahpæivæ
evening/night	ilta/yö	iltah/ewur

Months

January	tammikuu	tahmmikoo
February	helmikuu	haylmikoo
March	maaliskuu	marlisskoo
April	huhtikuu	hoohtikoo
May	toukokuu	toaookoakoo
June	kesäkuu	kaysækoo
July	heinäkuu	haynækoo
August	elokuu	ayloakoo
September	syyskuu	sewsskoo
October	lokakuu	loakahkoo
November	marraskuu	mahrrahsskoo
December	joulukuu	yoaoolookoo

| Merry Christmas! | Hyvää joulua! | hewvææ yoaoolooah! |
| Happy New Year! | Onnellista uutta vuotta! | oannayllisstah oottah vooattah |

FRENCH

Guide to Pronunciation

Letter	Approximate pronunciation	Symbol	Example	

Consonants

b, c, d, f, k, as in English
l, m, n, p, s,
t, v, x, z

ch	like **sh** in **sh**ut	sh	**ch**er**ch**er	shehrshay
ç	like **s** in **s**it	s	**ç**a	sah
g	1) before **e, i, y,** like **s** in plea**s**ure	zh	man**g**er	mahngzhay
	2) before **a, o, u,** like **g** in **g**o	g	**g**arçon	gahrsawng
gn	like **ni** in onion	ñ	li**gn**e	leeñ
h	always silent		**h**omme	om
j	like **s** in plea**s**ure	zh	**j**amais	zhahmeh
qu	like **k** in **k**ill	k	**qu**i	kee
r	rolled in the back of the mouth, rather like gargling	r	**r**ouge	roozh
w	usually like **v** in **v**oice	v	**w**agon	vahgawng

FRENCH

Vowels

a, à or â	between the a in hat and the a in father	ah	**mari**	mahree
é, er, et, e	like a in late	ay	**enchanté**	ahngshahngtay
è, ê, e + most consonants	like e in get	eh	**même**	mehm
e	sometimes (when at the end of a syllable or of a one-syllable word), like er in other (quite short)	er*	**me**	mer
i	like ee in meet	ee	**il**	eel
o	generally like o in hot but sometimes like o in wrote	o	**donner**	donay
ô	like o in wrote	oa	**Rhône**	roan
u	no equivalent in English. Round your lips and try to say ee; this should sound more or less correct	ew	**cru**	krew

Sounds spelt with two or more letters

ai, ay	can be pronounced as a in late	ay	**j'ai**	zhay
aient, ais, ait, aî	like e in get	eh	**chaîne**	shehn
(e)au	similar to o in wrote	oa	**chaud**	shoa
ei	like e in get	eh	**peine**	pehn
eu	like ur in fur, but with lips rounded, not spread	ur*	**peu**	pur
oi	like w followed by the a in hat	wah	**moi**	mwah
ou	like oo in look	oo	**nouveau**	noovoa
ui	approximately like wee in between	wee	**traduire**	trahdweer

Nasal sounds

The following sounds are pronounced through the mouth and the nose at the same time, very much like the twang found in speech in some parts of America or Britain.

an	something like arn in tarnish	ahng	**tante**	tahngt
en	generally like the previous sound	ahng	**enchanté**	ahngshahngtay

---

* The r should not be pronounced when reading this transcription.

ien	sounds like **yan** in **yan**k	yang	**bien**	byang
(a)in	approximately like **ang** in **rang**	ang	**instant**	angstahng
on	approximately like **orn** in **corn**	awng	**maison**	mayzawng
un	approximately like **ang** in **rang**	ang	**brun**	brang

Liaison

Normally, the final consonants are not pronounced in French. However, when a word ending in a consonant is followed by one beginning with a vowel, they are often run together, and the consonant is pronounced as if it began the following word. For instance, **nous** (*we*) is pronounced **noo**, but, in the sentence **"Nous avons un enfant"** (*We have a child*), the **s** of **nous** is pronounced, and the sentence sounds something like: **noozahvawngzangnahngfahng**. Another example: **"comment"** is pronounced **komahng**, but the **t** is pronounced in **"Comment allez-vous?"** (*How are you*), which sounds something like: **komahngtahlay voo**.

FRENCH

Some basic expressions

Yes.	**Oui.**	wee
No.	**Non.**	nawng
Please.	**S'il vous plaît.**	seel voo play
Thank you.	**Merci.**	mehrsee
Thank you very much.	**Merci beaucoup.**	mehrsee boakoo
That's all right.	**Il n'y a pas de quoi.**	eel nee ah pah der kwah

Greetings

Good morning.	**Bonjour.**	bawngzhoor
Good afternoon.	**Bonjour.**	bawngzhoor
Good evening.	**Bonsoir.**	bawngswahr
Good night.	**Bonne nuit.**	bon nwee
Good-bye.	**Au revoir.**	oa rervwahr
See you later.	**A bientôt.**	ah byangtoa
This is Mr....	**Voici Monsieur...**	vwahssee merssyur
This is Mrs....	**Voici Madame...**	vwahssee mahdahm
This is Miss...	**Voici Mademoiselle...**	vwahssee mahdmwahzehl
I'm very pleased to meet you.	**Enchanté.**	ahngshahngtay
How are you?	**Comment allez-vous?**	komahngtahlayvoo
Very well, thank you. And you?	**Très bien, merci. Et vous?**	treh byang mehrsee. ay voo
Fine.	**Bien.**	byang
Excuse me.	**Excusez-moi.**	ehkskewzaymwah

Questions

Where?	**Où?**	oo
Where is...?	**Où se trouve...?**	oo ser troov
Where are...?	**Où se trouvent...?**	oo ser troov
When?	**Quand?**	kahng

What?	**Quoi?**	kwah
How?	**Comment?**	komahng
How much?	**Combien?**	kawngbyang
How many?	**Combien?**	kawngbyang
Who?	**Qui?**	kee
Why?	**Pourquoi?**	poorkwah
Which?	**Lequel/Laquelle?**	lerkehl/lahkehl
What do you call this?	**Comment appelez-vous ceci?**	komahng ahperlayvoo serssee
What do you call that?	**Comment appelez-vous cela?**	komahng ahperlayvoo serlah
What does this mean?	**Que veut dire ceci?**	ker vur deer serssee
What does that mean?	**Que veut dire cela?**	ker vur deer serlah

Do you speak ... ?

Do you speak English?	**Parlez-vous anglais?**	pahrlayvoo ahngglay
Do you speak German?	**Parlez-vous allemand?**	pahrlayvoo ahlmahng
Do you speak French?	**Parlez-vous français?**	pahrlayvoo frahngsay
Do you speak Spanish?	**Parlez-vous espagnol?**	pahrlayvoo ehspahñol
Do you speak Italian?	**Parlez-vous italien?**	pahrlayvoo eetahlyang
Could you speak more slowly, please?	**Pourriez-vous parler plus lentement, s'il vous plaît?**	pooreeayvoo pahrlay plew lahngtermahng seel-vooplay
Please point to the phrase in the book.	**Montrez-moi la phrase dans le livre, s'il vous plaît.**	mawngtraymwah lah frahz dahng ler leevr seelvooplay
Just a minute. I'll see if I can find it in this book.	**Un instant. Je vais voir si je la trouve dans ce livre.**	angnangstahng. zher vay vwahr see zher lah troov dahng ser leevr
I understand.	**Je comprends.**	zher kawngprahng
I don't understand.	**Je ne comprends pas.**	zher ner kawngprahng pah

FRENCH

Can...?

Can I have...?	Puis-je avoir...?	pweezh ahvwahr
Can we have...?	Pouvons-nous avoir...?	poovawngnoo ahvwahr
Can you show me...?	Pouvez-vous m'indiquer...?	poovayvoo mangdeekay
Can you tell me...?	Pouvez-vous me dire...?	poovayvoo mer deer
Can you help me, please?	Pouvez-vous m'aider, s'il vous plaît?	poovayvoo mayday seelvooplay

Wanting

I'd like...	Je voudrais...	zher voodray
We'd like...	Nous voudrions...	noo voodreeawng
Please give me...	S'il vous plaît, donnez-moi...	seelvooplay donaymwah
Give it to me, please.	Donnez-le moi, s'il vous plaît.	donaylermwah seelvooplay
Please bring me...	S'il vous plaît, apportez-moi...	seelvooplay ahportaymwah
Bring it to me, please.	Apportez-le moi, s'il vous plaît.	ahportayler mwah seelvooplay
I'm hungry.	J'ai faim.	zhay fang
I'm thirsty.	J'ai soif.	zhay swahf
I'm tired.	Je suis fatigué.	zher swee fahteegay
I'm lost.	Je me suis perdu.	zher mer swee pehrdew
It's important.	C'est important.	saytangportahng
It's urgent.	C'est urgent.	saytewrzhahng
Hurry up!	Dépêchez-vous!	daypayshayvoo

It is/There is...

It is/It's...	C'est...	say
Is it...?	Est-ce...?	ehss
It isn't...	Ce n'est pas...	ser nay pah

There is/There are . . .	**Il y a . . .**	eel ee ah
Is there/Are there . . . ?	**Y a-t-il . . . ?**	ee ahteel
There isn't/There aren't . . .	**Il n'y a pas . . .**	eel nee ah pah
There isn't any/There aren't any.	**Il n'y en a pas.**	eel nee ahngnah pah

A few common words

big/small	**grand/petit**	grahng/pertee
quick/slow	**rapide/lent**	rahpeed/lahng
early/late	**tôt/tard**	toa/tahr
cheap/expensive	**bon marché/cher**	bawng mahrshay/shehr . . .
near/far	**près/loin**	pray/lwang
hot/cold	**chaud/froid**	shoa/frwah
full/empty	**plein/vide**	plang/veed
easy/difficult	**facile/difficile**	fahsseel/deefeesseel
heavy/light	**lourd/léger**	loor/layzhay
open/shut	**ouvert/fermé**	oovair/fehrmay
right/wrong	**juste/faux**	zhewst/foa
old/new	**ancien/nouveau**	ahngsyang/noovoa
old/young	**vieux/jeune**	vyur/zhurn
beautiful/ugly	**beau/laid**	boa/lay
good/bad	**bon/mauvais**	bawng/movay
better/worse	**meilleur/pire**	mayyurr/peer

Some prepositions and a few more useful words

at	**à**	ah
on	**sur**	sewr
in	**dans**	dahng
to	**à**	ah
from	**de**	der
inside	**dedans**	derdahng
outside	**dehors**	derawr
up	**en haut**	ahng oa
down	**en bas**	ahng bah
before	**avant**	ahvahng
after	**après**	ahpray
with	**avec**	ahvehk
without	**sans**	sahng
through	**à travers**	ah trahvehr
towards	**vers**	vehr
until	**jusqu'à**	zhewskah
during	**pendant**	pahngdahng
and	**et**	ay

FRENCH

or	**ou**	oo
not	**ne ... pas**	ner ... pah
nothing	**rien**	ryang
none	**aucun**	oakang
very	**très**	tray
also	**aussi**	oasee
soon	**bientôt**	byangtoa
perhaps	**peut-être**	purtehtr
here	**ici**	eesee
there	**là**	lah
now	**maintenant**	mangternahng
then	**alors**	ahlawr

FRENCH

Arrival

Your passport, please.	**Votre passeport, s'il vous plaît.**	votr pahsspawr seelvooplay
Here it is.	**Le voici.**	lervwahsee
Have you anything to declare?	**Avez-vous quelque chose à déclarer?**	ahvayvoo kehlkershoaz ah dayklahray
No, nothing at all.	**Non, rien du tout.**	nawng ryang dew too
Porter!	**Porteur!**	porturr
Can you help me with my luggage, please?	**Pouvez-vous prendre mes bagages, s'il vous plaît?**	poovayvoo prahngdr may bahgahzh seelvooplay
That's my suitcase.	**C'est ma valise.**	say mah vahleez
Where's the bus to the centre of town, please?	**Où est le bus qui va en ville, s'il vous plaît?**	oo ay ler bewss kee vah ahng veel seelvooplay
This way, please.	**Par ici, s'il vous plaît.**	pahr eessee seelvooplay

Changing money

| Can you change a traveller's cheque, please? | **Pouvez-vous changer un chèque de voyage, s'il vous plaît?** | poovayvoo shahngzhay ang shekh der vwahyahzh seelvooplay |
| Where's the nearest bank, please? | **Où est la banque la plus proche, s'il vous plaît?** | oo ay lah bahngk lah plew prosh seelvooplay |

Car rental

I'd like a car.	**Je voudrais une voiture.**	zher voodray ewn vwahtewr
For how long?	**Pour combien de temps?**	poor kawngbyang der tahng
A day/Four days/ A week/Two weeks.	**Un jour/Quatre jours/ Une semaine/Deux semaines.**	ang zhoor/kahtr zhoor/ewn sermehn/dur sermehn

Taxi

Where can I get a taxi?	**Où puis-je avoir un taxi?**	oo pweezh ahvwahr ang tahksee
What's the fare to . . . ?	**Quel est le tarif pour . . .?**	kehl ay ler tahreef poor
Take me to this address, please.	**Conduisez-moi à cette adresse, s'il vous plaît.**	kawngdweezaymwah ah seht ahdrehss seel-vooplay
I'm in a hurry.	**Je suis pressé.**	zher swee prehssay
Could you drive more slowly, please?	**Pourriez-vous conduire plus lentement, s'il vous plaît?**	pooreeayvoo kawngdweer plew lahngtermahng seel-vooplay

Hotel and other accommodation

My name is . . .	**Je m'appelle . . .**	zher mahpehl
Have you a reservation?	**Avez-vous fait réserver?**	ahvayvoo fay rayzehrvay
Yes, here's the confirmation.	**Oui, voici la confirmation.**	wee, vwahsee lah kawngfeermahsyawng
I'd like . . .	**J'aimerais . . .**	zhehmerray
I'd like a single room/a double room.	**J'aimerais une chambre pour une personne/pour deux personnes.**	zhehmerray ewn shahngbr poor ewn pehrson/poor dur pehrson
a room with a bath/with a shower	**une chambre avec bain/avec douche**	ewn shahngbr ahvehk bang/ahvehk doosh

How much?

What's the price per night/per week/per month?	Quel est le prix pour une nuit/pour une semaine/pour un mois?	kehl ay ler pree poor ewn nwee/poor ewn sermehn/poor ang mwah
May I see the room?	Puis-je voir la chambre?	pweezh vwahr lah shahngbr
I'm sorry, I don't like it.	Je regrette, elle ne me plaît pas.	zher rergreht ehl ner mer play pah
Yes, that's fine. I'll take it.	Oui, c'est bien. Je la prends.	wee say byang. zher lah prahng
What's my room number, please?	Quel est le numéro de ma chambre, s'il vous plaît?	kehl ay ler newmayroa der mah shahngbr seel-vooplay
Number 123.	Numéro 123.	newmayroa 123.

Service, please

Who is it?	Qui est-ce?	kee ehss
Just a minute.	Un instant, s'il vous plaît.	angnangstahng seel-vooplay
Come in! The door's open.	Entrez! La porte est ouverte.	ahngtray! lah port aytoovairt
May we have breakfast in our room?	Pouvons-nous prendre le petit déjeuner dans notre chambre?	poovawngnoo prahngdr le pertee dayzhurnay dahng notr shahngbr

Breakfast

I'll have ...	Je voudrais ...	zher voodray
I'll have some fruit juice.	Je voudrais un jus de fruit.	zher voodray ang zhew der frwee
a boiled egg	un œuf à la coque	angnurf ah lah kok
a fried egg	un œuf sur le plat	angnurf sewr ler plah
some bacon/some ham	du bacon/du jambon	dew baykern/dew zhahngbawng
some toast	des toasts	day toast
a pot of tea	du thé	dew tay
a cup of tea	une tasse de thé	ewn tahss der tay
some coffee	du café	dew kahfay
some chocolate	du chocolat	dew shokolah
more butter	davantage de beurre	dahvahngtahzh der burr
some hot water	de l'eau chaude	der loa shoad

Difficulties

The central heating doesn't work.	**Le chauffage central ne marche pas.**	ler shoafahzh sahngtrahl ner mahrsh pah
the light/the socket the tap/the toilet	**la lumière/la prise le robinet/les toilettes**	lah lewmyair/lah preez ler robeenay/lay twahleht
There's no hot water.	**Il n'y a pas d'eau chaude.**	eel nee ah pah doa shoad
May I see the manager, please?	**Puis-je voir le directeur, s'il vous plaît?**	pweezh vwahr ler deerehkturr seelvooplay

Telephone—Mail

There's a call for you.	**Il y a un appel pour vous.**	eel ee ah angnahpehl poor voo
Hold the line, please.	**Ne quittez pas, s'il vous plaît.**	ner keetay pah seelvooplay
Operator, I've been cut off.	**Mademoiselle, la communication a été coupée.**	mahdmwahzehl lah komewneekahsyawng ah aytay koopay
Did anyone telephone me?	**Est-ce qu'on m'a appelé?**	ehss kawng mah ahperlay
Is there any mail for me?	**Y a-t-il du courrier pour moi?**	ee ahteel dew kooreeay poor mwah
Are there any messages for me?	**Y a-t-il un message pour moi?**	ee ahteel ang mehssahzh poor mwah

Checking out

May I have my bill, please?	**Puis-je avoir ma note, s'il vous plaît?**	pweezh ahvwahr mah not seelvooplay
We're in a great hurry.	**Nous sommes très pressés.**	noo som tray prehssay
It's been a very enjoyable stay.	**Le séjour a été très agréable.**	ler sayzhoor ah aytay trayzahgrayahbl

Eating out

Good evening, sir/ Good evening, madam.	**Bonsoir, Monsieur/ Bonsoir, Madame.**	bawngswahr mersyur/ bawngswahr mahdahm

FRENCH

Good evening, I'd like a table for two, please.	**Bonsoir. Je voudrais une table pour deux personnes, s'il vous plaît.**	bawngswahr. zher voodray ewn tahbl poor dur pehrson seelvooplay
Do you have a fixed-price menu?	**Avez-vous un menu?**	ahvayvoo ang mernew
May I see the à la carte menu?	**Puis-je voir la carte?**	pweezh vwahr lah kahrt
May we have an ashtray, please?	**Pouvons-nous avoir un cendrier, s'il vous plaît?**	poovawngnoo ahvwahr ang sahngdreeay seelvooplay
some bread	**du pain**	dew pang
a fork	**une fourchette**	ewn foorsheht
a knife	**un couteau**	ang kootoa
a spoon	**une cuillère**	ewn kweeyair
a plate	**une assiette**	ewn ahssyeht
a glass	**un verre**	ang vair
a napkin	**une serviette**	ewn sehrvyeht
another chair	**une autre chaise**	ewn oatr shaiz
Where's the gentlemen's toilet (men's room)?	**Où sont les toilettes pour messieurs?**	oo sawng lay twahleht poor maysyur
Where's the ladies' toilet (ladies' room)?	**Où sont les toilettes pour dames?**	oo sawng lay twahleht poor dahm

Appetizers

I'd like some . . .	**Je voudrais . . .**	zher voodray
I'd like some assorted appetizers.	**Je voudrais des hors-d'œuvre variés.**	zher voodray day 'ordurvr vahreeay
orange juice	**un jus d'orange**	ang zhew dorahngzh
ham	**du jambon**	dew zhahngbawng
melon	**du melon**	der merlawng
pâté	**du pâté**	dew pahtay
smoked salmon	**du saumon fumé**	dew soamawng fewmay
shrimps (shrimp)	**des crevettes**	day krerveht

Soup

Have you any . . . ?	**Avez-vous . . . ?**	ahvayvoo
Have you any chicken soup?	**Avez-vous du potage au poulet?**	ahvayvoo dew potahzh oa poolay
vegetable soup	**une soupe de légumes**	ewn soop der laygewm
onion soup	**de la soupe à l'oignon**	der lah soop ah loñawng

Fish

I'd like some...	**J'aimerais ...**	zhehmerray
I'd like some fish.	**J'aimerais du poisson.**	zhehmerray dew pwahssawng
sole	**de la sole**	der lah sol
trout	**de la truite**	der lah trweet
lobster	**du homard**	dew omahr
crayfish	**des écrevisses**	day aykrerveess
prawns	**des langoustines**	day lahnggoosteen
I'd like it...	**Je l'aimerais ...**	zher lehmerray
I'd like it steamed.	**Je l'aimerais cuit à la vapeur.**	zher lehmerray kwee ah lah vahpurr
grilled	**grillé**	greeyay
boiled	**au court-bouillon**	oa koor booyawng
baked	**cuit au four**	kwee oa foor
fried	**frit**	free

Meat—Poultry—Game

I'd like some...	**Je voudrais ...**	zher voodray
I'd like some beef.	**Je voudrais du bœuf.**	zher voodray dew burf
a beef steak	**un bifteck**	ang beeftehk
some roast beef	**du rosbif**	dew roazbeef
a veal cutlet	**une côtelette de veau**	ewn koatleht de voa
mutton	**du mouton**	dew mootawng
lamb	**de l'agneau**	der lahñoa
a pork chop	**une côtelette de porc**	ewn koatleht der pawr
roast pork	**du rôti de porc**	dew roatee der pawr
hare	**du lièvre**	dew lyehvr
chicken	**du poulet**	dew poolay
roast chicken	**du poulet rôti**	dew poolay roatee
duck	**du canard**	dew kahnahr
How do you like your meat?	**Comment désirez-vous la viande?**	komahng dayzeerayvoo lah vyahngd
rare	**saignante**	sehñahngt
medium	**à point**	ah pwang
well done	**bien cuite**	byang kweet

Vegetables

What vegetables have you got?	**Quels légumes servez-vous?**	kehl laygewm sehrvayvoo
I'd like some . . .	**Je voudrais . . .**	zher voodray
I'd like some asparagus.	**Je voudrais des asperges.**	zher voodray dayzah-spehrzh
green beans	**des haricots verts**	day ahreekoa vair
mushrooms	**des champignons**	day shahngpeeñawng
carrots	**des carottes**	day kahrot
onions	**des oignons**	dayzoñawng
red cabbage	**du chou rouge**	dew shoo roozh
spinach	**des épinards**	dayzaypeenahr
rice	**du riz**	dew ree
peas	**des petits pois**	day pertee pwah
tomatoes	**des tomates**	day tomaht
green salad	**de la salade verte**	der lah sahlahd vairt
potatoes	**des pommes de terre**	day pom der tair

Desserts

Nothing more, thanks.	**Je ne veux plus rien, merci.**	zher ner vur plew ryang mehrsee
Just a small portion, please.	**Juste une petite portion, s'il vous plaît.**	zhewst ewn perteet por-syawng seelvooplay
Have you any ice-cream?	**Avez-vous des glaces?**	ahvayvoo day glahss
fruit salad	**une salade de fruits**	ewn sahlahd der frwee
fresh fruit	**des fruits frais**	day frwee fray
cheese	**du fromage**	dew fromahzh

Drink

What would you like to drink?	**Qu'aimeriez-vous boire?**	kehmerreeayvoo bwahr
I'll have a beer, please.	**J'aimerais une bière, s'il vous plaît.**	zhehmerray ewn byair seelvooplay
I'll have a whisky, please.	**Je voudrais un whisky, s'il vous plaît.**	zher voodray ang weeskee seelvooplay

Wine

I'd like a bottle of wine.	**Je voudrais une bouteille de vin.**	zher voodray ewn bootay der vang
red wine	**vin rouge**	vang roozh
rosé wine	**vin rosé**	vang roazay
white wine	**vin blanc**	vang blahng
Cheers!	**A votre santé!**	ah votr sahngtay

The bill (check)

May I have the bill (check) please?	**Puis-je avoir l'addition, s'il vous plaît?**	pweezh ahvwahr lahdee-ssyawng seelvooplay
Is service included?	**Le service est-il compris?**	ler sehrveess ayteel kawngpree
Everything's included.	**Tout est compris.**	tootay kawngpree
Thank you, that was a very good meal.	**Merci, c'était très bon.**	mehrsee saytay tray bawng

Travelling

Where's the railway station, please?	**Où se trouve la gare, s'il vous plaît?**	oo ser troov lah gahr seelvooplay
Where's the ticket office, please?	**Où est le guichet, s'il vous plaît?**	oo ay ler geeshay seelvooplay
I'd like a ticket to ...	**J'aimerais un billet pour ...**	zhehmerray ang beeyay poor
First or second class?	**Première ou deuxième classe?**	prermyair oo durzyehm klahss
First class, please.	**Première classe, s'il vous plaît.**	prermyair klahss seelvooplay
Single or return (one way or round-trip)?	**Aller simple ou aller et retour?**	ahlay sangpl oo ahlay ay rertoor
Do I have to change trains?	**Est-ce que je dois changer de train?**	ehss ker zher dwah shahngzhay der trang
What platform does the train leave from?	**De quel quai le train part-il?**	der kehl kay ler trang pahrteel
Where's the nearest underground (subway) station?	**Où est la station de métro la plus proche?**	oo ay lah stahsyawng der maytroa la plew prosh
Where's the bus station, please?	**Où est la gare routière, s'il vous plaît?**	oo ay lah gahr rootyair seelvooplay

FRENCH

When's the first bus to . . . ?	**A quelle heure est le premier autobus pour . . . ?**	ah kehl urr ay ler prer-myayroatoabewss poor
the last bus	**le dernier autobus**	ler dehrnyayroatoabewss
the next bus	**le prochain autobus**	ler proshehnoatoabewss
Please let me off at the next stop.	**S'il vous plaît, déposez-moi au prochain arrêt.**	seelvooplay daypoazay-mwah oa proshehnahray

Relaxing

What's on at the cinema (movies)?	**Que donne-t-on au cinéma?**	ker dontawng oa see-naymah
What's on at the theatre?	**Que joue-t-on au théâtre?**	ker zhootawng oa tayahtr
What time does the film begin?	**A quelle heure commence le film?**	ah kehl urr komahngss ler feelm
And the play?	**Et la pièce?**	ay lah pyehss
Are there any tickets for tonight?	**Reste-t-il encore des places pour ce soir?**	rehstteel ahngkawr day plahss poor ser swahr
Where can we go dancing?	**Où pouvons-nous aller danser?**	oo poovawngnoo ahlay dahngsay
Would you like to dance?	**Voulez-vous danser?**	voolayvoo dahngsay

Introductions

How do you do?	**Bonjour.**	bawngzhoor
How are you?	**Comment allez-vous?**	komahngtahlayvoo
Very well, thank you. And you?	**Très bien, merci. Et vous?**	tray byang mehrsee. ay voo
May I introduce Miss Philips?	**Puis-je vous présenter Mademoi-selle Philips?**	pweezh voo prayzahngtay mahdmwahzehl feeleeps
My name is . . .	**Je m'appelle . . .**	zher mahpehl
I'm very pleased to meet you.	**Je suis ravi de vous connaître.**	zher swee rahvee der voo konaitr

| How long have you been here? | **Depuis combien de temps êtes-vous ici?** | derpwee kawngbyang der tahng ehtvoo eesee |
| It was nice meeting you. | **Enchanté d'avoir fait votre connaissance.** | ahngshahngtay dahvwahr fay votr konaysahngss |

Dating

Would you like a cigarette?	**Voulez-vous une cigarette?**	voolayvoo ewn seegahreht
May I get you a drink?	**Puis-je vous offrir un verre?**	pweezh vooz offreer ang vair
Do you have a light, please?	**Avez-vous du feu, s'il vous plaît?**	ahvayvoo dew fur seelvooplay
Are you waiting for someone?	**Attendez-vous quelqu'un?**	ahtahngdayvoo kehlkang
Are you free this evening?	**Etes-vous libre ce soir?**	ehtvoo leebr ser swahr
Where shall we meet?	**Où nous retrouverons-nous?**	oo noo rertrooverrawngnoo
What time shall I meet you?	**A quelle heure vous verrai-je?**	ah kehl urr voo vairayzh
May I take you home?	**Puis-je vous ramener chez vous?**	pweezh voo rahmnay shay voo
Thank you, it's been a wonderful evening.	**Merci pour cette merveilleuse soirée.**	mehrsee poor seht mehrvayyurz swahray
What's your telephone number?	**Quel est votre numéro de téléphone?**	kehl ay votr newmayroa der taylayfon
Do you live alone?	**Habitez-vous seule?**	ahbeetayvoo surl
What time is your last train?	**A quelle heure est votre dernier train?**	ah kehl urr ay votr dairnyay trang
Good-night...	**Bonne nuit...**	bon nwee

Banks

| Where's the nearest bank, please? | **Où se trouve la banque la plus proche, s'il vous plaît?** | oo ser troov lah bahngk lah plew prosh seelvooplay |
| Where can I cash some traveller's cheques? | **Où puis-je toucher des chèques de voyage?** | oo pweezh tooshay day shehk der vwahyahzh |

FRENCH

What time does the bank open?	**A quelle heure la banque ouvre-t-elle?**	ah kehl urr lah bahngk oovrertehl
What time does it close?	**A quelle heure ferme-t-elle?**	ah kehl urr fairmtehl
I'm expecting some money from home. Has it arrived?	**J'attends de l'argent de la maison. Est-il arrivé?**	zhahtahng der lahrzhahng der lah mayzawng ayteel ahreevay
Can you give me some small change, please?	**Pouvez-vous me donner de la monnaie, s'il vous plaît?**	poovayvoo mer donay der lah monay seelvooplay

Shops, stores and services

Where is the nearest chemist's (pharmacy)?	**Où est la pharmacie la plus proche?**	oo ay lah fahrmahssee lah plew prosh
the nearest hairdresser's	**le coiffeur le plus proche**	le kwahfurr ler plew prosh
the photo shop	**le magasin de photographie**	le mahgahzang der foatoagrahfee
the jeweller's	**la bijouterie**	lah beezhooterree
the department store	**le grand magasin**	ler grahng mahgahzang
the police station	**le poste de police**	ler post der poleess
the garage	**le garage**	ler gahrahzh
How do I get there?	**Comment puis-je m'y rendre?**	komahng pweezh mee rahngdr
Is it within walking distance?	**Est-il possible d'y aller à pied?**	ayteel posseebl dee ahlay ah pyay

Service

Can you help me, please?	**Pouvez-vous m'aider, s'il vous plaît?**	poovayvoo mayday seelvooplay
Can you show me this? And that, too.	**Pouvez-vous me montrer ceci? Et cela aussi.**	poovayvoo mer mawngtray serssee? ay serlah oasee
It's too expensive/ too big/too small.	**C'est trop cher/trop grand/trop petit.**	say troa shair/troa grahng/troa pertee
Can you show me some more?	**Pouvez-vous me montrer un plus grand choix?**	poovayvoo mer mawngtray ang plew grahng shwah
something better	**quelque chose de mieux**	kehlker shoaz der myur
something cheaper	**quelque chose de meilleur marché**	kehlker shoaz der mayyurr mahrshay

How much is this? And that?	**Combien coûte ceci? Et cela?**	kawngbyang koot sersee ay serlah
It's not quite what I want.	**Ce n'est pas exactement ce que je désire.**	ser nay pah ehgzahktermahng ser ker zher dayzeer
I like it.	**Cela me plaît.**	serlah mer play

Chemist's (Pharmacy)

| I'd like something for a cold/for a cough/for travel sickness. | **J'aimerais quelque chose contre le rhume/contre la toux/contre le mal au cœur.** | zhehmerray kehlkershoaz kawngtr ler rewm/kawngtr lah too/kawngtr ler mahl oa kurr |
| Can you recommend something for hay-fever/for sunburn? | **Pouvez-vous m'indiquer quelque chose contre le rhume des foins/contre un coup de soleil?** | poovayvoo mangdeekay kehlker shoaz kawngtr ler rewm day fwang/kawngtr ang koo der solay |

Toiletry

May I have some razor blades?	**Puis-je avoir des lames de rasoir?**	pweezh ahvwahr day lahm de rahzwahr
some shaving cream some toothpaste	**de la crème à raser du dentifrice**	der lah krehm ah rahzay dew dahngteefreess
I'd like some soap.	**Je voudrais du savon.**	zher voodray dew sahvawng
some suntan oil	**de l'huile solaire**	der lweel solair

At the barber's

I'd like a haircut, please.	**Je voudrais me faire couper les cheveux, s'il vous plaît.**	zher voodray mer fair koopay lay shervur seelvooplay
Short/Leave it long.	**Courts/Laissez-les longs.**	koor/layssaylay lawng
A razor cut, please.	**Une coupe au rasoir, s'il vous plaît.**	ewn koop oa rahzwahr seelvooplay

At the hairdresser's

| I'd like a shampoo and set, please. | **J'aimerais un shampooing-mise en plis, s'il vous plaît.** | zhehmerray ang shahngpwangmeezahng plee seelvooplay |

FRENCH

I'd like a bleach.	**Je voudrais une dé-coloration.**	zher voodray ewn dayko-lorahsyawng
a permanent	**une permanente**	ewn pehrmahnahngt
a colour rinse	**un rinçage**	ang rangsahzh
a manicure	**une manucure**	ewn mahnewkewr

Photography

| I'd like a film for this camera. | **J'aimerais un film pour cet appareil.** | zhehmerray ang feelm poor seht ahpahray |
| This camera doesn't work. | **Cet appareil ne marche pas.** | seht ahpahray ner mahrsh pah |

At the post office

| Where's the nearest post office, please? | **Où est le bureau de poste le plus proche, s'il vous plaît?** | oo ay ler bewroa der post ler plew prosh seelvoo-play |
| I'd like to send this by express (special delivery)/by air mail. | **J'aimerais envoyer ceci par express/par avion.** | zhehmerray ahngvwahyay serssee pahr ehksprehss/pahr ahvyawng |

Service stations

Where is the nearest service station, please?	**Où est la station-service la plus proche, s'il vous plaît?**	oo ay lah stahs-syawngsehrveess lah plew prosh seelvooplay
Fill her up, please.	**Le plein, s'il vous plaît.**	ler plang seelvooplay
Check the oil, please.	**Contrôlez l'huile, s'il vous plaît.**	kawngtroalay lweel seel-vooplay
Would you check the tyres?	**Voudriez-vous véri-fier les pneus?**	voodreeayvoo vayreefeeay lay pnur

Street directions

Can you show me on the map where I am?	**Pouvez-vous me montrer sur la carte où je me trouve?**	poovayvoo mer mawngtray sewr lah kahrt oo zher mer troov
You're on the wrong road.	**Vous n'êtes pas sur la bonne route.**	voo neht pah sewr lah bon root
Go back to ...	**Retournez à ...**	rertoornay ah

| Go straight ahead. | **Continuez tout droit.** | kawngteeneway too drwah |
| It's on the left/on the right. | **C'est à gauche/à droite.** | saytah goash/ah drwaht |

Accidents

May I use your telephone?	**Puis-je utiliser votre téléphone?**	pweezh ewteeleezay votr taylayfon
Call a doctor quickly.	**Appelez vite un docteur.**	ahperlay veet ang dokturr
Call an ambulance.	**Appelez une ambulance.**	ahperlay ewn ahngbewlahngss
Please call the police.	**Appelez la police, s'il vous plaît.**	ahperlay lah poleess seel-vooplay

Numbers

zero	**zéro**	zayroa
one	**un**	ang
two	**deux**	dur
three	**trois**	trwah
four	**quatre**	kahtr
five	**cinq**	sangk
six	**six**	seess
seven	**sept**	seht
eight	**huit**	weet
nine	**neuf**	nurf
ten	**dix**	deess
eleven	**onze**	awngz
twelve	**douze**	dooz
thirteen	**treize**	traiz
fourteen	**quatorze**	kahtorz
fifteen	**quinze**	kangz
sixteen	**seize**	saiz
seventeen	**dix-sept**	deess-seht
eighteen	**dix-huit**	deez-weet
nineteen	**dix-neuf**	deez-nurf
twenty	**vingt**	vangt
twenty-one	**vingt et un**	vang-tay-ang
thirty	**trente**	trahngt
forty	**quarante**	kahrahngt
fifty	**cinquante**	sangkahngt
sixty	**soixante**	swahsahngt
seventy	**soixante-dix**	swahsahngtdeess
eighty	**quatre-vingts**	kahtrervang
ninety	**quatre-vingt-dix**	kahtrervangdeess
one hundred	**cent**	sahng
one thousand	**mille**	meel
ten thousand	**dix mille**	dee meel

FRENCH

Days

It's Sunday.	**C'est dimanche.**	say deemahngsh
Monday	**lundi**	langdee
Tuesday	**mardi**	mahrdee
Wednesday	**mercredi**	mehrkrerdee
Thursday	**jeudi**	zhurdee
Friday	**vendredi**	vahngdrerdee
Saturday	**samedi**	sahmdee
yesterday	**hier**	eeair
today	**aujourd'hui**	oazhoordwee
tomorrow	**demain**	dermang
morning/afternoon	**matin/après-midi**	mahtang/ahpraymeedee
evening/night	**soir/nuit**	swahr/nwee

Months

January	**janvier**	zhahngveeay
February	**février**	fayvreeay
March	**mars**	mahrss
April	**avril**	ahvreel
May	**mai**	may
June	**juin**	zhwang
July	**juillet**	zhweeyay
August	**août**	oot
September	**septembre**	sehptahngbr
October	**octobre**	oktobr
November	**novembre**	novahngbr
December	**décembre**	daysahngbr
Merry Christmas!	**Joyeux Noël! Bonne**	zhwahyur noaehl! bon
Happy New Year!	**Année!**	ahnay

GERMAN

Guide to Pronunciation

Letter	Approximate pronunciation	Symbol	Example	
Consonants				
f, h, k, l, m n, p, t, x	normally pronounced as in English			
b	1) at the end of a word, or between a vowel and a consonant, like **p** in u**p**	p	**ab**	ahp
	2) elsewhere as in English	b	**bis**	biss
c	1) before **e, i, ö,** and **ä,** like **ts** in hi**ts**	ts	**Celsius**	tsehlzeeuss
	2) elsewhere like **c** in **c**at	k	**Café**	kahfay
ch	like **ch** in Scottish lo**ch**	kh	**ich**	ikh
d	1) at the end of a word, or between a vowel and a consonant, like **t** in ea**t**	t	**bald**	bahlt
	2) elsewhere, like **d** in **d**o	d	**durstig**	durstikh
g	1) always hard as in **g**o, but, at the end of a word, often more like **ck** in ta**ck**	g	**gehen**	gayern
		k	**weg**	vehk
	2) when preceded by **i** at the end of a word, like Scottish lo**ch**	kh	**billig**	bilikh
j	like **y** in **y**es	y	**Juni**	yoonee
qu	like **k** followed by **v** in **v**at	kv	**Quark**	kvahrk
r	generally rolled in the back of the mouth	r	**warum**	vahrum

s	1) before or between vowels like **z** in **z**oo	z	**sie**	zee
	2) before **p** and **t**, at the beginning of a syllable like **sh** in **sh**ut	sh	**spät**	shpait
	3) elsewhere, like **s** in **s**it	s/ss	**es ist**	ehss ist
ß	always like **s** in **s**it	ss	**heiß**	highss
sch	like **sh** in **sh**ut	sh	**schnell**	shnehl
tsch	like **ch** in **ch**ip	ch	**deutsch**	doych
tz	like **ts** in hi**ts**	ts	**Platz**	plahts
v	like **f** in **f**or	f	**vier**	feer
w	like **v** in **v**ice	v	**wie**	vee
z	like **ts** in hi**ts**	ts	**zeigen**	tsighgern

Vowels

N.B. In German, vowels are generally long when followed by **h** or by one consonant and short when followed by two or more consonants.

a	1) short, like **u** in c**u**t	ah	**hat**	haht
	2) long, like **a** in c**a**r	ar*	**Abend**	arbernt
ä	1) short, like **e** in l**e**t	eh	**nächst**	nehkhst
	2) long, like **ai** in h**ai**r	ai	**spät**	sphait
e	1) short, like **e** in l**e**t	eh	**sprechen**	shprehkhern
	2) long, like **a** in l**a**te	ay	**gehen**	gayern
	3) in unstressed syllables, like a in about	er*	**bitte**	biter
			geben	gaybern
i	1) short, like **i** in h**i**t	i	**bis**	biss
	2) long, like **ee** in m**ee**t	ee	**ihm**	eem
ie	like **ee** in b**ee**	ee	**hier**	heer
o	1) short, like **o** in g**o**t	o	**voll**	fol
	2) long, like **o** in n**o**te	oa	**ohne**	oaner
ö	like **ur** in f**ur** (long or short)	ur*	**können**	kurnern
u	1) short, like **oo** in f**oo**t	u	**Nuß**	nuss
	2) long, like **oo** in m**oo**n	oo	**gut**	goot
ü	like French **u** in **u**ne; no English equivalent. Round your lips and try to say **ea** as in m**ea**n	ew	**über**	ewberr
y	like German **ü**	ew	**Symphonie**	zewmfoanee

Diphthongs

ai, ay, ei, ey	like **igh** in h**igh**	igh	**mein**	mighn
au	like **ow** in n**ow**	ow	**auf**	owf
äu, eu	like **oy** in b**oy**	oy	**neu**	noy

* The r should not be pronounced when reading this transcription.

Some basic expressions

Yes.	**Ja.**	yar
No.	**Nein.**	nighn
Please.	**Bitte.**	**bi**ter
Thank you.	**Danke.**	**dahng**ker
Thank you very much.	**Vielen Dank.**	**fee**lern dahngk
That's all right.	**Gern geschehen.**	gairn ger**shay**ern

Greetings

Good morning.	**Guten Morgen.**	**goo**tern **mor**gern
Good afternoon.	**Guten Tag.**	**goo**tern targ
Good evening.	**Guten Abend.**	**goo**tern **ar**bernt
Good night.	**Gute Nacht.**	**goo**ter nahkht
Good-bye.	**Auf Wiedersehen.**	owf **vee**derrzayern
See you later.	**Auf bald.**	owf bahlt
This is Mr....	**Das ist Herr ...**	dahss ist hair
This is Mrs....	**Das ist Frau ...**	dahss ist frow
This is Miss ...	**Das ist Fräulein ...**	dahss ist **froy**lighn
I'm very pleased to meet you.	**Sehr erfreut.**	zair ehr**froyt**
How are you?	**Wie geht es Ihnen?**	vee gayt ehss **ee**nern
Very well, thank you. And you?	**Sehr gut, danke. Und Ihnen?**	zair goot **dahng**ker. unt **ee**nern
Fine.	**Gut.**	goot
Excuse me.	**Verzeihung.**	fehr**tsig**hung

Questions

Where?	**Wo?**	voa
Where is ... ?	**Wo ist ... ?**	voa ist
Where are ... ?	**Wo sind ... ?**	voa zint
When?	**Wann?**	vahn
What?	**Was?**	vahss
How?	**Wie?**	vee
How much?	**Wieviel?**	vee**feel**
How many?	**Wie viele?**	vee**fee**ler

Who?	**Wer?**	vair
Why?	**Warum?**	vah**rum**
Which?	**Welcher/Welche/ Welches?**	**vehl**kherr/**vehl**kher/ **vehl**kherss
What do you call this?	**Wie heißt dies?**	vee highst deess
What do you call that?	**Wie heißt das?**	vee highst dahss
What does this mean?	**Was bedeutet dies?**	vahss ber**doy**tert deess
What does that mean?	**Was bedeutet das?**	vahss ber**doy**tert dahss

Do you speak ...?

Do you speak English?	**Sprechen Sie Englisch?**	shprehkhern zee ehnglish
Do you speak German?	**Sprechen Sie Deutsch?**	shprehkhern zee doych
Do you speak French?	**Sprechen Sie Französisch?**	shprehkhern zee frahnt**sur**zish
Do you speak Spanish?	**Sprechen Sie Spanisch?**	shprehkhern zee **shpar**nish
Do you speak Italian?	**Sprechen Sie Italienisch?**	shprehkhern zee itahly**ay**nish
Could you speak more slowly, please?	**Könnten Sie bitte langsamer sprechen?**	kurntern zee biter lahngzarmerr shprehkhern
Please point to the phrase in the book.	**Bitte zeigen Sie mir den Satz im Buch.**	biter tsighgern zee meer dayn zahts im bookh
Just a minute. I'll see if I can find it in this book.	**Einen Augenblick, ich sehe mal nach, ob ich es in diesem Buch finde.**	**igh**nern **ow**gernblik ikh zayer mahl nahkh op ikh ehss in **dee**zerm bookh finder
I understand.	**Ich verstehe.**	ikh fehr**shtay**er
I don't understand.	**Ich verstehe nicht.**	ikh fehr**shtay**er nikht

Can ...?

Can I have ...?	**Kann ich ... haben?**	kahn ikh ... **har**bern
Can we have ...?	**Können wir ... haben?**	kurnern veer ... **har**bern

Can you show me . . . ?	**Können Sie mir . . . zeigen?**	kurnern zee meer . . . tsighgern
Can you tell me . . . ?	**Können Sie mir sagen . . . ?**	kurnern zee meer zargern
Can you help me, please?	**Können Sie mir bitte helfen?**	kurnern zee meer biter hehlfern

Wanting

I'd like . . .	**Ich hätte gern . . .**	ikh hehter gairn
We'd like . . .	**Wir hätten gern . . .**	veer hehtern gairn
Please give me . . .	**Geben Sie mir bitte . . .**	gaybern zee meer biter
Give it to me, please.	**Bitte geben Sie es mir.**	biter gaybern zee ehss meer
Please bring me . . .	**Bringen Sie mir bitte . . .**	bringern zee meer biter
Bring it to me, please.	**Bitte bringen Sie es mir.**	biter bringern zee ehss meer
I'm hungry.	**Ich habe Hunger.**	ikh harber hunger
I'm thirsty.	**Ich habe Durst.**	ikh harber durst
I'm tired.	**Ich bin müde.**	ikh bin mewder
I'm lost.	**Ich habe mich verirrt.**	ikh harber mikh fehrirrt
It's important.	**Es ist wichtig.**	ehss ist vikhtik
It's urgent.	**Es ist dringend.**	ehss ist dringernt
Hurry up!	**Beeilen Sie sich!**	berighlern zee zikh

It is/There is . . .

It is/It's . . .	**Es ist . . .**	ehss ist
Is it . . . ?	**Ist es . . . ?**	ist ehss
It isn't . . .	**Es ist nicht . . .**	ehss ist nikht
There is/There are . . .	**Es gibt . . .**	ehss gibt
Is there/Are there . . . ?	**Gibt es . . . ?**	gibt ehss
There isn't/There aren't . . .	**Es gibt keinen/Es gibt keine/Es gibt kein . . .**	ehss gibt kighnern/ehss gibt kighner/ehss gibt kighn

GERMAN

There isn't any/	**Es gibt keinen/Es**	ehss gibt **kigh**nern/ehss
There aren't any.	**gibt keine/Es gibt**	gibt **kigh**ner/ehss gibt
	keins.	kighnss

A few common words

big/small	**groß/klein**	groass/klighn
quick/slow	**schnell/langsam**	shnehl/**lahng**zarm
early/late	**früh/spät**	frew/shpait
cheap/expensive	**billig/teuer**	bilikh/**toy**err
near/far	**nah/weit**	nar/vight
hot/cold	**heiß/kalt**	highss/kahlt
full/empty	**voll/leer**	fol/layr
easy/difficult	**leicht/schwierig**	lighkht/**shvee**rikh
heavy/light	**schwer/leicht**	shvair/lighkht
open/shut	**offen/geschlossen**	ofern/ger**shloss**ern
right/wrong	**richtig/falsch**	**rikh**tikh/fahlsh
old/new	**alt/neu**	ahlt/noy
old/young	**alt/jung**	ahlt/yung
beautiful/ugly	**schön/häßlich**	shurn/**hehss**likh
good/bad	**gut/schlecht**	goot/shlehkht
better/worse	**besser/schlechter**	**behss**err/**shlekh**terr

Some prepositions and a few more useful words

at	**an**	ahn
on	**auf**	owf
in	**in**	in
to	**zu**	tsoo
from	**von**	fon
inside	**drinnen**	**drin**nern
outside	**draußen**	**drow**ssern
up	**hinauf**	hin**owf**
down	**hinunter**	hin**un**ter
before	**vor**	fawr
after	**nach**	nahkh
with	**mit**	mit
without	**ohne**	**oa**ner
through	**durch**	doorkh
towards	**gegen**	**gay**gern
until	**bis**	biss
during	**während**	**vai**rernt
and	**und**	unt
or	**oder**	**oa**derr
not	**nicht**	nikht
nothing	**nichts**	nikhts
none	**kein**	kighn

very	**sehr**	zair
also	**auch**	owkh
soon	**bald**	bahlt
perhaps	**vielleicht**	feelighkht
here	**hier**	heer
there	**dort**	dort
now	**jetzt**	yehtst
then	**dann**	dahn

Arrival

Your passport, please.	**Ihren Paß, bitte.**	eerern pahss biter
Here it is.	**Hier, bitte.**	heer biter
Have you anything to declare?	**Haben Sie etwas zu vorzollen?**	harbern zee ehtvahss tsoo fehrtsolern
No, nothing at all.	**Nein, gar nichts.**	nighn garr nikhts
Porter!	**Gepäckträger!**	gerpehktraigerr
Can you help me with my luggage, please?	**Können Sie mir mit meinem Gepäck helfen, bitte?**	kurnern zee meer mit mighnerm gerpehk hehlfern biter
That's my suitcase.	**Das ist mein Koffer.**	dahss ist mighn koferr
Where's the bus to the centre of town, please?	**Wo ist der Bus zum Stadtzentrum, bitte?**	voa ist dehr buss tsum shtahttsehntrum biter
This way, please.	**Hier durch, bitte.**	heer doorkh biter

Changing money

| Can you change a traveller's cheque, please? | **Können Sie einen Reisescheck ein-lösen, bitte?** | kurnern zee ighnern righzershehk ighnlurzern biter |
| Where's the nearest bank, please? | **Wo ist die nächste Bank, bitte?** | voa ist dee nehkhster bahngk biter |

Car rental

I'd like a car.	**Ich möchte einen Wagen.**	ikh murkhter ighnern vargern
For how long?	**Für wie lange?**	fewr vee lahnger
A day/Four days/ A week/Two weeks.	**Einen Tag/Vier Tage/Eine Woche/ Zwei Wochen.**	ighnern targ/feer targer/ighner vokher/ tsvigh vokhern

GERMAN

Taxi

Where can I get a taxi?	**Wo finde ich ein Taxi?**	voa **finder** ikh ighn **tahksee**
What's the fare to ...?	**Was kostet es bis ...?**	vahss **kosstert** ehss biss
Take me to this address, please.	**Fahren Sie mich bitte zu dieser Adresse.**	**farrern** zee mikh **biter** tsoo **deezerr** ah**drehsser**
I'm in a hurry.	**Ich habe es eilig.**	ikh **harber** ehss **ighlikh**
Could you drive more slowly, please?	**Könnten Sie bitte langsamer fahren?**	**kurntern** zee **biter lahngzarmerr farrern**

Hotel and other accommodation

My name is ...	**Mein Name ist ...**	mighn **narmer** ist
Have you a reservation?	**Haben Sie vorbestellt?**	**harbern** zee **forbershtehlt**
Yes, here's the confirmation.	**Ja, hier ist die Bestätigung.**	yar heer ist dee ber**shtaitigung**
I'd like ...	**Ich hätte gern ...**	ikh **hehter** gairn
I'd like a single room/a double room.	**Ich hätte gern ein Einzelzimmer/ein Doppelzimmer.**	ikh **hehter** gairn ighn **ighntserltsimerr**/ighn **doperltsimerr**
a room with a bath/with a shower	**ein Zimmer mit Bad/mit Dusche**	ighn **tsimerr** mit bart/mit **dusher**

How much?

What's the price per night/per week/per month?	**Wieviel kostet es pro Nacht/pro Woche/pro Monat?**	vee**feel kosstert** ehss proa nahkht/proa **vokher**/proa **moanart**
May I see the room?	**Kann ich das Zimmer sehen?**	kahn ikh dahss **tsimerr zayern**
I'm sorry, I don't like it.	**Bedaure, es gefällt mir nicht.**	ber**dowrer** ehss ger**fehlt** meer nikht
Yes, that's fine. I'll take it.	**Ja, sehr gut. Ich nehme es.**	yar zair goot. ikh **naymer** ehss
What's my room number, please?	**Welche Zimmernummer habe ich, bitte?**	**vehlkher tsimerrnumerr harber** ikh **biter**
Number 123.	**Nummer 123.**	**numerr** 123

Service, please

Who is it?	**Wer ist da?**	vair ist dar
Just a minute.	**Einen Augenblick, bitte.**	**igh**nern **ow**gernblik **bi**ter
Come in! The door's open.	**Herein! Die Tür ist offen.**	hair**ighn**! dee tewr ist **o**fern
May we have breakfast in our room?	**Können wir in unserem Zimmer frühstücken?**	**kur**nern veer in **un**zererrem **tsi**merr **frew**shtewkern

Breakfast

I'll have . . .	**Ich möchte . . .**	ikh **murkh**ter
I'll have some fruit juice.	**Ich möchte einen Fruchtsaft.**	ikh **murkh**ter **igh**nern **frookh**tzahft
a boiled egg	**ein gekochtes Ei**	ighn ger**kokh**terss igh
a fried egg	**ein Spiegelei**	ighn **shpee**gerligh
some bacon/some ham	**Speck/Schinken**	shpehk/**shing**kern
some toast	**Toast**	toast
a pot of tea	**ein Kännchen Tee**	ighn **kehn**khern tay
a cup of tea	**eine Tasse Tee**	**igh**ner **tah**sser tay
some coffee	**Kaffee**	**kah**fay
some chocolate	**Schokolade**	shoakoa**lar**der
more butter	**noch etwas Butter**	nokh **eht**vahss **bu**terr
some hot water	**etwas heißes Wasser**	**eht**vahss **high**sserss **vah**sserr

Difficulties

The central heating doesn't work.	**Die Zentralheizung funktioniert nicht.**	dee tsehn**trarl**hightsung fungktseeoa**neert** nikht
the light/the socket	**das Licht/die Steckdose**	dahss likht/dee **shtehk**doazer
the tap/the toilet	**der Wasserhahn/die Toilette**	dair **vah**sserrharn/dee toy**leh**ter
There's no hot water.	**Es kommt kein warmes Wasser.**	ehss komt kighn **vahr**merss **vah**sserr
May I see the manager, please?	**Kann ich bitte den Direktor sprechen?**	kahn ikh **bi**ter dayn dee**rehk**tawr **shpreh**khern

Telephone—Mail

There's a call for you.	**Hier ist ein Anruf für Sie.**	heer ist ighn **ahn**roof fewr zee

GERMAN

Hold the line, please.	**Bitte bleiben Sie am Apparat.**	biter **bligh**bern zee ahm ahpah**rart**
Operator, I've been cut off.	**Fräulein, ich bin unterbrochen worden.**	**froy**lighn ikh bin unterr**brokh**ern **vor**dern
Did anyone telephone me?	**Hat mich jemand angerufen?**	haht mikh **yay**mahnt **ahn**gerroofern
Is there any mail for me?	**Ist Post für mich da?**	ist post fewr mikh dar
Are there any messages for me?	**Hat jemand eine Nachricht für mich hinterlassen?**	haht **yay**mahnt **igh**ner **nahkh**rikht fewr mikh hinter**lahss**ern

Checking out

May I have my bill, please?	**Kann ich bitte meine Rechnung haben?**	kahn ikh **bit**er **migh**ner **rehkh**nung **hah**bern
We're in a great hurry.	**Wir haben es sehr eilig.**	veer **hah**bern ehss zair **igh**likh
It's been a very enjoyable stay.	**Der Aufenthalt war sehr angenehm.**	dair **owf**ehnthahlt varr zair **ahn**gernaym

Eating out

Good evening, sir/Good evening, madam.	**Guten Abend, mein Herr/Guten Abend, gnädige Frau.**	**goot**ern **arb**ernt mighn hair/**goot**ern **arb**ernt **gnai**diger frow
Good evening. I'd like a table for two, please.	**Guten Abend. Ich hätte gern einen Tisch für zwei Personen, bitte.**	**goot**ern **arb**ernt. ikh **heh**ter gairn **igh**nern tish fewr tsvigh pehr**zo**anern **bit**er
Do you have a fixed-price menu?	**Haben Sie ein Menü?**	**harb**ern zee ighn meh**new**
May I see the à la carte menu?	**Kann ich die Speisekarte sehen?**	kahn ikh dee **shpigh**zerkahrter **zay**ern
May we have an ashtray, please?	**Können wir bitte einen Aschenbecher haben?**	**kurn**ern veer **bit**er **igh**nern **ahsh**ernbehkher **harb**ern
some bread	**etwas Brot**	**eht**vahss broat
a fork	**eine Gabel**	**igh**ner **garb**erl
a knife	**ein Messer**	ighn **mehss**err
a spoon	**einen Löffel**	**igh**nern **lurf**erl
a plate	**einen Teller**	**igh**nern **tehl**err

a glass	**ein Glas**	ighn glahss
a napkin	**eine Serviette**	**ighn**ner zairveee**ehter**
another chair	**noch einen Stuhl**	nokh **ighn**ern shtool
Where's the gentle-men's toilet (men's room)?	**Wo ist die Herren-toilette?**	voa ist dee **hehrern-**twahlehter
Where's the ladies' toilet (ladies' room)?	**Wo ist die Damen-toilette?**	voa ist dee **darmern-**twahlehter

Appetizers

I'd like some . . .	**Ich hätte gern . . .**	ikh **hehter** gairn
I'd like some assorted appetizers.	**Ich hätte gern gemischte Vor-speisen.**	ikh **hehter** gairn germish-ter **fawr**shpighzern
orange juice	**Orangensaft**	oa**rahng**zhernzahft
ham	**Schinken**	**shing**kern
melon	**Melone**	may**lo**aner
pâté	**Pastete**	pahss**tay**ter
smoked salmon	**geräucherten Lachs**	ger**roy**kherrtern lahks
shrimps (shrimp)	**Krevetten**	krer**veh**tern

Soup

Have you any . . . ?	**Haben Sie . . . ?**	**har**bern zee
Have you any chicken soup?	**Haben Sie Hühner-suppe?**	**har**bern zee **hewn**errzuper
vegetable soup	**Gemüsesuppe**	ger**mew**zerzuper
onion soup	**Zwiebelsuppe**	**tsvee**berlzuper

Fish

I'd like some . . .	**Ich hätte gern . . .**	ikh **hehter** gairn
I'd like some fish.	**Ich hätte gern Fisch.**	ikh **hehter** gairn fish
sole	**Seezunge**	**zayt**sunger
trout	**Forelle**	fo**rehler**
lobster	**Hummer**	**humerr**
crayfish	**Krebs**	**krayps**
prawns	**Garnelen**	gahr**nay**lern
I'd like it . . .	**Ich hätte es gern . . .**	ikh **hehter** ehss gairn
I'd like it steamed.	**Ich hätte es gern gedämpft.**	ikh **hehter** ehss gairn ger**dehmpft**
grilled	**gegrillt**	ger**grillt**
boiled	**gekocht**	ger**kokht**

GERMAN

| baked | **gebacken** | gerbahkern |
| fried | **in der Pfanne gebraten** | in dair **pfah**ner gerbrar-tern |

Meat—Poultry—Game

I'd like some . . .	**Ich hätte gern . . .**	ikh **hehter** gairn
I'd like some beef.	**Ich hätte gern Rindfleisch.**	ikh **hehter** gairn **rint**flighsh
a beef steak	**ein Beefsteak**	ighn **beef**stayk
some roast beef	**Roastbeef**	**rost**beef
a veal cutlet	**ein Kalbskotelett**	ighn **kahlps**kaoterleht
mutton	**Hammelfleisch**	**hah**merlflighsh
lamb	**Lammfleisch**	**lahm**flighsh
a pork chop	**ein Schweins-kotelett**	ighn **shvighns**koaterleht
roast pork	**Schweinebraten**	**shvigh**nerbrartern
hare	**Hase**	**harzer**
chicken	**Huhn**	hoon
roast chicken	**Brathühnchen**	**brart**hewnkhern
duck	**Ente**	**ehnter**
How do you like your meat?	**Wie möchten Sie Ihr Fleisch?**	vee **murkh**tern zee eer flighsh
rare	**halbroh**	**hahl**proa
medium	**mittel**	**miter**l
well done	**durchgebraten**	**doorkh**gerbrartern

Vegetables

What vegetables have you got?	**Was für Gemüse haben Sie?**	vahss fewr ger**mew**zer **har**bern zee
I'd like some . . .	**Ich hätte gern . . .**	ikh **hehter** gairn
I'd like some asparagus.	**Ich hätte gern Spargel.**	ikh **hehter** gairn **shparr**gerl
green beans	**grüne Bohnen**	**grew**ner **boa**nern
mushrooms	**Pilze**	**pil**tser
carrots	**Karotten**	kah**rotern**
onions	**Zwiebeln**	**tsvee**berln
red cabbage	**Rotkohl**	**roat**koal
spinach	**Spinat**	shp**inart**
rice	**Reis**	righss
peas	**Erbsen**	**airp**sern
tomatoes	**Tomaten**	toa**mar**tern
green salad	**grünen Salat**	**grew**nern zah**lart**
potatoes	**Kartoffeln**	kahr**tofer**ln

Desserts

Nothing more, thanks.	**Nein danke, nichts mehr.**	nighn **dahng**ker nikhts mair
Just a small portion, please.	**Nur eine kleine Portion, bitte.**	noor **ighn**er **kligh**ner portsee**oan** **bi**ter
Have you any ice-cream?	**Haben Sie Eis?**	**har**bern zee **igh**ss
fruit salad	**Obstsalat**	**oapst**zahlart
fresh fruit	**frisches Obst**	**frish**erss oapst
cheese	**Käse**	**kai**zer

Drink

What would you like to drink?	**Was möchten Sie gern trinken?**	vahss **murkh**tern zee gairn **tring**kern
I'll have a beer, please.	**Ich nehme ein Bier, bitte.**	ikh **nay**mer ighn beer **bi**ter
I'll have a whisky, please.	**Ich möchte einen Whisky, bitte.**	ikh **murkh**te **igh**nern **viss**kee **bi**ter

Wine

I'd like a bottle of wine.	**Ich möchte eine Flasche Wein.**	ikh **murkh**ter **igh**ner **flah**sher vighn
red wine	**Rotwein**	**roat**vighn
rosé wine	**Roséwein**	roa**zay**vighn
white wine	**Weißwein**	**vighss**vighn
Cheers!	**Zum Wohl!**	tsum voal

The bill (check)

May I have the bill (check) please?	**Die Rechnung, bitte.**	dee **rehkh**nung **bi**ter
Is service included?	**Ist Bedienung inbegriffen?**	ist berdee**nung** **in**bergrifern
Everything's included.	**Alles ist inbegriffen.**	**ah**lerss ist **in**bergrifern
Thank you, that was a very good meal.	**Danke, das Essen war sehr gut.**	**dang**ker dahss **eh**ssern varr zair goot

GERMAN

GERMAN

Travelling

Where's the railway station, please?	**Wo ist der Bahnhof, bitte?**	voa ist dair **barnhoaf** biter
Where's the ticket office, please?	**Wo ist der Fahrkartenschalter, bitte?**	voa ist dair **farrkahrternshahlterr** biter
I'd like a ticket to ...	**Ich möchte eine Fahrkarte nach ...**	ikh **murkhter** ighner **farrkahrter** nahhk
First or second class?	**Erste oder zweite Klasse?**	**airster oaderr tsvighter klahsser**
First class, please.	**Erste Klasse, bitte.**	**airster klahsser** biter
Single or return (one way or round-trip)?	**Einfach oder hin und zurück?**	**ighnfahkh oaderr** hin unt **tsurewk**
Do I have to change trains?	**Muß ich umsteigen?**	muss ikh **umshtighern**
What platform does the train leave from?	**Auf welchem Bahnsteig fährt der Zug ab?**	owf **vehlkherm barnshtighg** fairt dair **tsoog** ahp
Where's the nearest underground (subway) station?	**Wo ist die nächste U-Bahnstation?**	voa ist dee **nehkhster oobarnshtahtsioan**
Where's the bus station, please?	**Wo ist der Busbahnhof, bitte?**	voa ist dair **bussbarnhoaf** biter
When's the first bus to ...?	**Wann fährt der erste Bus nach ...?**	vahn fairt dair **ehrster** buss nahhk
the last bus	**der letzte Bus**	dair **lehtster** buss
the next bus	**der nächste Bus**	der **nehkhster** buss
Please let me off at the next stop.	**Bitte lassen Sie mich an der nächsten Haltestelle aussteigen.**	biter **lahssern** zee mikh ahn dair **nehkhstern hahltershtehler owssshtighern**

Relaxing

What's on at the cinema (movies)?	**Was gibt es im Kino zu sehen?**	vahss gibt ehss im **keenoa** tsoo **zayern**
What's on at the theatre?	**Was gibt es im Theater?**	vahss gibt ehss im **tayarter**
What time does the film begin? And the play?	**Wann beginnt der Film? Und das Stück?**	vahn **bergint** dair film? unt dahss **shtewk**

Are there any tickets for tonight?	**Gibt es noch Karten für heute abend?**	gibt ehss nokh **kahr**tern fewr **hoy**ter **arbernt**
Where can we go dancing?	**Wohin können wir tanzen gehen?**	voahin **kur**nern veer **tahn**tsern **gay**ern
Would you like to dance?	**Darf ich bitten?**	dahrf ikh **bi**tern

Introductions

How do you do?	**Guten Tag.**	**goo**tern targ
How are you?	**Wie geht es Ihnen?**	vee gayt ehss **ee**nern
Very well, thank you. And you?	**Sehr gut, danke. Und Ihnen?**	zair goot **dahng**ker. unt **ee**nern
May I introduce Miss Philips?	**Darf ich Fräulein Philips vorstellen?**	dahrf ikh **froy**lighn filips **for**shtehlern
My name is . . .	**Ich heiße . . .**	ikh **high**sser
I'm very pleased to meet you.	**Sehr erfreut.**	zair ehr**froyt**
How long have you been here?	**Wie lange sind Sie schon hier?**	vee **lahng**er zint zee shoan heer
It was nice meeting you.	**Es war mir ein Vergnügen.**	ehss varr meer ighn fehr**gnew**gern

Dating

Would you like a cigarette?	**Möchten Sie eine Zigarette?**	**murkh**tern zee **igh**ner tsigah**reh**ter
May I get you a drink?	**Darf ich Ihnen etwas zu trinken bestellen?**	dahrf ikh **ee**nern **eht**vahss; tsoo **tring**kern ber**shteh**lern
Do you have a light, please?	**Haben Sie Feuer, bitte?**	**hah**bern zee **foy**err **bi**ter
Are you waiting for someone?	**Warten Sie auf jemanden?**	**vahr**tern zee owf **yay**mahndern
Are you free this evening?	**Sind Sie heute abend frei?**	zint zee **hoy**ter **arbernt** frigh
Where shall we meet?	**Wo treffen wir uns?**	voa **treh**fern veer unss
What time shall I meet you?	**Wann treffe ich Sie?**	vahn **treh**fer ikh zee
May I take you home?	**Darf ich Sie nach Hause bringen?**	dahrf ikh zee nahkh **how**zer **bring**ern

GERMAN

GERMAN

Thank you, it's been a wonderful evening.	**Danke, es war ein wunderbarer Abend.**	dahngker ehss varr ighn vunderrbarrerr arbernt
What's your telephone number?	**Wie ist Ihre Telephonnummer?**	vee ist eerer tailaifoan-numerr
Do you live alone?	**Wohnen Sie allein?**	voanern zee ahlighn
What time is your last train?	**Wann fährt Ihr letzter Zug?**	vahn fairt eer lehtsterr tsoog
Good-night...	**Gute Nacht...**	gooter nahkht

Banks

Where's the nearest bank, please?	**Wo ist die nächste Bank, bitte?**	voa ist dee nehkhster bahngk biter
Where can I cash some traveller's cheques?	**Wo kann ich Reiseschecks ein-lösen?**	voa kahn ikh righzer-shehks ighnlurzern
What time does the bank open? What time does it close?	**Wann öffnet die Bank? Wann schließt sie?**	vahn urfnert dee bahngk? vahn shleest zee
I'm expecting some money from home. Has it arrived?	**Ich erwarte Geld von zu Hause. Ist es eingetroffen?**	ikh airvahrter gehlt fon tsoo howzer. ist ehss ighngertrofern
Can you give me some small change, please?	**Können Sie mir bitte Kleingeld geben?**	kurnern zee meer biter klighngehlt gaybern

Shops, stores and services

Where is the nearest chemist's (pharmacy)?	**Wo ist die nächste Apotheke?**	voa ist dee nehkhster ahpoatayker
the nearest hair-dresser's	**der nächste Friseur**	dair nehkhster frizurr
the photo shop	**das Photogeschäft**	dahss foatoagershehft
the jeweller's	**der Juwelier**	dair yooverleer
the department store	**das Warenhaus**	dahss varrernhowss
the police station	**die Polizeiwache**	dee poalitsighvahkher
the garage	**die Garage**	dee gahrarzher
How do I get there?	**Wie komme ich dorthin?**	vee komer ikh dorthin
Is it within walking distance?	**Kann man zu Fuß gehen?**	kahn mahn tsoo fooss gayern

Service

Can you help me, please?	**Können Sie mir helfen, bitte?**	kurnern zee meer **hehl**fern **bi**ter
Can you show me this? And that, too.	**Können Sie mir dies zeigen? Und das ebenfalls.**	kurnern zee meer deess tsigh**g**ern? unt dahss **ay**bernfahlss
It's too expensive/ too big/too small.	**Es ist zu teuer/zu groß/zu klein.**	ehss ist tsoo **toy**err/tsoo groass/tsoo klighn
Can you show me some more?	**Können Sie mir noch mehr zeigen?**	kurnern zee meer nokh mair **tsigh**gern
something better something cheaper	**etwas Besseres etwas Billigeres**	**eht**vahss **behs**serrerss **eht**vahss **bi**ligerrerss
How much is this? And that?	**Wieviel kostet dies? Und das?**	veefeel **koss**tert deess? unt dahss
It's not quite what I want.	**Es ist nicht ganz das, was ich möchte.**	ehss ist nikht gahnts dahss vahss ikh **murkh**ter
I like it.	**Es gefällt mir.**	ehss ger**fehlt** meer

Chemist's (Pharmacy)

I'd like something for a cold/for a cough/for travel sickness.	**Ich möchte etwas gegen eine Erkältung/gegen Husten/gegen Reisekrankheit.**	ikh **murkh**ter **eht**vahss **gay**gern **igh**ner ehr**kehl**tung/**gay**gern **hooss**tern/**gay**gern **righ**zerkrahngkhight
Can you recommend something for hay-fever/for sunburn?	**Können Sie mir etwas gegen Heufieber/gegen Sonnenbrand empfehlen?**	kurnern zee meer **eht**vahss **gay**gern **hoy**feeberr/ **gay**gern **zo**nernbrahnt ehmp**fay**lern

Toiletry

May I have some razor blades?	**Kann ich Rasierklingen haben?**	kahn ikh rah**zeer**klingern **har**bern
some shaving cream some toothpaste	**Rasiercreme Zahnpasta**	raze**er**kraym **tsarn**pahstah
I'd like some soap.	**Ich hätte gern Seife.**	ikh **heh**ter gairn **zigh**fer
some suntan oil	**Sonnenöl**	**zo**nernurl

At the barber's

I'd like a haircut, please.	**Ich möchte mir das Haar schneiden lassen, bitte.**	ikh **murkh**ter meer dahss harr **shnigh**dern **lahss**ern

GERMAN

| Short/Leave it long. | **Kurz/Lassen Sie es lang.** | koorts/**lahss**ern zee ehss lahng |
| A razor cut, please. | **Einen Messer-schnitt, bitte.** | **igh**nern **mehss**errshnit biter |

At the hairdresser's

I'd like a shampoo and set, please.	**Waschen und legen, bitte.**	**vah**shern unt **lay**gern biter
I'd like a bleach.	**Ich möchte eine Aufhellung.**	ikh **murkh**ter **igh**ner **owf**hehlung
a permanent	**eine Dauerwelle**	**igh**ner **dow**errvehler
a colour rinse	**eine Farbspülung**	**igh**ner **fahrp**shpewlung
a manicure	**eine Maniküre**	**igh**ner **mahni**kewrrer

Photography

| I'd like a film for this camera. | **Ich möchte einen Film für diese Kamera.** | ikh **murkh**ter **igh**nern film fewr **dee**zer **kah**merrah |
| This camera doesn't work. | **Diese Kamera ist defekt.** | **dee**zer **kah**merrah ist dai**fehkt** |

At the post office

| Where's the nearest post office, please? | **Wo ist das nächste Postamt, bitte?** | voa ist dahss **nehkh**ster **post**ahmt biter |
| I'd like to send this by express (special delivery)/by air mail. | **Ich möchte dies durch Eilboten/ mit Luftpost schicken.** | ikh **murkh**ter deess doorkh **ighl**boatern/ mit **luft**post **shik**ern |

Service stations

Where is the nearest service station, please?	**Wo ist die nächste Tankstelle, bitte?**	voa ist dee **nehkh**ster **tahngk**shtehler biter
Fill her up, please.	**Voll, bitte.**	fol biter
Check the oil, please.	**Kontrollieren Sie bitte den Ölstand.**	kontro**leer**ern zee biter dayn **url**shtahnt
Would you check the tyres?	**Würden Sie bitte die Reifen prüfen?**	**vewr**dern zee biter dee **righ**fern **prewf**ern

Street directions

Can you show me on the map where I am?	Können Sie mir auf der Karte zeigen, wo ich bin?	kurnern zee meer owf dair kahrter tsighgern voa ikh bin
You're on the wrong road.	Sie sind auf der falschen Straße.	zee zint owf dair fahlshern shtrarsser
Go back to...	Fahren Sie zurück nach...	farrern zee tsoorewk nahkh
Go straight ahead.	Fahren Sie geradeaus.	farrern zee gerrarderowss
It's on the left/on the right.	Es ist linker Hand/rechter Hand.	ehss ist lingker hahnt/rehkhterr hahnt

Accidents

May I use your telephone?	Darf ich Ihr Telephon benutzen?	dahrf ikh eer tailaifoan bernewtsern
Call a doctor quickly.	Rufen Sie schnell einen Arzt.	roofern zee shnehl ighnern ahrtst
Call an ambulance.	Rufen Sie einen Krankenwagen.	roofern zee ighnern krahngkernvargern
Please call the police.	Rufen Sie bitte die Polizei.	roofern zee biter dee poalitsigh

Numbers

zero	null	nool
one	eins	ighnss
two	zwei	tsvigh
three	drei	drigh
four	vier	feer
five	fünf	fewnf
six	sechs	zehks
seven	sieben	zeebern
eight	acht	ahkht
nine	neun	noyn
ten	zehn	tsayn
eleven	elf	ehlf
twelve	zwölf	tsvurlf
thirteen	dreizehn	drightsayn
fourteen	vierzehn	feertsayn
fifteen	fünfzehn	fewnftsayn
sixteen	sechzehn	zehkhtsayn
seventeen	siebzehn	zeeptsayn
eighteen	achtzehn	ahkhtsayn
nineteen	neunzehn	noyntsayn

GERMAN

twenty	**zwanzig**	tsvahntsikh
twenty-one	**einundzwanzig**	ighnunttsvahntsikh
thirty	**dreißig**	drighssikh
forty	**vierzig**	feertsikh
fifty	**fünfzig**	fewnftsikh
sixty	**sechzig**	zehkhtsikh
seventy	**siebzig**	zeeptsikh
eighty	**achtzig**	ahkhtsikh
ninety	**neunzig**	noyntsikh
one hundred	**hundert**	hunderrt
one thousand	**tausend**	towzernt
ten thousand	**zehntausend**	tsayntowzernt

Days

It's Sunday.	**Es ist Sonntag.**	ehss ist zontark
Monday	**Montag**	moantark
Tuesday	**Dienstag**	deensstark
Wednesday	**Mittwoch**	mitvokh
Thursday	**Donnerstag**	donerrsstark
Friday	**Freitag**	frightark
Saturday	**Sonnabend**	zonarbernt
yesterday	**gestern**	gehssterrn
today	**heute**	hoyter
tomorrow	**morgen**	morgern
morning/afternoon	**Vormittag/Nach-mittag**	formitark/nahkhmitark
evening/night	**Abend/Nacht**	arbernt/nahkht

Months

January	**Januar**	yahnooarr
February	**Februar**	faybrooarr
March	**März**	mairts
April	**April**	ahpril
May	**Mai**	migh
June	**Juni**	yoonee
July	**Juli**	yoolee
August	**August**	owgust
September	**September**	zehptehmberr
October	**Oktober**	oktoaberr
November	**November**	noavehmberr
December	**Dezember**	daytsehmberr
Merry Christmas!	**Fröhliche Weihnach-ten! Glückliches Neues Jahr!**	frurlikher vighnahkhtern!
Happy New Year!		glewklikherss noyerss yarr

GREEK

Guide to Pronunciation

Letter	Approximate pronunciation	Symbol	Example	

Vowels

α	like the vowel in car, but pronounced further forward in the mouth	ah	άρωμα	**ah**romah
ε	like **e** in sell	eh	μέρα	**meh**rah
η, ι, υ	like **ee** in meet	ee	κύριος	**kee**reeoss
ο, ω	like **o** in got	o	παρακαλώ	pahrahkahl**o**

Consonants

β	like **v** in vine	v	βιβλίο	vee**vl**eeo
γ	1) before α, ο, ω, ου, and consonants, a voiced version of the **ch** sound in Scottish loch	ĝ	μεγάλος	meh**ĝah**loss
	2) before ε, αι, η, ι, υ, ει, οι, like **y** in yet	y	γεμάτος	yeh**mah**toss
δ	like **th** in this	dh	δέν	**dh**ehn
ζ	like **z** in zoo	z	ζεστός	**z**estoss
θ	like **th** in thing	th	θά	**th**ah
κ	like **k** in kit	k	καλός	**k**ah**l**oss
λ	like **l** in lemon	l	λάθος	**l**ah**th**oss
μ	like **m** in man	m	μέσα	**meh**ssah

ν	like **n** in **n**ew	n	νέος	**neh**oss
ξ	like **x** in si**x**	ks	ἔξω	**ehk**so
π	like **p** in **p**ot	p	πρός	pross
ρ	like **r** in **r**ed	r	πρίν	preen
σ, ς	1) before β, γ, δ, ζ, μ, ν, ρ, like **z** in **z**oo	z	κόσμος	**koz**moss
	2) elsewhere, like **s** in **s**ee	s/ss	στό	sto
τ	like **t** in **t**ea	t	τότε	**tot**eh
φ	like **f** in **f**ive	f	φέρτε	**fehr**teh
χ	like **ch** in Scottish lo**ch**	kh	ἄσχημος	**ahss**kheemoss
ψ	like **ps** in dro**psy**	ps	διψῶ	dhee**pso**

Groups of letters

αι	like **e** in g**e**t	eh	εἶναι	**ee**neh
ει, οι	like **ee** in s**ee**	ee	πεῖτε	**pee**teh
ου	like **oo** in r**oo**t	oo	μοῦ	moo
αυ	similar to **ave** in h**ave**	ahv	αὐτό	ahv**to**
ευ	like **ev** in l**ev**el	ehv	Εὐρώπη	ehvro**pee**
γγ	like **ng** in li**ng**er	ngg	Ἀγγλία	ahng**glee**ah
γκ	1) at the beginning of a word like **g** in **g**o	g	γκαμήλα	gah**mee**lah
	2) in the middle of a word, like **ng** in li**ng**er	ngg	ἄγκυρα	**ahng**geerah
γξ	like **nks** in li**nks**	ngks	φάλαγξ	fah**lahngks**
γχ	like **ng** followed by the **ch** of Scottish lo**ch**	ngkh	μελαγ-χολία	mehlahng-**kholee**ah
μπ	1) at the beginning of a word like **b** in **b**eer	b	μπορείτε	bo**ree**teh
	2) in the middle of a word like **mb** in lu**mb**er	mb	᾿Ολυμπος	o**leem**boss
ντ	1) at the beginning of a word, like **d** in **d**ear	d	ντομάτα	do**mah**tah
	2) in the middle of a word, like **nd** in u**nd**er	nd	κέντρο	**kehn**dro
τζ	like **ds** in see**ds**	dz	τζάκι	**dzah**kee

Accent marks

These are written in various ways, e.g., ὰ, ά, or ᾶ, but all of them indicate the stressed syllable. The signs for the "breathing" of initial vowels (α, ἀ) can be ignored. A diaeresis (two dots) written over a letter means that the letter is pronounced separately from the previous one, e.g., καιρός is pronounced keh**ross**, but in Κάϊρο, the α and ι are pronounced separately, **kah**eero.

The alphabet

Here are the characters which comprise the Greek alphabet. The column at left shows the printed capital and small letters, while written letters are shown in the center column. The column at right gives you the name of these letters as pronounced by Greeks.

Α	α	*A*	*α*	**ahl**fah
Β	β	*B*	*b*	**vee**tah
Γ	γ	*Γ*	*γ*	**ghah**mah
Δ	δ	*Δ*	*δ*	**dhehl**tah
Ε	ε	*E*	*ε*	**eh**pseelon
Ζ	ζ	*Z*	*ζ*	**zee**tah
Η	η	*H*	*n*	**ee**tah
Θ	θ	*θ*	*θ*	**thee**tah
Ι	ι	*I*	*ι*	**yee**otah
Κ	κ	*K*	*u*	**kah**pah
Λ	λ	*Λ*	*λ*	**lahm**dhah
Μ	μ	*M*	*μ*	mee
Ν	ν	*N*	*r*	nee
Ξ	ξ	*Ξ*	*ξ*	ksee
Ο	ο	*O*	*o*	o**mee**kron
Π	π	*Π*	*ω*	pee
Ρ	ρ	*P*	*ρ*	ro
Σ	σ ς	*Σ*	*ς s*	**seegh**mah
Τ	τ	*T*	*τ*	tahf
Υ	υ	*Y*	*υ*	**ee**pseelon
Φ	φ	*Φ*	*φ*	fee
Χ	χ	*X*	*χ*	khee
Ψ	ψ	*Ψ*	*ψ*	psee
Ω	ω	*Ω*	*ω*	o**mehg**hah

Some basic expressions

Yes.	Ναί.	neh
No.	῎Οχι.	okhee
Please.	Παρακαλῶ.	pahrahkahlo
Thank you.	Εὐχαριστῶ.	ehvkahreesto
Thank you very much.	Εὐχαριστῶ πολύ.	ehvkahreesto polee
That's all right.	Τίποτα.	teepotah

Greetings

Good morning.	Καλημέρα.	kahleemehrah
Good afternoon.	Καλησπέρα.	kahleespehrah
Good evening.	Καλησπέρα.	kahleespehrah
Good night.	Καληνύκτα.	kahleeneektah
Good-bye.	᾿Αντίο.	ahndeeo
See you later.	Εἰς τό ἐπανιδεῖν.	eess to ehpahneedheen
This is Mr. . . .	῾Ο κύριος . . .	o keereeoss
This is Mrs. . . .	῾Η κυρία . . .	ee keereeah
This is Miss . . .	῾Η δεσποινίς . . .	ee dhehspeeneess
I'm very pleased to meet you.	Χαίρομαι πού σᾶς γνωρίζω.	khehromeh poo sahss gnoreezo
How are you?	Τί κάνετε;	tee kahnehteh
Very well, thank you.	Πολύ καλά, εὐχαριστῶ.	polee kahlah ehvkahreesto
And you?	Καί ἐσεῖς;	keh ehsseess
Fine.	Πολύ καλά.	polee kahlah
Excuse me.	Μέ συγχωρεῖτε.	meh seengkhoreeteh

Questions

Where?	Ποῦ;	poo
Where is . . . ?	Ποῦ εἶναι . . . ;	poo eeneh
Where are . . . ?	Ποῦ εἶναι . . . ;	poo eeneh
When?	Πότε;	poteh
What?	Τί;	tee

How?	Πῶς;	poss
How much?	Πόσο;	**posso**
How many?	Πόσα;	**possah**
Who?	Ποιός;	pee**oss**
Why?	Γιατί;	yeeah**tee**
Which?	Ποιός/Ποιά/Ποιό;	pee**oss**/pee**ah**/pee**o**
What do you call this?	Πῶς λέγεται αὐτό;	poss **leh**yehteh ahv**to**
What do you call that?	Πῶς λέγεται ἐκεῖνο;	poss **leh**yehteh ehkee**no**
What does this mean?	Τί σημαίνει αὐτό;	tee see**meh**nee ahv**to**
What does that mean?	Τί σημαίνει ἐκεῖνο;	tee see**meh**nee ehkee**no**

Do you speak...?

Do you speak English?	Μιλᾶτε Ἀγγλικά;	mee**lah**teh ahnggleekah
Do you speak German?	Μιλᾶτε Γερμανικά;	mee**lah**teh yehrmahnee**kah**
Do you speak French?	Μιλᾶτε Γαλλικά;	mee**lah**teh ġahleekah
Do you speak Spanish?	Μιλᾶτε Ἰσπανικά;	mee**lah**teh eespahneekah
Do you speak Italian?	Μιλᾶτε Ἰταλικά;	mee**lah**teh eetahleekah
Could you speak more slowly, please?	Μπορεῖτε νά μιλᾶτε πιό ἀργά, παρακαλῶ;	bo**ree**teh nah mee**lah**teh peeo ahrġah pahrahkahlo
Please point to the phrase in the book.	Παρακαλῶ δεῖξτε τή φράση στό βιβλίο.	pahrahkahlo **dheek**steh tee **frah**ssee sto veevleeo
Just a minute. I'll see if I can find it in this book.	Ἕνα λεπτό. Θά δῶ ἄν μπορῶ, νά τό βρῶ σ'αὐτό τό βιβλίο.	ehnah lehpto. thah dho ahn boro nah to vro s ahvto to veevleeo
I understand.	Καταλαβαίνω.	kahtahlah**veh**no
I don't understand.	Δέν καταλαβαίνω.	dhehn kahtahlah**veh**no

GREEK

Can...?

Can I have...?	Μπορῶ νά ἔχω...;	boro nah ehkho
Can we have...?	Μποροῦμε νά ἔχουμε...;	boroomeh nah eh-khoomeh
Can you show me...?	Μπορεῖτε νά μοῦ δείξετε...;	boreeteh nah moo dheeksteh
Can you tell me...?	Μπορεῖτε νά μοῦ πῆτε...;	boreeteh nah moo peeteh
Can you help me, please?	Μπορεῖτε νά μέ βοηθήσετε, παρακαλῶ;	boreeteh nah meh voeetheesehteh, pahrahkahlo

Wanting

I'd like...	Θά ἤθελα...	thah eethehlah
We'd like...	Θά θέλαμε...	thah thehlahmeh
Please give me...	Παρακαλῶ δῶστε μου...	pahrahkahlo dhossteh moo
Give it to me, please.	Δῶστε μοῦ το, παρακαλῶ.	dhossteh moo to pahrahkahlo
Please bring me...	Παρακαλῶ, φέρτε μου...	pahrahkahlo fehrteh moo
Bring it to me, please.	Φέρτε μοῦ το, παρακαλῶ.	fehrteh moo to pahrahkahlo
I'm hungry.	Πεινῶ.	peeno
I'm thirsty.	Διψῶ.	dheepso
I'm tired.	Εἶμαι κουρασμένος.	eemeh koorahsmehnoss
I'm lost.	Χάθηκα.	kahtheekah
It's important.	Εἶναι σοβαρό.	eeneh sovahro
It's urgent.	Εἶναι ἐπεῖγον.	eeneh ehpeegon
Hurry up!	Γρήγορα!	greegorah

It is/There is...

It is/It's...	Εἶναι...	eeneh
Is it...?	Εἶναι...;	eeneh
It isn't...	Δέν εἶναι...	dhehn eeneh
There is/There are...	Ὑπάρχει/ Ὑπάρχουν...	eepahrkhee/eepahrkhoon

Is there/Are there . . . ?	Ὑπάρχει/ Ὑπάρχουν . . . ;	eepahrkhee/eepahrkhoon
There isn't/There aren't . . .	Δέν ὑπάρχει/Δέν ὑπάρχουν . . .	dhehn eepahrkhee/ dhehn eepahrkhoon
There isn't any/ There aren't any.	Δέν ὑπάρχει καθόλου/Δέν ὑπάρχουν καθόλου.	dhehn eepahrkhee kahtholoo/dhehn eepahrkhoon kahtholoo

A few common words

big/small	μεγάλος/μικρός	mehgahloss/meekross
quick/slow	γρήγορος/ἀργός	greegoross/ahrgoss
early/late	νωρίς/ἀργά	noreess/ahrgah
cheap/expensive	φτηνός/ἀκριβός	fteenoss/ahkreevoss
near/far	κοντά/μακρυά	kondah/mahkreeah
hot/cold	ζεστός/κρύος	zehstoss/kreeoss
full/empty	γεμᾶτος/ἄδειος	yehmahtoss/ahdheeoss
easy/difficult	εὔκολος/δύσκολος	ehvkoloss/dheeskoloss
heavy/light	βαρύς/ἐλαφρός	vahreess/ehlahfross
open/shut	ἀνοικτός/κλειστός	ahneektoss/kleestoss
right/wrong	σωστός/λάθος	sostoss/lahthoss
old/new	παλιός/καινούργιος	pahleeoss/kehnooryeeoss
old/young	γέρος/νέος	yehros/nehoss
beautiful/ugly	ὡραῖος/ἄσχημος	orehoss/ahsskheemoss
good/bad	καλός/κακός	kahloss/kahkoss
better/worse	καλύτερος/χειρότερος	kahleetehross/kheerotehross

Some prepositions and a few more useful words

at	στό	sto
on	ἐπάνω	ehpahno
in	μέσα	mehssah
to	πρός	pross
from	ἀπό	ahpo
inside	μέσα	mehssah
outside	ἔξω	ehkso
up	ἐπάνω	ehpahno
down	κάτω	kahto
before	᾽πρίν	preen
after	μετά	mehtah
with	μέ	meh
without	χωρίς	khoreess
through	ἀνάμεσα	ahnahmehssah
towards	πρός	pross
until	μέχρι	mehkhree
during	κατά τή διάρκεια	katah tee dheeahrkeeah
and	καί	keh

GREEK

or	ἤ	ee
not	δέν	dhehn
nothing	τίποτε	teepoteh
none	κανένα	kahnehnah
very	πολύ	polee
also	ἐπίσης	ehpeesseess
soon	σύντομα	seendomah
perhaps	ἴσως	eessoss
here	ἐδῶ	ehdho
there	ἐκεῖ	ehkee
now	τώρα	torah
then	τότε	toteh

Arrival

Your passport, please.	Τό διαβατήριό σας, παρακαλῶ.	to dheeahvahteereeo sahss pahrahkahlo
Here it is.	'Ορίστε.	oreesteh
Have you anything to declare?	Ἔχετε κάτι νά δηλώσετε;	ehkhehteh kahtee nah dheelosehteh
No, nothing at all.	'Οχι, τίποτε.	okhee teepoteh
Porter!	'Αχθοφόρε.	ahkhthoforeh
Can you help me with my luggage, please?	Μπορεῖτε νά μέ βοηθήσετε μέ τίς ἀποσκευές μου, παρακαλῶ;	boreeteh nah meh voeetheessehteh meh teess ahposkehvehss moo pahrahkahlo
That's my suitcase.	Αὐτή εἶναι ἡ βαλίτσα μου.	ahftee eeneh ee vahleetsah moo
Where's the bus to the centre of town, please?	Ποῦ εἶναι τό λεωφορεῖο γιά τό κέντρο τῆς πόλεως, παρακαλῶ;	poo eeneh to lehoforeeo yeeah to kehndro teess polehoss pahrahkahlo
This way, please.	'Από ἐδῶ, παρακαλῶ.	ahpo ehdho pahrahkahlo

Changing money

| Can you change a traveller's cheque, please? | Μπορεῖτε νά ἀλλάξετε ἕνα τράβελερ τσέκ, παρακαλῶ; | boreeteh nah ahlahksehteh ehnah trahvehlehr tsehk pahrahkahlo |
| Where's the nearest bank, please? | Ποῦ εἶναι ἡ πλησιέστερη τράπεζα, παρακαλῶ; | poo eeneh ee pleesseeehstehree trahpehzah pahrahkahlo |

Car rental

I'd like a car.	Θά ἤθελα ἕνα αὐτοκίνητο.	thah **eeth**ehlah **eh**nah ahfto**kee**neeto
For how long?	Γιά πόσο καιρό;	yeeah **po**sso keh**ro**
A day/Four days/ A week/Two weeks.	Μία ἡμέρα/ Τέσσερεις ἡμέρες/ Μία ἑβδομάδα/ Δύο ἑβδομάδες.	**mee**ah ee**meh**rah/ **tehs**sehreess eemehrehss/ **mee**ah ehvdhomahdhah/ **dhee**o ehvdhomahdhehss

Taxi

Where can I get a taxi?	Ποῦ μπορῶ νά βρῶ ἕνα ταξί;	poo bo**ro** nah vro **eh**nah tah**ksee**
What's the fare to . . . ?	Ποιά εἶναι ἡ τιμή γιά . . . ;	peeah **ee**neh ee tee**mee** yeeah
Take me to this address, please.	Πηγαίνετέ με σ'αὐτή τή διεύθυνσι, παρακαλῶ.	pee**yeh**nehteh meh sahf**tee** tee dheeehftheensee pahrahkahlo
I'm in a hurry.	Εἶμαι βιαστικός.	**ee**meh veeahstee**koss**
Could you drive more slowly, please?	Μπορεῖτε νά ὁδηγῆτε πιό ἀργά, παρακαλῶ;	bo**ree**teh nah odhee**yee**teh peeoo ah**rġah** pahrahkahlo

Hotel and other accommodation

My name is . . .	Τό ὄνομά μου εἶναι . . .	to **o**nomah moo **ee**neh
Have you a reservation?	Ἔχετε κρατήσει δωμάτιο;	**ehk**hehteh krah**tee**ssee dhomahteeo
Yes, here's the confirmation.	Μάλιστα, ἰδού ἡ διαβε βαίωση.	**mah**leestah ee**dhoo** ee dheeahveh**veh**hossee
I'd like . . .	Θά ἤθελα . . .	thah **ee**thehlah
I'd like a single room/a double room.	Θά ἤθελα ἕνα μονό δωμάτιο/ἕνα διπλό δωμάτιο.	thah **ee**thehlah **eh**nah mono dho**mah**teeo/**eh**nah dhee**plo** dho**mah**teeo
a room with a bath/ with a shower	ἕνα δωμάτιο μέ μπάνιο/μέ ντούς	**eh**nah dho**mah**teeo meh **bah**neeo/meh dooss

How much?

| What's the price per night/per week/per month? | Ποιά εἶναι ἡ τιμή γιά μία νύχτα/μία ἑβδομάδα/ἕνα μῆνα; | peeah **ee**neh ee tee**mee** yeeah **mee**ah **neek**htah/ **mee**ah ehvdhomahdhah/ **eh**nah **mee**nah |
| May I see the room? | Μπορῶ νά δῶ τό δωμάτιο; | bo**ro** nah dho to dho**mah**teeo |

GREEK

I'm sorry, I don't like it.	Μέ συγχωρεῖτε, δέν μοῦ ἀρέσει.	meh seenkhor**ee**teh dhehn moo ah**reh**ssee
Yes, that's fine. I'll take it.	Ναί, εἶναι καλό. Θά τό πάρω.	neh **ee**neh kah**lo**. thah to **pah**ro
What's my room number, please?	Ποιός εἶναι ὁ ἀριθμός τοῦ δωματίου μου, παρακαλῶ;	pee**oss ee**neh o ahreeth**moss** too dhomah**tee**oo moo pahrahkah**hlo**
Number 123.	Νούμερο 123.	**noo**mehro 123

Service, please

Who is it?	Ποιός εἶναι;	pee**oss ee**neh
Just a minute.	Ἕνα λεπτό.	**eh**nah leh**pto**
Come in! The door's open.	Ὁρίστε. Ἡ πόρτα εἶναι ἀνοικτή.	or**ee**steh. ee **por**tah **ee**neh ah**neek**tee
May we have breakfast in our room?	Μποροῦμε νά πάρουμε τό πρόγευμα στό δωμάτιό μας;	bo**roo**meh nah **pah**roomeh to **pro**yehvmah sto dho**mah**teeo mahss

Breakfast

I'll have . . .	Θά πάρω . . .	thah **pah**ro
I'll have some fruit juice.	Θά πάρω ἕνα χυμό φρούτων.	thah **pah**ro **eh**nah khee**mo froo**ton
a boiled egg	ἕνα βραστό αὐγό	**eh**nah vrah**sto** ahv**go**
a fried egg	ἕνα τηγανιτό αὐγό	**eh**nah teeyahnee**to** ahv**go**
some bacon/some ham	χοιρομέρι/ζαμπόν	kheero**meh**ree zahm**bon**
some toast	μερικά τόστ	mehree**kah** tost
a pot of tea	τσάϊ	**tsah**ee
a cup of tea	ἕνα φλυτζάνι τσάϊ	**eh**nah fleent**zah**nee **tsah**ee
some coffee	καφέ	kah**feh**
some chocolate	κακάο	kah**kah**o
more butter	περισσότερο βούτυρο	pehree**sso**tehro **voo**teero
some hot water	ζεστό νερό	zeh**sto** neh**ro**

Difficulties

| The central heating doesn't work. | Ἡ κεντρική θέρμανση δέν δουλεύει. | ee kehndree**kee thehr**mahnsee dhehn dhoo**leh**vee |
| the light/the socket the tap/the toilet | τό φῶς/ἡ πρίζα τό ρομπινέ/ἡ τουαλέττα | to foss/ee **pree**zah to rombee**neh**/ee tooah**leh**tah |

| There's no hot water. | Δέν ἔχει ζεστό νερό. | dhenn **ehkhee** zeh**sto** nehro |
| May I see the manager, please? | Μπορῶ νά δῶ τόν διευθυντή, παρακαλῶ; | boro nah dho ton dheeehftheen**dee** pahrahkah**lo** |

Telephone—Mail

There's a call for you.	Σας ζητοῦν στό τηλέφωνο.	sahss zee**toon** sto teelehfono
Hold the line, please.	Περιμένετε στό ἀκουστικό σας, παρακαλῶ.	pehree**meh**nehteh sto ahkoostee**ko** sahss pahrahkah**lo**
Operator, I've been cut off.	Δεσποινίς μέ διέκοψαν.	dhehspee**neess** meh dhee**ehk**opsahn
Did anyone telephone me?	Μοῦ τηλεφώνησε κανείς;	moo teelehfon**eess**eh kah**neess**
Is there any mail for me?	Ὑπάρχουν γράμματα γιά μένα;	eepahr**khoon** **grah**mahtah yeeah **meh**nah
Are there any messages for me?	Ὑπάρχουν παραγγελίες γιά μένα;	eepahr**khoon** pahrzhnggehlee**eh**ss yeeah **meh**nah

Checking out

May I have my bill, please?	Μπορῶ νά ἔχω τόν λογαριασμό, παρακαλῶ;	boro nah **ehk**ho ton lo**g**ahreeah**zmo** pahrahkah**lo**
We're in a great hurry.	Εἴμαστε πολύ βιαστικοί.	**ee**mahsteh polee veeah-**stee**kee
It's been a very enjoyable stay.	Ἡ διαμονή ἦταν πολύ εὐχάριστη.	eedheeahmon**ee** **ee**tahn polee ehf**khah**reestee

Eating out

Good evening, sir/ Good evening, madam.	Καλησπέρα, κύριε/Καλησπέρα, κυρία.	kahlees**peh**rah, **keer**eeeh/kahlees**peh**rah keer**ee**ah
Good evening. I'd like a table for two, please.	Καλησπέρα. Θά ἤθελα ἕνα τραπέζι γιά δύο, παρακαλῶ.	kahlees**peh**rah. thah **ee**thehlah **eh**nah trah**peh**zee yeeah **dhee**o pahrahkah**lo**
Do you have a fixed-price menu?	Ἔχετε φαγητό μέ καθωρισμένη τιμή;	**ehk**hehteh fahyee**to** meh kahthoreez**meh**nee tee**mee**

GREEK

May I see the à la carte menu?	Μπορῶ νά δῶ τό μενοῦ ἀ-λά-κάρτ;	boro nah dho to meh**noo** ahlah**kahrt**
May we have an ashtray, please?	Μπορούμε νά ἔχου-με ἕνα στακτο-δοχείο, παρακαλῶ;	bo**roo**meh nah **eh**khoo-meh **eh**nah stahktodho-**khee**o pahrahkah**lo**
some bread	ψωμί	pso**mee**
a fork	ἕνα πειρούνι	**eh**nah peer**oo**nee
a knife	ἕνα μαχαίρι	**eh**nah mah**kheh**ree
a spoon	ἕνα κουτάλι	**eh**nah koo**tah**lee
a plate	ἕνα πιάτο	**eh**nah pee**ah**to
a glass	ἕνα ποτήρι	**eh**nah po**tee**ree
a napkin	ἕνα τραπεζομάν-τηλο	**eh**nah trahpehzo**mahn**-deelo
another chair	μία καρέκλα ἀκόμη	**mee**ah kah**reh**klah ah**ko**meh
Where's the gentle-men's toilet (men's room)?	Ποῦ εἶναι οἱ τουαλέττες τῶν ἀνδρῶν;	poo **ee**neh ee tooah**leh**tehss ton ahn**dhron**
Where's the ladies' toilet (ladies' room)?	Ποῦ εἶναι οἱ τουαλέττες τῶν γυναικῶν;	poo **ee**neh ee tooah**leh**tehss ton yeeneh**kon**

Appetizers

I'd like some ...	Θά ἤθελα ...	thah **ee**thehlah
I'd like some assorted appetizers.	Θά ἤθελα μία ποικιλία ὀρεκτικῶν.	thah **ee**thehlah **mee**ah peekee**lee**ah orehktee**kon**
orange juice	ἕνα χυμό πορτοκαλιοῦ	**eh**nah **khee**mo por-tokah**lee**oo
ham	ζαμπόν	zahm**bon**
melon	πεπόνι	peh**po**nee
pâté	πατέ	pah**teh**
smoked salmon	καπνιστό σολωμό	kahpnee**sto** solo**mo**
shrimps (shrimp)	γαρίδες	ǵah**ree**dhehss

Soup

Have you any ...?	Ἔχετε ...;	**eh**khehteh
Have you any chicken soup?	Ἔχετε κοτόσουπα;	**eh**khehteh kotossoopah
vegetable soup	χορτόσουπα	khor**tos**soopah
onion soup	κρεμμυδόσουπα	krehmee**dhos**soopah

Fish

I'd like some . . .	Θά ἤθελα . . .	thah eethehlah
I'd like some fish.	Θά ἤθελα ψάρι.	thah eethehlah psahree
sole	γλῶσσα	glosah
trout	πέστροφα	pehstrofah
lobster	ἀστακό	ahstahko
crayfish	καραβίδες	kahrahveedhehss
prawns	καβούρια	kahvooreeah
I'd like it . . .	Θά τό ἤθελα . . .	thah to eethehlah
I'd like it steamed.	Θά τό ἤθελα στόν ἀτμό.	thah to eethehlah ston ahtmo
grilled	ψητό	pseeto
boiled	βραστό	vrahsto
baked	μαγειρευμένο	mahyeerehvmehno
fried	τηγανιτό	teegahneeto

Meat—Poultry—Game

I'd like some . . .	Θά ἤθελα . . .	thah eethehlah
I'd like some beef.	Θά ἤθελα μοσχάρι.	thah eethehlah mosskhahree
a beef steak	μία μπριζόλα	meeah breezolah
some roast beef	ροζ-μπήφ	rozbeef
a veal cutlet	μία μοσχαρίσια μπριζόλα	meeah mosskhahreesseeah breezolah
mutton	ἀρνί	ahrnee
lamb	ἀρνάκι γάλακτος	ahrnahkee galahktoss
a pork chop	μία χοιρινή μπριζόλα	meeah kheereenee breezolah
roast pork	ψητό χοιρινό	pseeto kheereeno
hare	λαγό	lahgo
chicken	κοτόπουλο	kotopoolo
roast chicken	κοτόπουλο ψητό	kotopoolo pseeto
duck	πάπια	pahpeeah
How do you like your meat?	Πῶς θέλετε τό κρέας σας;	poss thehlehteh to krehahss sahss
rare	λίγο ψημένο	leego pseemehno
medium	μέτριο	mehtreeo
well done	καλοψημένο	kahlopseemehno

Vegetables

What vegetables have you got?	Τί λαχανικά ἔχετε;	tee lahkhahneekah ehkhehteh
I'd like some . . .	Θά ἤθελα . . .	thah eethehlah

GREEK

I'd like some asparagus.	Θά ήθελα σπαράγγια.	thah **ee**thehlah spah**rahng**geeah
green beans	φασόλια φρέσκα	fah**ssoo**leeah **fresh**skah
mushrooms	μανιτάρια	mahnee**tah**reeah
carrots	καρόττα	kah**rot**tah
onions	κρεμμύδια	kreh**mee**dheeah
red cabbage	κόκκινο λάχανο	**ko**keeno **lah**khahno
spinach	σπανάκι	spah**nah**kee
rice	ρύζι	**ree**zee
peas	μπιζέλια	bee**zeh**leeah
tomatoes	τομάτες	toh**mah**tehss
green salad	πράσινη σαλάτα	**prah**sseenee sahl**ah**tah
potatoes	πατάτες	pah**tah**tehss

Desserts

Nothing more, thanks.	Τίποτε άλλο, εὐχαριστῶ.	**tee**poteh **ah**lo ehfkhahree**sto**
Just a small portion, please.	Μία μικρή μερίδα, παρακαλῶ.	**mee**ah meek**ree** meh**ree**dhah pahrahkah**lo**
Have you any ice-cream?	Ἔχετε παγωτά;	**eh**khehteh pah**go**tah
fruit salad	φρουτοσαλάτα	frootossahl**ah**tah
fresh fruit	φρέσκα φροῦτα	**fresh**skah **froo**tah
cheese	τυρί	tee**ree**

Drink

What would you like to drink?	Τί θά θέλατε νά πιῆτε;	tee thah **theh**lahteh nah pee**ee**eteh
I'll have a beer, please.	Θά πάρω μία μπύρα, παρακαλῶ.	thah **pah**ro **mee**ah **bee**rah pahrahkah**lo**
I'll have a whisky, please.	Θά πάρω ἕνα οὔισκυ, παρακαλῶ.	thah **pah**ro **eh**nah **oo**eeskee pahrahkah**lo**

Wine

I'd like a bottle of wine.	Θά ήθελα ἕνα μπουκάλι κρασί.	thah **ee**thehlah **eh**nah boo**kah**lee krah**ssee**
red wine	κόκκινο κρασί	**ko**keeno krah**ssee**
rosé wine	ρόζέ κρασί	ro**zeh** krah**ssee**
white wine	ἄσπρο κρασί	**ah**spro krah**ssee**
Cheers!	Στήν ὑγειά σας!	steen eey**eeah** sahss

The bill (check)

May I have the bill (check) please?	Μπορῶ νά ἔχω τό λογαριασμό, παρακαλῶ;	boro nah **eh**kho to loğahreeahz**mo** pahrahkah**lo**
Is service included?	Τό φιλοδώρημα περιλαμβάνεται;	to feelo**dho**reemah pehreelahm**vah**nehteh
Everything's included.	'Ολα περιλαμβάνονται.	**o**lah pehreelahm**vah**nondheh
Thank you, that was a very good meal.	Εὐχαριστῶ, τό γεῦμα ἦταν πολύ καλό.	ehfkahree**sto** to **yeh**vmah eetahn polee kah**lo**

Travelling

Where's the railway station, please?	Ποῦ εἶναι ὁ σιδηρο-δρομικός σταθμός, παρακαλῶ;	poo **ee**neh o seedheerodhromee**koss** stahth**moss** pahrahkah**lo**
Where's the ticket office, please?	Ποῦ εἶναι τό γραφεῖο ἐκδόσεως εἰσιτηρίων, παρακαλῶ;	poo **ee**neh to ğrah**fee**o ehk**dho**ssehoss eesseetee**ree**on pahrahkah**lo**
I'd like a ticket to...	Θά ἤθελα ενα εἰσιτήριο γιά...	thah **ee**thehlah ehnah eesseeteereeo yeeah
First or second class?	Πρώτη ἤ δευτέρα θέση;	protee ee dhehf**te**hrah **theh**ssee
First class, please.	Πρώτη θέση, παρακαλῶ.	pro**tee theh**ssee pahrahkah**lo**
Single or return (one way or round-trip)?	'Απλῆ διαδρομή ἤ μετ'ἐπιστροφῆς;	ah**plee** dheeahdhro**mee** ee mehtehpeestro**feess**
Do I have to change trains?	Πρέπει νά ἀλλάξω τραῖνο;	**preh**pee nah ah**lah**kso **treh**no
What platform does the train leave from?	'Από ποιά ἀποβάθρα φεύγει τό τραῖνο;	ah**po** peeah ahpo**vah**thrah **feh**vyee to **treh**no
Where's the nearest underground (subway) station?	Ποῦ εἶναι ὁ πλη-σιέστερος σταθμός τοῦ 'Ηλεκτρικοῦ;	poo **ee**neh o pleessee**eh**stehross stahth**moss** too eelehktree**koo**
Where's the bus station, please?	Ποῦ εἶναι ο σταθμός τῶν λεωφορείων παρακαλῶ;	poo **ee**neh o stahth**moss** ton lehofo**ree**oo pahrahkah**lo**

GREEK

When's the first bus to . . . ?	Πότε εἶναι τό πρῶτο λεωφορεῖο γιά . . . ;	**poteh eeneh** to **proto** lehoforeeo yeeah
the last bus	τό τελευταῖο λεωφορεῖο	to tehlehfteho lehoforeeo
the next bus	τό ἐπόμενο λεωφορεῖο	to ehpomehno lehoforeeo
Please let me off at the next stop.	Παρακαλῶ, θέλω νά κατεβῶ στήν ἐπομένη στάση.	pahrahkahlo thehlo nah kahtehvo steen ehpomehnee stahssee

Relaxing

What's on at the cinema (movies)?	Τί παίζουν στόν κινηματογράφο;	tee **peh**zoon ston keeneemahto**grah**fo
What's on at the theatre?	Τί παίζουν στό θέατρο;	tee **peh**zoon sto **the**hahtro
What time does the film begin? And the play?	Τί ὥρα ἀρχίζει τό φίλμ; Καί τό ἔργο;	tee orah ahr**khee**zee to feelm? keh to **ehr**go
Are there any tickets for tonight?	Ὑπάρχουν εἰσητήρια γι'ἀπόψε;	eepahrkhoon eessee**teer**eeah yeeah**pop**seh
Where can we go dancing?	Ποῦ μποροῦμε νά πᾶμε νά χορέψουμε;	poo bor**oo**meh nah **pah**meh nah kho**reh**psoomeh
Would you like to dance?	Θά θέλατε νά χορέψετε;	thah **theh**lahteh nah kho**reh**psehteh

Introductions

How do you do?	Πῶς εἶσθε;	poss **ees**theh
How are you?	Τί κάνετε;	tee **kah**nehteh
Very well, thank you. And you?	Πολύ καλά, εὐχαριστῶ. Καί ἐσεῖς;	polee kah**lah** ehfkhah**rees**to. keh eh**seess**
May I introduce Miss Philips?	Μπορῶ νά σᾶς συστήσω τή δεσποινίδα Φίλιπς;	boro nah sahss see**stees**so tee dhehspee**need**dhah Philips
My name is . . .	Ὀνομάζομαι . . .	ono**mah**zomeh
I'm very pleased to meet you.	Χαίρω πολύ πού σᾶς γνωρίζω.	**kheh**ro polee poo sahss gno**ree**zo
How long have you been here?	Πόσο καιρό εἶσθε ἐδῶ;	**poso** keh**ro ees**theh eh**dho**
It was nice meeting you.	Χάρηκα πού σᾶς γνώρισα.	**khah**reekah poo sahss **gno**reessah

Dating

Would you like a cigarette?	Θά θέλατε ἔνα τσιγάρο;	thah **theh**lahteh **eh**nah tseeᶃahro
May I get you a drink?	Μπορῶ νά σᾶς φέρω ἕνα ποτό;	boro nah sahss **feh**ro **eh**nah poto
Do you have a light, please?	Ἔχετε φωτιά, παρακαλῶ;	**eh**khehteh foteeah pahrahkahlo
Are you waiting for someone?	Περιμένετε κάποιον;	pehree**meh**nehteh **kah**peeon
Are you free this evening?	Εἶσθε ἐλεύθερη ἀπόψε;	**ees**theh ehlehf**theh**ree ah**pop**seh
Where shall we meet?	Ποῦ θά συναντηθοῦμε;	poo thah seenahndeeth**oo**meh
What time shall I meet you?	Τί ὥρα θά σᾶς συναντήσω;	tee **o**rah thah sahss seenahn**dees**so
May I take you home?	Μπορῶ νά σᾶς πάω στό σπίτι σας;	boro nah sahss **pah**o sto **spee**tee sahss
Thank you, it's been a wonderful evening.	Εὐχαριστῶ, ἦταν μία ὑπέροχη βραδιά.	ehfkahree**sto ee**tahn **mee**ah eepeh**ro**khee vrahdhee**ah**
What's your telephone number?	Ποιός εἶναι ὁ ἀριθμός τοῦ τηλεφώνου σας;	pee**oss ee**neh o ahreeth**moss** too teelehfonoo sahss
Do you live alone?	Μένετε μόνη σας;	**meh**nehteh **mo**nee sahss
What time is your last train?	Τί ὥρα εἶναι τό τελευταῖο τραῖνο σας;	tee **o**rah **ee**neh to tehlehf**teh**o **treh**no sahss
Good-night . . .	Καληνύκτα . . .	kahleeneektah

Banks

Where's the nearest bank, please?	Ποῦ εἶναι ἡ πλησιέστερη τράπεζα, παρακαλῶ;	poo **ee**neh ee pleesseeeh**steh**ree **trah**pehzah pahrahkahlo
Where can I cash some traveller's cheques?	Ποῦ μπορῶ νά ἐξαργυρώσω μερικά τράβελερς τσέκ;	poo boro nah ehksahryee**ro**sso mehree**kah trah**vehlehrs tsehk
What time does the bank open? What time does it close?	Τί ὥρα ἀνοίγει ἡ τράπεζα; Τί ὥρα κλείνει;	tee orah ah**nee**yee ee **trah**pehzah? tee **o**rah **klee**nee

| I'm expecting some money from home. Has it arrived? | Περιμένω χρήματα ἀπό τό σπίτι. Μήπως ἦλθαν; | pehreemehno khreemahtah ahpo to speetee. meeposs eelthahn |
| Can you give me some small change, please? | Μπορεῖτε νά μοῦ δώσετε μερικά κέρματα, παρακαλῶ; | boreeteh nah moo dhossehteh mehreekah kehrmahtah pahrahkahlo |

Shops, stores and services

Where is the nearest chemist's (pharmacy)?	Ποῦ εἶναι τό πλησιέστερο φαρμακεῖο;	poo eeneh to pleesseeehstehro fahrmahkeeo
the nearest hair-dresser's	τό πλησιέστερο κουρεῖο	to pleesseeehstehro kooreeo
the photo shop	τό φωτογραφεῖο	to fotograhfeeo
the jeweller's	τό κοσμηματο-πωλεῖο	to kozmeemahtopoleeo
the department store	τό ἐμπορικό κατάστημα	to ehmboreeko kahtahsteemah
the police station	τό ἀστυνομικό τμῆμα	to ahsteenomeeko tmeemah
the garage	τό γκαράζ	to gahrahz
How do I get there?	Πῶς νά πάω ἐκεῖ;	poss nah paho ehkee
Is it within walking distance?	Μπορῶ νά πάω μέ τά πόδια;	boro nah paho meh tah podheeah

Service

Can you help me, please?	Μπορεῖτε νά μέ βοηθήσετε, παρακαλῶ;	boreeteh nah meh voeetheessehteh pahrahkahlo
Can you show me this? And that, too.	Μπορεῖτε νά μοῦ δείξετε αὐτό; Καί ἐκεῖνο ἐπίσης.	boreeteh nah moo dheeksehteh ahfto? keh ehkeeno ehpeesseess
It's too expensive/too big/too small.	Εἶναι πολύ ἀκριβό/πολύ μεγάλο/πολύ μικρό.	eeneh polee ahkreevo/polee mehgahlo/polee meekro
Can you show me some more?	Μπορεῖτε νά μοῦ δείξετε περισσότερα;	boreeteh nah moo dheeksehteh pehreessotehrah
something better	κάτι καλύτερο	kahtee kahleetehro
something cheaper	κάτι φθηνότερο	kahtee ftheenotehro

How much is this? And that?	Πόσο κοστίζει αὐτό; Καί ἐκεῖνο;	**po**sso ko**stee**zee ah**fto**? keh eh**kee**eno
It's not quite what I want.	Δέν εἶναι ἀκριβῶς αὐτό πού θέλω.	dhehn **ee**neh ahkree**voss** ah**fto** poo **theh**lo
I like it.	Μοῦ ἀρέσει.	moo ah**reh**see

Chemist's (Pharmacy)

| I'd like something for a cold/for a cough/for travel sickness. | Θά ἤθελα κάτι γιά τό κρύωμα/γιά τό βήχα/γιά τή ναυτία. | thah **ee**thehlah **kah**tee yee**ah** to **kree**omah/yee**ah** to **vee**khah/yee**ah** tee nahf**tee**ah |
| Can you recommend something for hay-fever/for sunburn? | Μπορεῖτε νά μοῦ συστήσετε κάτι γιά τόν ὑψηλό πυρετό/ γιά τά ἐγκαύματα τοῦ ἡλίου; | bo**ree**teh nah moo sees**tee**ssehteh **kah**tee yee**ah** ton eep**see**lo peereh**to**/ yee**ah** tah ehng**gahv**mahtah too eelee**oo** |

Toiletry

May I have some razor blades?	Μπορῶ νά ἔχω μερικά ξυραφάκια ξυρίσματος;	bo**ro** nah **eh**kho mehree**kah** kseerah**fah**keeah kseer**eez**mahtoss
some shaving cream	κρέμα ξυρίσματος	**kreh**mah kseer**eez**mahtoss
some toothpaste	ὀδοντόπαστα	odhon**do**pahstah
I'd like some soap.	Θά ἤθελαἕνα σαπούνι.	thah **ee**thehlah **eh**nah sah**poo**nee
some suntan oil	λάδι ἡλίου	**lah**dhee eelee**oo**

At the barber's

I'd like a haircut, please.	Θά ἤθελα νά μοῦ κόψετε τά μαλλιά παρακαλῶ.	thah **ee**thehlah nah moo **ko**psehteh tah mahlee**ah** pahrahkah**hlo**
Short/Leave it long.	Κοντά/Ἀφῆστε τα μακρυά.	kon**dah**/ah**fee**steh tah mahkree**ah**
A razor cut, please.	Κόψιμο μέ ξυράφι, παρακαλῶ.	**ko**pseemo meh kseer**ah**fee pahrahkah**lo**

At the hairdresser's

| I'd like a shampoo and set, please. | Θά ἤθελα λούσιμο καί μίξ-αν-πλί, παρακαλῶ. | thaht **ee**thehlah **loo**seemo keh meezahn**plee** pahrahkah**hlo** |

GREEK

I'd like a bleach.	Θά ήθελα μία ντεκολορασιόν.	thah **ee**thehlah **mee**ah dehkolorahsee**on**
a permanent	μία περμανάντ	**mee**ah pehrmah**nahnd**
a colour rinse	ένα ντεκαπάζ	**ehn**ah dehkah**pahz**
a manicure	μανικιούρ	mahneekee**oor**

Photography

I'd like a film for this camera.	Θά ήθελα ένα φίλμ γι'αύτή τή μηχανή.	thah **ee**thehlah **ehn**ah feelm yeeah**ftee** tee meek**hah**nee
This camera doesn't work.	Αύτή ή μηχανή δέν δουλεύει.	ah**ftee** ee meek**hah**nee dhehn dhoo**leh**vee

At the post office

Where's the nearest post office, please?	Πού είναι τό πλησιέστερο ταχυδρομείο, παρακαλώ;	poo **ee**neh to pleessee**eh**stehro tahkhee-dhro**mee**o pahrahkah**lo**
I'd like to send this by express (special delivery)/by air mail.	Θά ήθελα νά στείλω αύτό έξπρές/άεροπορικώς.	thah **ee**thehlah nah **stee**lo ah**fto** ehks**prehss**/ aehroporee**koss**

Service stations

Where is the nearest service station, please?	Πού είναι τό πλησιέστερο πρατήριο βενζίνης, παρακαλώ;	poo **ee**neh to pleessee**eh**stehro prah**tee**-reeo vehn**zee**neess pahrahkah**lo**
Fill her up, please.	Νά τό γεμίσετε, παρακαλώ.	nah to yeh**mee**ssehteh pahrahkah**lo**
Check the oil, please.	Έλέγξατε τό λάδι, παρακαλώ.	eh**lehnk**sahteh to **lah**dhee pahrahkah**lo**
Would you check the tyres?	Θά μπορούσατε νά έλέγξετε τά λάστιχα;	thah bor**oo**ssahteh nah eh**lehnk**sehteh tah **lah**steekhah

Street directions

Can you show me on the map where I am?	Μπορείτε νά μού δείξετε στό χάρτη πού είμαι;	bor**ee**teh nah moo **dhee**ksehteh sto **khahr**tee poo **ee**meh
You're on the wrong road.	Έχετε πάρει λάθος δρόμο.	**ehk**hehteh **pah**ree **lah**thoss **dhro**mo

Go back to . . .	Γυρίστε πίσω στό . . .	yeereesteh peesso sto
Go straight ahead.	Νά πᾶτε εὐθεία.	nah pahteh ehftheeah
It's on the left/on the right.	Εἶναι ἀριστερά/ δεξιά.	eeneh ahreestehrah/ dhehkseeah

Accidents

May I use your telephone?	Μπορῶ νά χρησιμοποιήσω τό τηλέφωνό σας;	boro nah khreesseemopeeeesso to teelehfono sahss
Call a doctor quickly.	Καλέστε ἕνα γιατρό γρήγορα.	kahlehsteh ehnah yeeahtro greeǵorah
Call an ambulance.	Καλέστε ἕνα ἀσθενοφόρο.	kahlehsteh ehnah ahsthehnoforo
Please call the police.	Παρακαλῶ καλέστε τήν ἀστυνομία.	pahrahkahlo kahlehsteh teen ahsteenomeeah

Numbers

zero	μηδέν	meedhehn
one	ἕνα	ehnah
two	δύο	dheeo
three	τρία	treeah
four	τέσσερα	tehsehrah
five	πέντε	pehndeh
six	ἕξη	ehksee
seven	ἑπτά	ehptah
eight	ὀκτώ	okto
nine	ἐννέα	ehnnehah
ten	δέκα	dhehkah
eleven	ἕντεκα	ehndehkah
twelve	δώδεκα	dhodhehkah
thirteen	δεκατρία	dhehkahtreeah
fourteen	δεκατέσσερα	dhehkahtehsehrah
fifteen	δεκαπέντε	dhehkahpehndeh
sixteen	δεκαέξη	dhehkahehksee
seventeen	δεκαεπτά	dhehkahehptah
eighteen	δεκαοκτώ	dhehkahokto
nineteen	δεκαεννέα	dhehkahehnnehah
twenty	εἴκοσι	eekossee
twenty-one	εἴκοσι ἕνα	eekossee ehnah
thirty	τριάντα	treeahndah
forty	σαράντα	sharahndah
fifty	πενήντα	pehneendah
sixty	ἐξῆντα	eekseendah
seventy	ἑβδομῆντα	ehvdhomeendah

GREEK

eighty	ὀγδόντα	oǵdhondah
ninety	ἐνενήντα	ehnehneendah
one hundred	ἑκατό	ehkahto
one thousand	χίλια	kheeleeah
ten thousand	δέκα χιλιάδες	dhehkah kheeleeahdhehss

Days

It's Sunday.	Εἶναι Κυριακή.	eeneh keereeahkee
Monday	Δευτέρα	dhehftehrah
Tuesday	Τρίτη	treetee
Wednesday	Τετάρτη	tertahrtee
Thursday	Πέμπτη	pehmptee
Friday	Παρασκευή	pahrahskehvee
Saturday	Σάββατο	shavahto
yesterday	χθές	khthehss
today	σήμερα	seemehrah
tomorrow	αὔριο	ahvreeo
morning/afternoon	πρωΐ/ἀπόγευμα	proee/ahpoyehvmah
evening/night	βράδυ/νύκτα	vrahdhee/neektah

Months

January	Ἰανουάριος	eeahnooahreeoss
February	Φεβρουάριος	fehvrooahreeoss
March	Μάρτιος	mahrteeoss
April	Ἀπρίλιος	ahpreeleeoss
May	Μάϊος	maheeoss
June	Ἰούνιος	eeooneeoss
July	Ἰούλιος	eeooleeoss
August	Αὔγουστος	ahvgoostoss
September	Σεπτέμβριος	sehptehmvreeoss
October	Ὀκτώβριος	oktovreeoss
November	Νοέμβριος	noehmvreeoss
December	Δεκέμβριος	dhehkehmvreeoss
Merry Christmas!	Καλά Χριστούγεννα.	kahlah khreestooyehnah
Happy New Year!	Εὐτυχισμένος ὁ καινούργιος χρόνος.	ehfteekheezmehnoss o kehnooryeeoss khronoss

GREEK

ITALIAN

Guide to Pronunciation

Letter	Approximate pronunciation	Symbol	Example	

Consonants

b, d, f, k, l, m, n, p, q, t, v	are pronounced as in English			
c	1) before **e** and **i**, like **ch** in chip	ch	**cerco**	**chayr**koa
	2) elsewhere, like **c** in cat	k	**conto**	**koan**toa
ch	like **c** in cat	k	**che**	kay
g	1) before **e** and **i**, like **j** in jet	j	**leggero**	layd**jair**oa
	2) elsewhere, like **g** in go	g	**grande**	**grahn**day
gh	like **g** in go	g	**ghiaccio**	geeahtchoa
gl	like **lli** in million	ly	**gli**	lyee
gn	like **ni** in onion	ñ	**bagno**	**bah**ñoa
h	always silent		**ha**	ah

r	trilled like a Scottish **r**	r	caro	**kar**roa
s	1) generally like **s** in sit	s/ss	casa	**kar**ssah
			questo	koo**ay**stoa
	2) sometimes like **z** in zoo	z	viso	**vee**zoa
sc	1) before **e**, **i**, like **sh** in shut	sh	uscita	oo**shee**tah
	2) elsewhere, like **sk** in skin	sk	scarpa	**skahr**pah
z or zz	1) generally like **ts** in hits	ts	grazie	**grah**tseeay
	2) sometimes like **ds** in roads	dz	romanzo	roa**mahnd**zoa

Vowels

a	1) short, like a in car, but shorter	ah	gatto	**gaht**toa
	2) long, like **a** in car (but without any r-sound)	ar	casa	**kar**ssah
e	1) can always be pronounced like **ay** in gay	ay	sera	**say**rah
	2) in correct speech, it is sometimes pronounced like **e** in get or, when long, more like **ai** in hair	eh	bello	**behl**loa
		ai	bene	**bai**nay
i	like the **ee** in meet	ee	vini	**vee**nee
o	1) can always be pronounced like **oa** in goat	oa	sole	**soa**lay
	2) in correct speech, it is sometimes pronounced like **o** in got, or when long, more like **aw** in law	o	notte	**not**tay
		aw	rosa	**raw**zah
u	like the **oo** in foot	oo	fumo	**foo**moa

Two or more vowels

In groups of vowels, **a**, **e**, and **o** are strong vowels, and **i** and **u** are weak vowels. When two strong vowels are next to each other, they are pronounced as two separate syllables, e.g., *beato* = bay**ah**toa. When a strong and weak vowel are next to each other, the weak one is pronounced more quickly and with less stress (less loudly) than the strong one, e.g., *piede* = pee**ay**day; such sounds are diphthongs and constitute only one syllable. If the weak vowel is stressed, then it is pronounced as a separate syllable, e.g., *due* = **doo**ay. Two weak vowels together are pronounced as a diphthong, and it is generally the second one that is more strongly stressed, e.g., *guida* = goo**ee**dah.

Stressing of words

Generally, the vowel of the next to the last syllable is stressed. When a final vowel is stressed, it has an accent written over it *(più)*. Normally an accent is used only when the stress falls on a final vowel, and not when it falls on syllables before the next to the last one.

Some basic expressions

Yes.	**Sì.**	see
No.	**No.**	no
Please.	**Per favore.**	pair fahvoaray
Thank you.	**Grazie.**	**grah**tseeay
Thank you very much.	**Mille grazie.**	**mee**llay **grah**tseeay
That's all right.	**Prego.**	**pray**goa

Greetings

Good morning.	**Buon giorno.**	bwon **joar**noa
Good afternoon.	**Buon giorno.**	bwon **joar**noa
Good evening.	**Buona sera.**	**bwo**nah sayrah
Good night.	**Buona notte.**	**bwo**nah nottay
Good-bye.	**Arrivederci.**	ahreevay**dair**chee
See you later.	**A più tardi.**	a pyoo **tahr**dee
This is Mr....	**Questo è il signor...**	kooa**yss**toa ay eel seeñor
This is Mrs....	**Questa è la signora...**	kooa**yss**tah ay lah seeñoarah
This is Miss...	**Questa è la signorina...**	kooa**yss**tah ay lah seeñoa**ree**nah
I'm very pleased to meet you.	**Piacere.**	peeah**chay**ray
How are you?	**Come sta?**	**koa**may stah
Very well, thank you.	**Molto bene. Grazie.**	**moal**toa **bai**nay. **grah**tseeay
And you?	**E lei?**	ay **la**iee
Fine.	**Bene.**	**bai**nay
Excuse me.	**Mi scusi.**	mee **skoo**zee

Questions

Where?	**Dove?**	**doa**vay
Where is...?	**Dov'è...?**	doa**vai**
Where are...?	**Dove sono...?**	**doa**vay **soa**noa

When?	**Quando?**	kwahndoa
What?	**Cosa?**	kawssah
How?	**Come?**	koamay
How much?	**Quanto?**	kwahntoa
How many?	**Quanti?**	kwahntee
Who?	**Chi?**	kee
Why?	**Perchè?**	pehrkay
Which?	**Quale?**	kwarlay
What do you call this?	**Come si chiama questo?**	koamay see keearmah kooaysstoa
What do you call that?	**Come si chiama quello?**	koamay see keearmah kooaylloa
What does this mean?	**Cosa significa questo?**	kawssah seeñeefeekah kooaystoa
What does that mean?	**Cosa significa quello?**	kawssah seeñeefeekah kooaylloa

ITALIAN (vertical text in left margin)

Do you speak . . . ?

Do you speak English?	**Parla inglese?**	pahrlah eengglayssay
Do you speak German?	**Parla tedesco?**	pahrlah taydayskoa
Do you speak French?	**Parla francese?**	pahrlah frahnchayzay
Do you speak Spanish?	**Parla spagnolo?**	pahrlah spahñoaloa
Do you speak Italian?	**Parla italiano?**	pahrlah eetahlyarnoa
Could you speak more slowly, please?	**Può parlare più adagio, per piacere?**	pwo pahrlarray peeoo ahdarjoa pair peeahchayray
Please point to the phrase in the book.	**Per favore, mi indichi la frase nel libro.**	pair fahvoaray mee eendeekee lah frarzay nehl leebroa
Just a minute. I'll see if I can find it in this book.	**Un momento. Vedo se posso trovarla nel libro.**	oon moamayntoa. vaydoa say posssoa troavarrlah nayl leebroa
I understand.	**Capisco.**	kahpeesskoa
I don't understand.	**Non capisco.**	noan kahpeesskao

Can...?

Can I have...?	**Posso avere...?**	**posss**soa ahvay**ray**
Can we have...?	**Possiamo avere...?**	posss**eear**moa ahvay**ray**
Can you show me...?	**Può indicarmi...?**	pwo eendee**karr**mee
Can you tell me...?	**Può dirmi...?**	pwo **deer**mee
Can you help me, please?	**Può aiutarmi, per piacere?**	pwo ighoo**tarr**mee pair peeah**chay**ray

Wanting

I'd like...	**Vorrei...**	vor**raiee**
We'd like...	**Vorremmo...**	vor**rehm**moa
Please give me...	**Per favore, mi dia...**	pair fah**voa**ray mee **dee**ah
Give it to me, please.	**Me lo dia, per favore.**	may loa **dee**ah pair fah**voa**ray
Please bring me...	**Per favore, mi porti...**	pair fah**voa**ray mee **por**tee
Bring it to me, please.	**Me lo porti, per favore.**	may loa **por**tee pair fah**voa**ray
I'm hungry.	**Ho fame.**	oa **far**may
I'm thirsty.	**Ho sete.**	oa **say**tay
I'm tired.	**Sono stanco.**	**soa**noa **stahng**koa
I'm lost.	**Mi sono perso.**	mee **soa**noa **pehr**soa
It's important.	**È importante.**	ay eempor**tahn**tay
It's urgent.	**È urgente.**	ay oor**jehn**tay
Hurry up!	**Si affretti!**	see ahf**frayt**tee

It is/There is...

It is/It's...	**È...**	ai
Is it...?	**È...?**	ai
It isn't...	**Non è...**	noan ai
There is/There are...	**C'è/Ci sono...**	chai/chee **soa**noa
Is there/Are there...?	**C'è/Ci sono...?**	chai/chee **soa**noa

ITALIAN

| There isn't/There aren't... | **Non c'è/Non ci sono...** | noan chai/noan chee soanoa |
| There isn't any/There aren't any. | **Non ce n'è/Non ce ne sono.** | noan chay nai/noan chay nay soanoa |

A few common words

big/small	**grande/piccolo**	grahnday/peekkoaloa
quick/slow	**rapido/lento**	rarpeedoa/lehntoa
early/late	**presto/tardi**	prehsstoa/tahrdee
cheap/expensive	**economico/costoso**	aykoanawmeekoa/kosstoasoa
near/far	**vicino/lontano**	veecheenoa/lontarnoa
hot/cold	**caldo/freddo**	kahldoa/frayddoa
full/empty	**pieno/vuoto**	peeaynoa/vooawtoa
easy/difficult	**facile/difficile**	farcheelay/deefeecheelay
heavy/light	**pesante/leggero**	paysahntay/laydjairoa
open/shut	**aperto/chiuso**	ahpehrtoa/keeoossoa
right/wrong	**giusto/sbagliato**	joosstoa/zbahlyartoa
old/new	**vecchio/nuovo**	vehkkeeoa/nooawvoa
old/young	**vecchio/giovane**	vehkkeeoa/joavahnay
beautiful/ugly	**bello/brutto**	behlloa/broottoa
good/bad	**buono/cattivo**	booawnoa/kahtteevoa
better/worse	**migliore/peggiore**	meelyoaray/paydjoaray

Some prepositions and a few more useful words

at	**a**	ah
on	**sopra**	soaprah
in	**in**	een
to	**a**	ah
from	**da**	dah
inside	**dentro**	dayntroa
outside	**fuori**	fooawree
up	**sù**	soo
down	**giù**	joo
before	**prima di**	preemah dee
after	**dopo di**	dawpoa dee
with	**con**	kon
without	**senza**	sayntsah
through	**attraverso**	ahttrahvehrsoa
towards	**verso**	vehrsoa
until	**fino a**	feenoa ah
during	**durante**	doorahntay
and	**e**	ay
or	**o**	oa
not	**non**	noan
nothing	**niente**	neeehntay
none	**nessuno**	naysssoonoa

ITALIAN

very	molto	moaltoa
also	anche	ahngkay
soon	presto	prehsstoa
perhaps	forse	forsay
here	qui	kooee
there	là	lah
now	ora	oarah
then	poi	poy

Arrival

Your passport, please.	Il passaporto, per favore.	eel pahsssahportoa pair fahvoaray
Here it is.	Eccolo.	ehkkoaloa
Have you anything to declare?	Ha qualcosa da dichiarare?	ah kwahlkawssah dah deekeeahrarray
No, nothing at all.	No. Non ho nulla.	noa noan oa noollah
Porter!	Facchino!	fahkkeenoa
Can you help me with my luggage, please?	Può prendere le mie valige, per favore?	pwo prehndayray lay meeay vahleejay pair fahvoaray
That's my suitcase.	Quella è la mia valigia.	kooayllah ai lah meeah vahleejah
Where's the bus to the centre of town, please?	Dov'è l'autobus per il centro della città, per favore?	doavai lowtoabooss pair eel chehntroa dayllah cheettah pair fahvoaray
This way, please.	Da questa parte, per piacere.	dah kooaysstah pahrtay pair peeahchayray

Changing money

| Can you change a traveller's cheque, please? | Può cambiarmi un traveller's cheque, per favore? | pwo kahmbeearrmee oon "traveller's cheque" pair fahvoaray |
| Where's the nearest bank, please? | Dov'è la banca più vicina, per favore? | doavai lah bahngkah peeoo veecheenah pair fahvoaray |

Car rental

I'd like a car.	Vorrei un'automobile.	vorraiee oon owtoamawbeelay
For how long?	Per quanto tempo?	pair kooahntoa tehmpoa
A day/Four days/ A week/Two weeks.	Un giorno/Quattro giorni/Una settimana/Due settimane.	oon joarnoa/kooahttroa joarnee/oonah sayteemarnah/dooay saytteemarnay

ITALIAN

Taxi

Where can I get a taxi?	**Dove posso trovare un tassi?**	doavay **poss**soa troavarray oon tahs**see**
What's the fare to . . . ?	**Quanto costa la corsa per . . . ?**	**kwahn**toa **koss**tah lah **kor**sah pair
Take me to this address, please.	**Mi porti a questo indirizzo, per favore.**	mee **por**tee ah koo**ayss**toa eendee**reet**tsoa pair fah**voa**ray
I'm in a hurry.	**Ho fretta.**	oa **fray**ttah
Could you drive more slowly, please?	**Può guidare più adagio, per favore?**	pwo gooee**dar**ray pee**oo** ah**dar**joa pair fah**voa**ray

Hotel and other accommodation

My name is . . .	**Mi chiamo . . .**	mee kee**ar**moa
Have you a reservation?	**Ha fatto la prenotazione?**	ah **faht**toa lah praynoatahtsee**oa**nay
Yes, here's the confirmation.	**Sì; ecco la conferma.**	see **ehk**koa lah kon**fehr**mah
I'd like . . .	**Vorrei . . .**	vor**raie**
I'd like a single room/a double room.	**Vorrei una camera singola/per due persone.**	vor**raie** **oo**nah **kar**mayrah **seeng**goalah/pair **dooay** payr**soa**nay
a room with a bath/with a shower	**una camera con bagno/con doccia**	**oo**nah **kar**mayrah kon **bah**ñoa/kon **dot**chah

How much?

What's the price per night/per week/per month?	**Qual è il prezzo per una notte/per una settimana/per un mese?**	kwah**lai** eel **preht**tsoa pàir **oo**nah **not**tay/pair **oo**nah saytteemar**nah**/pair oon **may**ssay
May I see the room?	**Posso vedere la camera?**	**poss**soa vay**day**ray lah **kar**mayrah
I'm sorry, I don't like it.	**Mi dispiace: non è di mio gradimento.**	mee despee**ar**chay noan ai dee **mee**oa grahdee**mayn**toa
Yes, that's fine. I'll take it.	**Sì, va bene. La prendo.**	see vah **bai**nay lah **prayn**doa
What's my room number, please?	**Qual è il numero della mia camera?**	kwah**lai** eel **noo**mayroa **dayl**lah **mee**ah **kar**mayrah
Number 123.	**Numero 123.**	**noo**mayroa 123

Service, please

Who is it?	Chi è?	kee ai
Just a minute.	Un momento, per favore.	oon moamayntoa pair fahvoaray
Come in! The door's open.	Avanti! La porta è aperta.	ahvahntee lah portah ai ahpehrtah
May we have breakfast in our room?	Possiamo fare la prima colazione in camera?	possseearmoa farray lah preemah koalahtseeoanay een karmayran

Breakfast

I'll have...	Vorrei...	vorraiee
I'll have some fruit juice.	Vorrei un succo di frutta.	vorraiee oon sookkoa dee froottah
a boiled egg	un uovo alla "coque"	oon ooawvoa ahllah kok
a fried egg	un uovo al tegame	oon ooawvoa ahl taygarmay
some bacon/some ham	della pancetta affumicata/del prosciutto	dayllah pahnchehttah ahffoomeekartah/dayl proashoottoa
some toast	del pane tostato	dayl parnay toasstartoa
a pot of tea	del tè	dayl tay
a cup of tea	una tazza di tè	oonah tahttsah dee tay
some coffee	del caffè	dayl kahffay
some chocolate	della cioccolata	dayllah choakkoalartah
more butter	un altro po'di burro	oon ahltroa po dee boorroa
some hot water	dell'acqua calda	daylahkkooah kahldah

Difficulties

The central heating doesn't work.	Il riscaldamento centrale non funziona.	eel reesskahldahmayntoa chayntrarlay noan foontseeoanah
the light/the socket	la luce/la presa	lah loochay/lah praysah
the tap/the toilet	il rubinetto/il gabinetto	eel roobeenayttoa/eel gahbeenayttoa
There's no hot water.	Non c'è acqua calda.	noan chai ahkkooah kahldah
May I see the manager, please?	Posso vedere il direttore, per piacere?	possoa vaydayray eel deerayttoaray pair peeahchayray

ITALIAN

Telephone—Mail

There's a call for you.	C'è una telefonata per lei.	chai oonah taylayfoanartah pair laiee
Hold the line, please.	Resti in linea, per piacere.	rehsstee een leenayah pair peeahchayray
Operator, I've been cut off.	Signorina, mi hanno interrotto.	seeñoareenah mee ahnnoa eentehrrottoa
Did anyone telephone me?	Mi ha telefonato qualcuno?	mee ah taylayfoanartoa kwahlkoonoa
Is there any mail for me?	C'è posta per me?	chai posstah pair may
Are there any messages for me?	Ci sono comunicazioni per me?	chee soanoa komooneekahtseeoanee pair may

Checking out

May I have my bill, please?	Posso avere il mio conto, per favore?	posssoa ahvayray eel meeoa koantoa pair fahvoaray
We're in a great hurry.	Abbiamo molta fretta.	ahbbeearmoa moaltah frayttah
It's been a very enjoyable stay.	È stato un soggiorno molto piacevole.	ai startoa oon soadjoarnoa moaltoa peeahchayvoalay

Eating out

Good evening, sir/ Good evening, madam.	Buona sera, signore/Buona sera, signora.	bwonah sayrah seeñoaray/bwonah sayrah seeñoarrah
Good evening. I'd like a table for two, please.	Buona sera. Vorrei una tavola per due, per favore.	bwonah sayrah. vorraiee oonah tarvoalah pair dooay pair fahvoaray
Do you have a fixed-price menu?	Avete un menu a prezzo fisso?	ahvaytay oon maynoo ah prehttsoa feesssoa
May I see the à la carte menu?	Posso vedere il menu a scelta?	posssoa vaydayray eel maynoo ah shayltah
May we have an ashtray, please?	Posso avere un portacenere, per favore?	posssoa ahvayray oon portahchaynayray pair fahvoaray
some bread	un po'di pane	oon po dee parnay
a fork	una forchetta	oonah forkehttah
a knife	un coltello	oon koaltehlloa

a spoon	un cucchiaio	oon kookkeeighoa
a plate	un piatto	oon peeahttoa
a glass	un bicchiere	oon beekkeeairay
a napkin	un tovagliolo	oon toavahlyawloa
another chair	un'altra sedia	oonahltrah saideeah
Where's the gentlemen's toilet (men's room)?	Dove sono i gabinetti per uomini?	doavay soanoa ee gahbeenayttee pair ooomeenee
Where's the ladies' toilet (ladies' room)?	Dove sono i gabinetti per signore?	doavay soanoa ee gahbeenayttee pair seeñoaray

Appetizers

I'd like some . . .	Vorrei . . .	vorraiee
I'd like some assorted appetizers.	Vorrei degli antipasti assortiti.	vorraiee daylyee ahnteepahsstee ahssorteettee
orange juice	un succo d'arancia	oon sookkoa dahrahnchah
ham	del prosciutto	day proashoottoa
melon	del melone	dayl mayloanay
pâté	del pâté	dayl pahtay
smoked salmon	del salmone affumicato	dayl sahlmoanay ahffoomeekartoa
shrimps (shrimp)	dei gamberetti	daiee gahmbayrayttee

Soup

Have you any . . . ?	Ha . . . ?	ah
Have you any chicken soup?	Ha un brodo di pollo?	ah oon brawdoa dee poalloa
vegetable soup	una minestra di verdure	oonah meenehsstrah dee vehrdooray
onion soup	una minestra di cipolle	oonah meenehsstrah dee cheepoallay

Fish

I'd like some . . .	Vorrei . . .	vorraiee
I'd like some fish.	Vorrei del pesce.	vorraiee dayl payshay
sole	della sogliola	dayllah sawlyoalah
trout	delle trote	dayllay trawtay
lobster	un'aragosta	oon ahrahgoasstah
crayfish	dei gamberi d'acqua dolce	daiee gahmbayree dahkkooah dolchay
prawns	dei gamberi	daiee gahmbayree

ITALIAN

I'd like it...	**Li vorrei ...**	lee vorraiee
I'd like it steamed.	**Li vorrei al vapore.**	lee vorraiee ahl vahpoaray
grilled	**alla griglia**	ahllah greelyah
boiled	**bolliti**	bolleetee
baked	**al forno**	ahl fornoa
fried	**fritti**	freettee

Meat—Poultry—Game

I'd like some...	**Vorrei ...**	vorraiee
I'd like some beef.	**Vorrei del manzo.**	vorraiee dayl **mahn**dzoa
a beef steak	**una bistecca di manzo**	oonah bee**stayk**kah dee **mahn**dzoa
some roast beef	**un arrosto di manzo**	oon ahr**roass**toa dee **mahn**dzoa
a veal cutlet	**una cotoletta di vitello**	oonah koatoa**layt**tah dee vee**tehl**loa
mutton	**del montone**	dayl moan**toa**nay
lamb	**dell'agnello**	dayl ah**ñehl**loa
a pork chop	**una braciola di maiale**	oonah brah**choa**lah dee mi**ghar**lay
roast pork	**un arrosto di maiale**	oon ahr**ross**toa dee mi**ghar**lay
hare	**della lepre**	**day**llah lai**pray**
chicken	**del pollo**	dayl **poal**loa
roast chicken	**del pollo arrosto**	dayl **poal**loa ahr**roass**toa
duck	**dell'anatra**	dayl **ar**nahtrah
How do you like your meat?	**Come vuole la carne?**	**koa**may voo**aw**lay lah **kahr**nay
rare	**al sangue**	ahl **sahn**gooay
medium	**non troppo cotta**	noan **trop**poa **kot**tah
well done	**ben cotta**	bain **kot**tah

Vegetables

What vegetables have you got?	**Quali legumi ha?**	**koo**arlee lay**goo**mee ah
I'd like some...	**Vorrei ...**	vorraiee
I'd like some asparagus.	**Vorrei degli asparagi.**	vorraiee **day**lyee ahspar**rah**jee
green beans	**dei fagiolini**	daiee fahjoa**lee**nee
mushrooms	**dei funghi**	daiee **foong**gee
carrots	**delle carote**	**day**llay kah**raw**tay
onions	**delle cipolle**	**day**llay chee**poal**lay
red cabbage	**dei cavoli rossi**	daiee **kah**voalee **ross**see

spinach	**degli spinaci**	**day**lyee speen**ar**chee
rice	**del riso**	dayl **ree**soa
peas	**dei piselli**	daiee pee**seh**llee
tomatoes	**dei pomodori**	daiee poamoa**daw**ree
green salad	**dell'insalata**	dayl eensah**lar**tah
potatoes	**delle patate**	**day**llay pah**tar**tay

Desserts

Nothing more, thanks.	**Nient'altro. Grazie.**	neeehntahltroa **grah**tseeay
Just a small portion, please.	**Solo una piccola porzione, per favore.**	soaloa oonah peek**koal**ah portseeoanay pair fah**voa**ray
Have you any ice-cream?	**Ha un gelato?**	ah oon jay**lar**toa
fruit salad	**una macedonia**	oonah mahchay**daw**neeah
fresh fruit	**della frutta fresca**	**day**llah **froot**tah **frayss**kah
cheese	**del formaggio**	dayl for**mahd**joa

Drink

What would you like to drink?	**Cosa desidera da bere?**	**kaw**ssah day**zee**dayrah dah **bay**ray
I'll have a beer, please.	**Mi dia una birra, per piacere.**	mee **dee**ah oonah **beer**rah pair peeah**chay**ray
I'll have a whisky, please.	**Mi dia un whisky, per favore.**	mee **dee**ah oon whisky (**wiss**kee) pair fah**voa**ray

Wine

I'd like a bottle of wine.	**Vorrei una bottiglia di vino.**	vor**raie**e oonah bot**tee**lyah dee **vee**noa
red wine	**di vino rosso**	dee **vee**noa **roass**soa
rosé wine	**di rosé**	dee roa**zay**
white wine	**di vino bianco**	dee **vee**noa bee**ahng**koa
Cheers!	**Salute!**	sah**loo**tay

The bill (check)

| May I have the bill (check) please? | **Posso avere il mio conto, per piacere?** | **poss**soa ah**vay**ray eel **mee**oa **koan**toa pair peeah**chay**ray |
| Is service included? | **È compreso il servizio?** | ai koam**pray**zoa eel sayr**veet**seeoa |

ITALIAN

Everything's included.	**Tutto compreso.**	**toot**toa koam**pray**zoa
Thank you, that was a very good meal.	**Grazie. Abbiamo mangiato molto bene.**	**graht**seeay ahbbee**ar**moa mahn**jar**toa **moal**toa **bai**nay

Travelling

Where's the railway station, please?	**Dove si trova la stazione, per favore?**	**doa**vay see **traw**vah lah stahtsee**oa**nay pair fah**voa**ray
Where's the ticket office, please?	**Dove si trova lo sportello dei biglietti, per favore?**	**doa**vay see **traw**vah loa spor**tehl**loa **dai**ee beelyayt**tee** pair fah**voa**ray
I'd like a ticket to ...	**Vorrei un biglietto per ...**	vor**raiee** oon beelyayt**toa** pair
First or second class?	**Di prima o di seconda classe?**	dee **pree**mah oa dee say**koan**dah **klahss**say
First class, please.	**Di prima classe, per piacere.**	dee **pree**mah **klahss**say pair peeah**chay**ray
Single or return (one way or round-trip)?	**Andata o andata e ritorno?**	ahn**dar**tah oa ahn**dar**tah ay reetor**noa**
Do I have to change trains?	**Devo cambiare treno?**	**day**voa kahmbee**ar**ray **tray**noa
What platform does the train leave from?	**Da che binario parte il treno?**	dah kay beenar**reeoa** **pahr**tay eel **tray**noa
Where's the nearest underground (subway) station?	**Dov'è la più vicina stazione della metropolitana?**	doa**vai** lah peeoo vee**chee**nah stahtsee**oa**nay **dayl**lah may-troapoalee**tar**nah
Where's the bus station, please?	**Dov'è la stazione degli autobus, per piacere?**	doa**vai** lah stahtsee**oa**nay **day**lyee **ow**toabooss pair peeah**chay**ray
When's the first bus to ...?	**Quando passa il primo autobus per ...?**	**kwahn**doa **pahss**sah eel **pree**moa **ow**toabooss pair
the last bus/the next bus	**l'ultimo autobus/il prossimo autobus**	**lool**teemoa **ow**toabooss/ eel **prosss**eemoa **ow**toabooss
Please let me off at the next stop.	**Mi faccia scendere alla prossima fermata, per piacere.**	mee **faht**chah **shayn**dayray **ahl**lah **prosss**seemah fehr**mar**tah pair peeah**chay**ray

Relaxing

What's on at the cinema (movies)?	Cosa danno al cinema?	kawssah dahnnoa ahl cheenaymah
What's on at the theatre?	Cosa danno al teatro?	kawssah dahnnoa ahl tayartroa
What time does the film begin? And the play?	A che ora incomincia il film? E la rappresentazione?	ah kay oarah eengkoa-meencheeah eel feelm? ay lah rahppprayssayntah-tseeoanay
Are there any tickets for tonight?	Ci sono ancora posti liberi per questa sera?	chee soanoa ahngkoarah poastee leebayree pair kooaysstah sayrah
Where can we go dancing?	Dove possiamo andare a ballare?	doavay possseearmoa ahndarray ah bahllarray
Would you like to dance?	Vuole ballare?	vooawlay bahllarray

Introductions

How do you do?	Buon giorno.	bwon joarnoa
How are you?	Come sta?	koamay stah
Very well, thank you. And you?	Molto bene, grazie. E lei?	moaltoa bainay grahtseeay. ay laiee
May I introduce Miss Philips?	Posso presentarle la signorina Philips?	posssoa prayzayntarrlay lah seenoareenah Philips
My name is...	Mi chiamo...	mee keearmoa
I'm very pleased to meet you.	Sono molto lieto di fare la sua conoscenza.	soanoa moaltoa leeaytoa dee farray lah sooah koanoashehntsah
How long have you been here?	Da quanto tempo è qui?	dah kwahntoa tehmpoa ai kooee
It was nice meeting you.	Sono lieto di aver fatto la sua conoscenza.	soanoa leeaytoa dee ahvayr fahttoa lah sooah koanoashehntsah

Dating

Would you like a cigarette?	Accetta una sigaretta?	ahtchayttah oonah seegahrayttah
May I get you a drink?	Posso offrirle da bere?	posssoa offffreerlay dah bayray

ITALIAN

ITALIAN

Do you have a light, please?	**Mi fa accendere, per piacere?**	mee fah aht**chehn**dayray pair peeah**chay**ray
Are you waiting for someone?	**Attende qualcuno?**	aht**tehn**day kooahl-**koo**noa
Are you free this evening?	**È libera, stasera?**	ai lee**bay**rah stah**say**rah
Where shall we meet?	**Dove possiamo incontrarci?**	**doa**vay posss**seear**moa eengkon**trarr**chee
What time shall I meet you?	**A che ora la vedrò?**	ah kay **o**arah lah vay**droa**
May I take you home?	**Posso accompa-gnarla a casa?**	posss**soa** ahkkoampah-**ñarr**lah ah **kars**sah
Thank you, it's been a wonderful evening.	**Grazie! È stata una magnifica serata.**	**grah**tseeay! ai **star**tah **oo**nah mañee**fee**kah say-**rar**tah
What's your telephone number?	**Qual è il suo nu-mero di telefono?**	kwah**lai** eel **soo**oa **noo**mayroa dee tay**lai**foanoa
Do you live alone?	**Vive sola?**	**vee**vay **soa**lah
What time is your last train?	**A che ora parte il suo ultimo treno?**	ah kay **o**arah **pahr**tay eel **soo**oa **ool**teemoa **tray**noa
Good-night ...	**Buona notte ...**	**bwo**nah **not**tay

Banks

Where's the nearest bank, please?	**Dov'è la banca più vicina, per favore?**	doa**vai** lah **bahng**kah **peeoo** vee**chee**nah pair fah**voa**ray
Where can I cash some traveller's cheques?	**Dove posso cam-biare un traveller's cheque?**	**doa**vay posss**soa** kahm-bee**ar**ray oon "traveller's cheque"
What time does the bank open/What time does it close?	**A che ora apre la banca/A che ora chiude?**	ah kay **o**arah **ah**pray la **bahng**kah/ah kay **o**arah **keeoo**oday
I'm expecting some money from home. Has it arrived?	**Aspetto del denaro da casa. È arrivato?**	ah**spayt**toa dayl day**nar**roa dah **kars**sah. ai ahr-ree**var**toa
Can you give me some small change, please?	**Potrebbe darmi della moneta spic-ciola, per favore?**	poa**trayb**bay **darr**mee **day**lah moa**nay**tah **speet**choa-lah pair fah**voa**ray

Shops, stores and services

Where is the nearest chemist's (pharmacy)?	**Dov'è la più vicina farmacia?**	doavai lah peeoo veecheenah fahrmahcheeah
the nearest hairdresser's	**il parrucchiere più vicino**	eel pahrrookkeeairay peeoo veecheenoa
the photo shop	**il fotografo**	eel foatawgrahfoa
the jeweller's	**la gioielleria**	lah joyayllayreeah
the department store	**il grande magazzino**	eel **grahn**day mahgahd**dzee**noa
the police station	**la questura (il posto di polizia)**	lah kooaysstoorah (eel **poass**toa dee poaleetseeah)
the garage	**l'autorimessa**	lowtoareemaysssah
How do I get there?	**Come ci si può arrivare?**	**koa**may chee see pwo ahrreevarray
Is it within walking distance?	**Ci si può andare anche a piedi?**	chee see pwo ahn**dar**ray **ahng**kay ah peeaydee

Service

Can you help me, please?	**Può aiutarmi, per piacere?**	pwo ighootarrmee pair peeahchayray
Can you show me this? And that, too.	**Può mostrarmi questo? E anche quello.**	pwo moasstrarrmee kooaysstoa? ay ahngkay kooaylloa
It's too expensive/too big/too small.	**È troppo caro/troppo grande/troppo piccolo.**	ay troppoa karroa/troppoa grahnday/troppoa peekkoaloa
Can you show me some more?	**Mi può mostrare una scelta più ampia?**	mee pwo moasstrarray oonah shayltah peeoo ahmpeeah
something better	**qualcosa migliore**	kwahlkawssah meelyoaray
something cheaper	**qualcosa di più economico**	kwahlkawssah dee peeoo aykoanawmeekoa
How much is this? And that?	**Quanto costa questo? E quello?**	kwahntoa kosstah kooaysstoa? ay kooaylloa
It's not quite what I want.	**Non è proprio quello che volevo.**	noan ay prawpreeoa kooaylloah kay voalayvoa
I like it.	**Questo mi piace.**	kooaysstoa mee peearchay

ITALIAN

Chemist's (Pharmacy)

I'd like something for a cold/for a cough/for travel sickness.	Vorrei qualcosa per il raffreddore/per la tosse/per il mal di moto.	vorraiee kwahlkawssah pair eel rahffrayddoaray/ pair lah toasssay/pair eel mahl dee mawtoa
Can you recommend something for hay-fever/for sunburn?	Puo consigliarmi qualcosa per la febbre del fieno/per una scottatura di sole?	pwo koanseelyarrmee kwahlkawssah pair lah faybbray dayl feeehnoa/ pair oonah skottahtoorah dee soalay

Toiletry

May I have some razor blades?	Potrei avere delle lamette da barba?	poatraiee ahvayray dayllay lahmayttay dah bahrbah
some shaving cream	una crema da barba	oonah kraimah dah bahrbah
some toothpaste	un dentifricio	oon daynteefreechoa
I'd like some soap.	Vorrei una saponetta.	vorraiee oonah sahpoanayttah
some suntan oil	dell'olio per la tintarella	dayl awlyoa pair lah teentahrehllah

At the barber's

I'd like a haircut, please.	Vorrei farmi tagliare i capelli, per favore.	vorraiee farrmee tahlyarray ee kahpayllee pair fahvoaray
Short/Leave it long.	Corti/Li lasci lunghi.	koartee/lee lahshee loonggee
A razor cut, please.	Un taglio col rasoio, per piacere.	oon tarlyoa koal rahsaweeoa pair peeahchayray

At the hairdresser's

I'd like a shampoo and set, please.	Vorrei uno shampoo e una messa in piega, per piacere.	vorraiee oonoa ''shampoo'' ay oonah maysssah een peeaigah pair peeahchayray
I'd like a bleach.	Vorrei una decolorazione.	vorraiee oona daykoaloarahtseeoanay
a permanent	una permanente	oonah payrmahnehntay
a colour rinse	un ''cachet''	oon kahshay
a manicure	una manicure	oonah mahneekooray

Photography

| I'd like a film for this camera. | **Vorrei un rullino per questa macchina fotografica.** | vorraiee oon roolleenoa pair kooaysstah mahk-keenah foatoagrarfeekah |
| This camera doesn't work. | **Questa macchina fotografica non funziona.** | kooaysstah mahkkeenah foatoagrarfeekah noan foontseeoanah |

At the post office

| Where's the nearest post office, please? | **Dove si trova l'ufficio postale più vicino, per favore?** | doavay see trawvah looffeechoa poasstarlay peeoo veecheenoa pair fahvoaray |
| I'd like to send this by express (special delivery)/by air mail. | **Vorrei spedire questo per espresso/per via aerea.** | vorraiee spaydeeray kooaysstoa pair ayssprehssoa/pair veeah ahairayah |

Service stations

Where is the nearest service station, please?	**Dove si trova la più vicina stazione di rifornimento, per favore?**	doavay see trawvah lah peeoo veecheenah stah-tseeoanay dee reefornee-mayntoa pair fahvoaray
Fill her up, please.	**Faccia il pieno, per favore.**	fahtchah eel peeainoa pair fahvoaray
Check the oil, please.	**Controlli l'olio, per favore.**	koantroallee lawlyoa pair fahvoaray
Would you check the tyres?	**Vorrebbe controllare le gomme?**	vorraybbay koantroallarray lay gommay

Street directions

Can you show me on the map where I am?	**Può indicarmi sulla carta dove mi trovo?**	pwo eendeekarrmee sool-lah kahrtah doavay mee trawvoa
You're on the wrong road.	**È sulla strada sbagliata.**	ay soollah strardah zbahlyartah
Go back to ...	**Ritorni a ...**	reetoarnee ah
Go straight ahead.	**Continui diritto.**	koanteenooee deereettoa
It's on the left/on the right.	**È a sinistra/a destra.**	ai ah seeneesstrah/ah dehstrah

Accidents

May I use your telephone?	**Potrei usare il suo telefono?**	poatra**ie** oo**zar**ray eel **soo**oa tayla**i**foanoa
Call a doctor quickly.	**Chiami subito un medico.**	kee**ar**mee **soo**beetoa oon **mai**deekoa
Call an ambulance.	**Chiami un'auto-ambulanza.**	kee**ar**mee oon owtoaahm-boo**lahnt**sah
Please call the police.	**Per piacere, chiami la polizia.**	pair peeah**chay**ray kee**ar**mee lah poalee**tseeah**

Numbers

zero	**zero**	**dzay**roa
one	**uno**	**oo**noa
two	**due**	**doo**ay
three	**tre**	tray
four	**quattro**	koo**ahtt**roa
five	**cinque**	**cheeng**kooay
six	**sei**	**seh**ee
seven	**sette**	**seht**tay
eight	**otto**	**ott**oa
nine	**nove**	**naw**vay
ten	**dieci**	**dee**aichee
eleven	**undici**	**oon**deechee
twelve	**dodici**	**doa**deechee
thirteen	**tredici**	**tray**deechee
fourteen	**quattordici**	koo**ahtt**ordeechee
fifteen	**quindici**	koo**ee**ndeechee
sixteen	**sedici**	**say**deechee
seventeen	**diciassette**	deechah**sss**eht**tay**
eighteen	**diciotto**	dee**chott**oa
nineteen	**diciannove**	deechah**naw**vay
twenty	**venti**	**vayn**tee
twenty-one	**ventuno**	vayn**too**noa
thirty	**trenta**	**trayn**tah
forty	**quaranta**	koo**a**rahntah
fifty	**cinquanta**	cheengkoo**a**hntah
sixty	**sessanta**	saysss**a**hntah
seventy	**settanta**	sayt**tahn**tah
eighty	**ottanta**	oat**tahn**tah
ninety	**novanta**	noa**vahn**tah
one hundred	**cento**	**chehn**toa
one thousand	**mille**	**meel**lay
ten thousand	**diecimila**	deeehchee**mee**lah

Days

It's Sunday.	**È domenica.**	ai doa**may**neekah
Monday	**lunedì**	loonay**dee**
Tuesday	**martedì**	mahrtay**dee**
Wednesday	**mercoledì**	mehrkoalay**dee**
Thursday	**giovedì**	joavay**dee**
Friday	**venerdì**	vaynayr**dee**
Saturday	**sabato**	**sar**bahtoa
yesterday	**ieri**	ee**ai**ree
today	**oggi**	**od**jee
tomorrow	**domani**	doa**mar**nee
morning/afternoon	**mattino/pomeriggio**	mah**ttee**noa/poamay**reed**joa
evening/night	**sera/notte**	**say**rah/**not**tay

Months

January	**gennaio**	jay**nigh**oa
February	**febbraio**	fehb**brigh**oa
March	**marzo**	**mahr**tsoa
April	**aprile**	ah**pree**lay
May	**maggio**	**mahd**joa
June	**giugno**	**joo**ñoa
July	**luglio**	**lool**yoa
August	**agosto**	ah**goass**toa
September	**settembre**	say**ttehm**bray
October	**ottobre**	oa**ttoa**bray
November	**novembre**	noa**vehm**bray
December	**dicembre**	dee**chehm**bray
Merry Christmas!	**Buon Natale!**	bwon nah**tar**lay!
Happy New Year!	**Buon Anno!**	bwon **ahn**noa

NORWEGIAN

Guide to Pronunciation

Letter	Approximate pronunciation	Symbol	Example	

Consonants

b, d, f, h, m, n, p, t, v	as in English			
g	1) before **i**, **y** or **ei**, like **y** in **yet**	y	**g**i	yee
	2) otherwise, like **g** in **go**	g	**g**ate	**ga**rter
j, gj, hj, lj	like **y** in **yet**	y	**j**a	yar
			hjem	yehm
k	1) before **i**, **y** or **j**, like **ch** in German i**ch**, or something like **ch** in Scottish lo**ch**; it is similar to the first sound of **h**uge	kh	**k**irke	**kheer**ker
			kyst	khewst
	2) otherwise like **k** in **k**it	k	**k**affe	**kah**ffer
l	always as in lee, never as in bell	l	ta**l**e	**tar**ler

r	in southwestern Norway, it is pronounced in the back of the mouth (as in French), elsewhere it is slightly rolled in the front of the mouth	r	**rask**	rahsk

N.B. In the groups **rd**, **rl**, **rn** and **rt**, the **r** tends not to be pronounced but influences the pronunciation of the following consonant, which is then pronounced with the tongue behind the upper teeth ridge (turned upwards at the front). We don't use a special symbol for this retroflex pronunciation of **d**, **l**, **n** or **t**.

rs	is generally pronounced like **sh** in **sh**ut in eastern Norway	sh	**norsk**	noshk
s	always as in **s**o	s/ss	**rose**	**roo**sser
sj, skj, sk	when followed by **i**, **y**, **ø** or **øy**, like **sh** in **sh**ut	sh	**sjø**	shur
			ski	shee

N.B. The letters **c**, **q**, **w**, **z** are only found in foreign words, and tend to be pronounced as in the language of origin.

Vowels

In Norwegian, vowels in stressed syllables are long when followed by, at most, one pronounced consonant. They are generally short when followed by two or more consonants.

a	1) when long, like **a** in c**a**r	ar*	**dag**	darg
	2) when short, fairly like **u** in cut or **o** in American college	ah	**vaske**	**vah**sker
e	1) when long, like **ay**, in s**ay**, but a pure sound, *not* a diphthong	ay	**se**	say
	2) when short, like **e** in g**e**t	eh	**penn**	pehn
	3) when followed by **r**, like **a** in b**a**d; long or short	ææ / æ	**her** **sterk**	hææer stæerk
	4) when unstressed, like **er** in other	er*	**nese**	**nay**sser
i	1) when long, like **ee** in s**ee**, but with the tongue more raised, and the lips more drawn back at the sides	ee	**ti**	tee
	2) when short, like **ee** in m**ee**t	i	**drikke**	**drik**ker
o	1) when long, like **oo** in s**oo**n, but with the lips more rounded (when followed by **-rt**, **-st**, **-m** and **-nd**, it can be short)	oo	**god**	goo

---

* The **r** should not be pronounced when reading this transcription.

	2) when short, generally like **o** in hot	o	**tolv**	tol
u	1) something like the **ew** in few, or Scottish **oo** in good; you will find it very hard to distinguish from Norwegian **y**, so we use the same symbol for both	ew	**mur**	mewr
	2) in some words, like **oo** in foot	oo	**nummer**	noommerr
y	put your tongue in the position for the **ee** in bee, and then round your lips as for the **oo** in pool: the vowel you pronounce like this should be more or less correct	ew	**by** **tynn**	bew tewn
æ	1) before **r** like **a** in bad; usually long but sometimes short	ææ æ	**lære** **lærd**	læærer læd
	2) otherwise, like **ay** in say	ay	**hæl**	hayl
ø	like **u** in fur; either long or short	ur*	**dør** **søtt**	durr surt
å	1) when long, like **aw** in saw	aw	**på**	paw
	2) when short (rare), more like **o** in hot	o	**gått**	got

Diphthongs

au	this sounds like **ow** in now, but, in fact, the first part is a Norwegian ø-sound	ow	**sau**	sow
ei	like **ay** in say but often reminiscent of **igh** in sigh	ay	**vei**	vay
øy	fairly like **oy** in boy	oy	**høy**	hoy

Silent letters

1) The letter **g** is generally silent in the endings **-lig** and **-ig**.
2) The letter **d** is generally silent after **l** or **n** or after **r** at the end of a word (with lengthening of the vowel) or often after a long vowel, e.g. ho**ld**e, lan**d**, går**d**.
3) The letter **t** is silent in the definite form (''the'') of neuter nouns (e.g., eple**t**) and in the pronoun de**t**.
4) The letter **v** is silent in a few words, e.g., sel**v**, tol**v**, hal**v**, søl**v**.

---

* The **r** should not be pronounced when reading this transcription.

NORWEGIAN

Some basic expressions

Yes.	**Ja.**	yar
No.	**Nei.**	nay
Please.	**Vennligst.**	**vehn**ligst
Thank you.	**Takk.**	tahk
Thank you very much.	**Mange takk.**	**mahng**er tahk
That's all right.	**Ingen årsak.**	**ing**ern **aws**hahk

Greetings

Good morning.	**God morgen.**	goo **maw**ern
Good afternoon.	**God dag.**	goo darg
Good evening.	**God kveld./ God aften.**	goo kvehl/goo **ahf**tern
Good night.	**God natt.**	goo naht
Good-bye.	**Adjø.**	ah**dyur**
See you later.	**På gjensyn.**	paw **yehn**sewn
This is Mr....	**Dette er herr ...**	**deht**ter ær hær
This is Mrs....	**Dette er fru ...**	**deht**ter ær frew
This is Miss...	**Dette er frøken ...**	**deht**ter ær **frur**kern
I'm very pleased to meet you.	**Det gleder meg å treffe Dem.**	day **glay**derr may aw **treh**ffer dehm
How are you?	**Hvordan står det til?**	**voor**dahn stawr day til
Very well, thank you. And you?	**Bare bra, takk. Og med Dem?**	**barr**er brar tahk. awg may(d) dehm
Fine.	**Fint.**	fint
Excuse me.	**Unnskyld.**	**ewn**shewl

Questions

Where?	**Hvor?**	voor
Where is ... ?	**Hvor er ... ?**	voor ær
Where are ... ?	**Hvor er ... ?**	voor ær
When?	**Når?**	nawr

What?	**Hva?**	var
How?	**Hvordan?**	**voor**dahn
How much?	**Hvor mye?**	voor **mewer**
How many?	**Hvor mange?**	voor **mahnger**
Who?	**Hvem?**	vehm
Why?	**Hvorfor?**	**voor**for
Which?	**Hvilken?**	**vil**kern
What do you call this?	**Hva heter dette?**	var **hay**terr **deht**ter
What do you call that?	**Hva heter det?**	var **hay**terr day
What does this mean?	**Hva betyr dette?**	var ber**tewr deht**ter
What does that mean?	**Hva betyr det?**	var ber**tewr** day

Do you speak . . . ?

Do you speak English?	**Snakker De engelsk?**	**snahk**kerr dee **ehng**erlsk
Do you speak German?	**Snakker De tysk?**	**snahk**kerr dee tewsk
Do you speak French?	**Snakker De fransk?**	**snahk**kerr dee frahnsk
Do you speak Spanish?	**Snakker De spansk?**	**snahk**kerr dee spahnsk
Do you speak Italian?	**Snakker De italiensk?**	**snahk**kerr de itah**lee**ehnsk
Could you speak more slowly, please?	**Kunne De snakke litt saktere?**	**kewn**ner dee **snahk**ker lit **sahk**terrer
Please point to the phrase in the book.	**Kunne De peke på setningen i boken.**	**kewn**ner dee **pay**ker paw **seht**ningern ee **boo**kern
Just a minute. I'll see if I can find it in this book.	**Et øyeblikk. Jeg skal se om jeg kan finne det i denne boken.**	eht **oyer**blik. yay skal say om yay karn **fin**ner day ee **dehn**ner **boo**kern
I understand.	**Jeg forstår.**	yay for**shtawr**
I don't understand.	**Jeg forstår ikke.**	yay for**shtawr ik**ker

Can...?

Can I have...?	**Kan jeg få...?**	kahn yay faw
Can we have...?	**Kan vi få...?**	kahn vee faw
Can you show me...?	**Kan De vise meg...?**	kahn dee **vee**sser may
Can you tell me...?	**Kan De si meg...?**	kahn dee see may
Can you help me, please?	**Kan De være så vennlig å hjelpe meg?**	kahn dee **væææ**rer saw **vehn**lee aw **yehl**per may

Wanting

I'd like...	**Jeg vil gjerne ha...**	yay vil **yææ**ner har
We'd like...	**Vi ville gjerne ha...**	vee **vi**ler **yææ**ner har
Please give me...	**Vennligst, gi meg...**	**vehn**ligst yee may
Give it to me, please.	**Vennligst, gi det til meg.**	**vehn**ligst yee day til may
Please bring me...	**Vennligst, hent...til meg.**	**vehn**ligst hehnt...til may
Bring it to me, please.	**Vennligst, hent det til meg.**	**vehn**ligst hehnt day til may
I'm hungry.	**Jeg er sulten.**	yay ær **sewl**tern
I'm thirsty.	**Jeg er tørst.**	yay ær tursht
I'm tired.	**Jeg er trett.**	yay ær treht
I'm lost.	**Jeg har gått meg vill.**	yay har got may vil
It's important.	**Det er viktig.**	day ær **vik**tee
It's urgent.	**Det haster.**	day **hahss**terr
Hurry up!	**Skynd Dem!**	shewn dehm

It is/There is...

It is/It's...	**Det er...**	day ær
Is it...?	**Er det...?**	ær day
It isn't...	**Det er ikke...**	day ær **ik**ker
There is/There are...	**Det finnes...**	day **fin**nerss
Is there/Are there...?	**Finnes det...?**	**fin**nerss day

There isn't/There aren't...	**Det finnes ikke ...**	day finnerss ikker
There isn't any/ There aren't any.	**Det finnes ingen.**	day finnerss ingern

A few common words

big/small	**stor/liten**	stoor/leetern
quick/slow	**hurtig/langsom**	hewtee/lahngsom
early/late	**tidlig/sen**	teelee/sayn
cheap/expensive	**billig/dyr**	billee/dewr
near/far	**nær/langt borte**	næær/lahngt boorter
hot/cold	**varm/kald**	vahrm/kahl
full/empty	**full/tom**	fewl/tom
easy/difficult	**lett/vanskelig**	leht/vahnskerlee
heavy/light	**tung/lett**	tewng/leht
open/shut	**åpen/lukket**	awpern/lookkert
right/wrong	**riktig/gal**	riktee/garl
old/new	**gammel/ny**	gahmmerl/new
old/young	**gammel/ung**	gahmmerl/oong
beautiful/ugly	**pen/stygg**	payn/stewg
good/bad	**god/dårlig**	goo/dawrlee
better/worse	**bedre/verre**	baydrer/værrer

Some prepositions and a few more useful words

at	**ved**	vay(d)
on	**på**	paw
in	**i**	ee
to	**til**	til
from	**fra**	frar
inside	**innenfor**	innernfor
outside	**utenfor**	ewternfor
up	**opp**	op
down	**ned**	nay(d)
before	**før**	furr
after	**etter**	ehtterr
with	**med**	may(d)
without	**uten**	ewtern
through	**gjennom**	yehnnom
towards	**mot**	moot
until	**til**	til
during	**i løpet av**	ee lurpert ahv
and	**og**	aw(g)
or	**eller**	ehllerr
not	**ikke**	ikker
nothing	**ingenting**	ingernting

NORWEGIAN

none	**ingen**	**ingern**
very	**veldig**	**vehl**dee
also	**også**	**aws**saw
soon	**snart**	snahrt
perhaps	**kanskje**	**kahn**sher
here	**her**	hæær
there	**der**	dæær
now	**nå**	naw
then	**da**	dar

Arrival

Your passport, please.	**Passet Deres, takk.**	**pahss**ser **day**rerss tahk
Here it is.	**Vær så god.**	væær saw goo
Have you anything to declare?	**Har De noe å for-tolle?**	harr dee **noo**er aw for-**tol**ler
No, nothing at all.	**Nei, ingen ting.**	nay **ingern**ting
Porter!	**Bærer!**	**bæær**err
Can you help me with my luggage, please?	**Kan De hjelpe meg med bagasjen?**	kahn dee **yehl**per may may(d) bah**gar**shern
That's my suitcase.	**Det er min koffert.**	day ær meen **koo**fferrt
Where's the bus to the centre of town, please?	**Hvor tar man bus-sen inn til sentrum?**	voor tarr mahn **bewss**ssern in til **sehn**trewm
This way, please.	**Denne vei.**	**dehn**ner vay

Changing money

| Where's the nearest bank, please? | **Hvor ligger nærmeste bank?** | voor **ligg**err **næær**merster bahnk |
| Can you change a traveller's cheque, please? | **Kan De innløse en reisesjekk?** | kahn dee **in**lursser ayn **righ**ssershehk |

Car rental

I'd like a car.	**Jeg vil gjerne leie en bil.**	yay vil **yæær**ner **lay**er ayn beel
For how long?	**Hvor lenge?**	voor **lehng**ger
A day/Four days/ A week/Two weeks.	**En dag/Fire dager/ En uke/To uker.**	ayn darg/**feer**er **darg**err/ ayn **ew**ker/too **ew**kerr

Taxi

Where can I get a taxi?	**Hvor kan jeg få tak i en drosje?**	voor kahn yay faw tark ee ayn **drosh**er
What's the fare to ... ?	**Hva koster det til ... ?**	var **koss**terr day til
Take me to this address, please.	**Vennligst, kjør meg til denne adressen.**	**vehn**ligst khurr may til **dehn**ner ah**drehss**sern
I'm in a hurry.	**Jeg har det travelt.**	yay harr day **trarv**erlt
Could you drive more slowly, please?	**Kunne De kjøre litt saktere?**	**kewn**ner dee **khurr**er lit **sahk**terrer

Hotel and other accommodation

My name is ...	**Mitt navn er ...**	mit nahvn ær
Have you a reservation?	**Har De reservert?**	harr dee raysehr**vayrt**
Yes, here's the confirmation.	**Ja, her er bekreftelsen.**	yar hææær ær berkrehf**terl**ssern
I'd like ...	**Jeg vil gjerne ha ...**	yay vil **yææ**ner har
I'd like a single room/a double room.	**Jeg vil gjerne ha et enkeltrom/et dobbeltrom.**	yay vil **yææ**ner har eht **ehng**kerltroom/eht **dob**berltroom
a room with a bath/ with a shower	**et rom med bad/ med dusj**	eht room may(d) bard/ may(d) dewsh

How much?

What's the price per night/per week/per month?	**Hva koster det for en natt/for en uke/for en måned?**	var **koss**terr day for ayn naht/for ayn **ew**ker/for ayn **maw**nerd
May I see the room?	**Kan jeg få se rommet?**	kahn yay faw say **room**mert
I'm sorry, I don't like it.	**Jeg beklager, men jeg liker det ikke.**	yay ber**klar**gerr mayn yay **lee**kerr day **ik**ker
Yes, that's fine. I'll take it.	**Ja, det er bra. Jeg tar det.**	yar day ær brar. yay tarr day
What's my room number, please?	**Hvilket værelsenummer har jeg?**	**vil**kert **væææ**rerlssernoommerr harr yay
Number 123.	**Nummer 123.**	**noom**merr 123

Service, please

Who is it?	**Hvem er det?**	vehm ær day
Just a minute.	**Et øyeblikk.**	eht oyerblik
Come in! The door's open.	**Kom inn! Døren er åpen.**	kom in. durrern ær awpern
May we have break-fast in our room?	**Kan vi få frokost på rommet?**	kahn vee faw frookoost paw roommer

Breakfast

I'll have ...	**Jeg vil gjerne ha ...**	yay vil yææner har
I'll have some fruit-juice.	**Jeg vil gjerne ha litt fruktsaft.**	yay vil yææner har lit frewktsahft
a boiled egg	**et kokt egg**	eht kookt ehg
a fried egg	**et speilegg**	eht spaylehg
some bacon/some ham	**litt bacon/litt skinke**	lit baykern/lit shingker
some toast	**litt ristet loff**	litt risstert loof
a pot of tea	**en kanne te**	ayn kahnner tay
a cup of tea	**en kopp te**	ayn kop tay
some coffee	**kaffe**	kahffer
some chocolate	**sjokolade**	shookoolarder
more butter	**mer smør**	mair smurr
some hot water	**litt varmt vann**	lit vahrmt vahn

Difficulties

The central heating doesn't work.	**Sentralvarmen vir-ker ikke.**	sehntrarlvahrmern veerker ikker
the light/the socket	**lyset/støpslet**	lewsser/sturpsler
the tap/the toilet	**vannkranen/ toalettet**	vahnkrarnern/twahlehtter
There's no hot water.	**Det er ikke noe varmt vann.**	day ær ikker nooer vahrmt vahn
May I see the manager, please?	**Kan jeg få snakke med direktøren?**	kahn yay faw snahkker may(d) deerehkturrern

Telephone—Mail

There's a call for you.	**Det er telefon til Dem.**	day ær taylerfoon til dehm
Hold the line, please.	**Ikke legg på røret.**	ikker lehg paw rurrer

Operator, I've been cut off.	**Frøken, jeg er blitt avbrutt.**	frurkern yay ær blit ahvbrewt
Did anyone telephone me?	**Har noen ringt til meg?**	harr **noo**ern ringt til may
Is there any mail for me?	**Er det noe post til meg?**	ær day **noo**er post til may
Are there any messages for me?	**Er det noen beskjed til meg?**	ær day **noo**ern ber**shay(d)** til may

Checking out

May I have my bill, please?	**Kan jeg få regningen, takk.**	kahn yay faw **ray**ningern tahk
We're in a great hurry.	**Vi har det svært travelt.**	vee harr day svæt **trar**verlt
It's been a very enjoyable stay.	**Det har vært et meget hyggelig opphold.**	day harr væt eht **may**gert **hewg**gerlee ophol

Eating out

Good evening, sir/ Good evening, madam.	**God aften.**	goo **ahf**tern
Good evening. I'd like a table for two, please.	**God aften. Jeg vil gjerne ha et bord for to, takk.**	goo **ahf**tern. yay vil **yææ**ner har eht boor for too tahk
Do you have a fixed-price menu?	**Har De en fastsatt meny?**	harr dee ayn **fahst**saht meh**new**
May I see the à la carte menu?	**Kan jeg få se spisekartet?**	kahn yay faw say **spees**ser**kahr**ter
May we have an ashtray, please?	**Kan vi få et askebeger?**	kahn vee faw eht **ahs**ker**bay**gerr
some bread	**litt brød**	lit brur(d)
a fork	**en gaffel**	ayn **gahf**ferl
a knife	**en kniv**	ayn kneev
a spoon	**en skje**	ayn shay
a plate	**en tallerken**	ayn tahl**lær**kern
a glass	**et glass**	eht glahss
a napkin	**en serviett**	ayn sær**vieht**
another chair	**en stol til**	ayn stool til

NORWEGIAN

| Where's the gentle-men's toilet (men's room)? | **Hvor er herre-toalettet?** | voor ær **hæ**rerr-twahlehtter |
| Where's the ladies' toilet (ladies' room)? | **Hvor er dametoalettet?** | voor ær **dar**mer-twahlehtter |

Appetizers

I'd like some ...	**Jeg vil gjerne ha ...**	yay vil **yææ**ner har
I'd like some assorted appetizers.	**Jeg vil gjerne ha noen assorterte hors-d'œuvres.**	yay vil **yææ**ner har **noo**ern ahssor**tair**ter or**durv**r
orange juice	**appelsinsaft**	ahpperlss**een**ssahft
ham	**skinke**	**shing**ker
melon	**melon**	meh**loon**
pâté	**postei**	poos**stay**
smoked salmon	**røkelaks**	**rur**kerlahks
shrimps (shrimp)	**reker**	**ray**kerr

Soup

Have you any ...?	**Har De ...?**	harr dee
Have you any chicken soup?	**Har De hønse-suppe?**	harr dee **hurn**ssersssewpper
vegetable soup	**grønnsaksuppe**	**grurn**ssahksewpper
onion soup	**løksuppe**	**lurk**sewpper

Fish

I'd like some ...	**Jeg vil gjerne ha ...**	yay vil **yææ**ner har
I'd like some fish.	**Jeg vil gjerne ha fisk.**	yay vil **yææ**ner har fisk
sole	**sjøtunge**	**shur**toonger
trout	**ørret**	**urr**rert
lobster	**hummer**	**hoom**merr
crayfish	**kreps**	krehps
prawns	**store reker**	**stoo**rer **ray**kerr
I'd like it ...	**Jeg vil gjerne ha det ...**	yay vil **yææ**ner har day
I'd like it steamed.	**Jeg vil gjerne ha det dampet.**	yay vil **yææ**ner har day **dahm**pert
grilled	**grillstekt**	**gril**staykt
boiled	**kokt**	kookt
baked	**ovnstekt**	**ovn**staykt
fried	**stekt**	staykt

Meat—Poultry—Game

I'd like some . . .	**Jeg vil gjerne ha . . .**	yay vil **yææ**ner har
I'd like some beef.	**Jeg vil gjerne ha oksekjøtt.**	yay vil **yææ**ner har **ook**serkhurt
a beef steak	**en biff**	ayn bif
some roast beef	**roastbiff**	**roast**bif
a veal cutlet	**en kalvekotelett**	ayn **kahl**verkotterleht
mutton	**fårekjøtt**	**fawr**erkhurt
lamb	**lammekjøtt**	**lahm**merkhurt
a pork chop	**en svinekotelett**	ayn **svee**nerkotterleht
roast pork	**svinestek**	**svee**nerstayk
hare	**hare**	**harr**er
chicken	**kylling**	**khew**lling
roast chicken	**stekt kylling**	staykt **khew**lling
duck	**and**	ahn
How do you like your meat?	**Hvordan vil De ha kjøttet tilberedt?**	**voor**dahn vil dee har **khurt**tert **til**berreht
rare	**blodig**	**bloo**dee
medium	**medium**	**may**diewm
well done	**godt stekt**	got staykt

Vegetables

What vegetables have you got?	**Hvilke grønnsaker har De?**	**vil**ker **grurns**sakerr harr dee
I'd like some . . .	**Jeg vil gjerne ha . . .**	yay vil **yææ**ner har
I'd like some asparagus.	**Jeg vil gjerne ha asparges.**	yay vil **yææ**ner har ah**spar**gerss
green beans	**grønne bønner**	**grur**nner **burn**nerr
mushrooms	**sopp**	sop
carrots	**gulrøtter**	**gewl**rurtterr
onions	**løk**	lurk
red cabbage	**rødkål**	**rurd**kawl
spinach	**spinat**	spin**art**
rice	**ris**	rees
peas	**erter**	**æ**terr
tomatoes	**tomater**	too**mart**err
green salad	**grønn salat**	grurn sah**lart**
potatoes	**poteter**	poo**tayt**err

Desserts

Nothing more, thanks.	**Takk, jeg er forsynt.**	tahk yay ær fo**shewnt**

Just a small portion, please.	**Bare en liten porsjon.**	barrer ayn **lee**tern **poo**shoon
Have you any ice-cream?	**Har De iskrem?**	harr dee **ee**skrehm
fruit salad	**fruktsalat**	**frewkt**sahlart
fresh fruit	**frisk frukt**	frisk frewkt
cheese	**ost**	oost

Drink

What would you like to drink?	**Hva vil De ha å drikke?**	var vil dee har aw **drik**ker
I'll have a beer, please.	**Jeg vil gjerne ha en øl.**	yay vil **yææ**ner har ayn url
I'll have a whisky, please.	**Jeg vil gjerne ha en whisky.**	yay vil **yææ**ner har ayn **wiss**kee

Wine

I'd like a bottle of wine.	**Jeg vil gjerne ha en flaske vin.**	yay vil **yææ**ner har ayn **flah**sker veen
red wine	**rødvin**	**rur(d)**vin
rosé wine	**rosévin**	roa**say**vin
white wine	**hvitvin**	**veet**vin
Cheers!	**Skål!**	skawl

The bill (check)

May I have the bill (check) please?	**Kan jeg få regningen, takk!**	karn yay faw **ray**ningern tahk
Is service included?	**Er service inkludert?**	ær **sehr**viss ing-klew**dai(r)t**
Everything's included.	**Alt er inkludert.**	ahlt ær ingklew**dai(r)t**
Thank you, that was a very good meal.	**Takk, det var et utmerket måltid.**	tahk day varr eht **ewt**mærkert **mawl**tid

Travelling

Where's the railway station, please?	**Hvor ligger jernbanestasjonen?**	voor **lig**gerr **yææn**barner-**stahs**hoonern
Where's the ticket office, please?	**Hvor er billettkontoret?**	voor ær bil**leht**koontoorer
I'd like a ticket to ...	**Jeg vil gjerne ha en billett til ...**	yay vil **yææ**ner har ayn bil**leht** til

First or second class?	Første eller annen klasse?	furshter ehllerr ahnnern klahssser
First class, please.	Første, takk.	furshter tahk
Single or return (one way or round-trip)?	Enveis eller tur-retur?	aynvayss ehller tewr-rertewr
Do I have to change trains?	Må jeg bytte tog?	maw yay bewtter tawg
What platform does the train leave from?	Fra hvilken plattform går toget?	frar vilkern plahtform gawr tawger
Where's the nearest underground (sub-way) station?	Hvor ligger nærmeste under-grunnsstasjon?	voor liggerr nærmersster ewnnergrennwnsstahshoon
Where's the bus station, please?	Hvor er buss-stasjonen?	voor ær bewss-stahshoonern
When's the first bus to . . . ?	Når går den første bussen til . . . ?	nawr gawr dayn furshter bewsssern til
the last bus the next bus	den siste bussen den neste bussen	dayn sisster bewsssern dayn nehsster bewsssern
Please let me off at the next stop.	Vil De slippe meg av på neste stop-pested?	vil dee slipper may ahv paw nehsster stopper-stehd

Relaxing

What's on at the cinema (movies)?	Hva går på kino?	var gawr paw kheenoo
What's on at the theatre?	Hva går på teatret?	var gawr paw tayartrer
What time does the film begin? And the play?	Når begynner filmen? Og stykket?	nawr beryewnnerr filmern? awg stewkker
Are there any tickets for tonight?	Er det noen billetter igjen til i kveld?	ær day nooern billehtterr eeyern til ee kvehl
Where can we go dancing?	Hvor kan vi gå for å danse?	voor kahn vee gaw for aw dahnser
Would you like to dance?	Vil De danse?	vil dee dahnser

Introductions

| How do you do? | God dag. | goo darg |
| How are you? | Hvordan står det til? | voordahn stawr day til |

Very well, thank you. And you?	**Bare bra, takk. Og med Dem?**	**bar**rer brar tahk. awg may(d) dehm
May I introduce Miss Philips?	**Kan jeg få presentere frøken Philips?**	kahn yay faw praysahng-tayrerl frurkern Philips
My name is...	**Mitt navn er...**	mit nahvn ær
I'm very pleased to meet you.	**Det gleder meg å treffe Dem.**	day **glay**derr may aw **treff**fer dehm
How long have you been here?	**Hvor lenge har De vært her?**	voor **lehng**er harr dee vært hær
It was nice meeting you.	**Det var hyggelig å treffe Dem.**	day varr **hewg**gerlee aw **treff**fer dehm

Dating

Would you like a cigarette?	**Vil De ha en sigarett?**	vil dee har ayn sigah**reht**
May I get you a drink?	**Kan jeg by Dem på en drink?**	kahn yay bew dehm paw ayn drink
Do you have a light, please?	**Unnskyld, har De en fyrstikk?**	**ewn**shewl harr dee ayn **few**shtik
Are you waiting for someone?	**Venter De på noen?**	**vehn**terr dee paw **noo**ern
Are you free this evening?	**Er De ledig i kveld?**	ær dee **lay**dee ee kvehl
Where shall we meet?	**Hvor skal vi møtes?**	voor skahl ve **mur**terss
What time shall I meet you?	**Når skal jeg møte Dem?**	nawr skahl yay **mur**ter dehm
May I take you home?	**Kan jeg få følge Dem hjem?**	kahn yay faw **fur**ler dehm yehm
Thank you, it's been a wonderful evening.	**Mange takk, det har vært en hyggelig kveld.**	**mahng**er tahk day harr vært ayn **hewg**gerlee kvehl
What's your telephone number?	**Hva er telefonnummeret Deres?**	var ær tayler**foon**-noommerrer **day**rerss
Do you live alone?	**Bor De alene?**	boor dee ah**lay**ner
What time is your last train?	**Når går det siste toget Deres?**	nawr gawr day **siss**ter **taw**ger **day**rerss
Good-night...	**God natt...**	goo naht

Banks

Where's the nearest bank, please?	**Unnskyld, hvor ligger nærmeste bank?**	ewnshewl voor **lig**gerr **nær**merster bahnk
Where can I cash some traveller's cheques?	**Hvor kan jeg innløse noen reisesjekker?**	voor kahn yay **in**lursser **noo**ern **righ**ssershehkkerr
What time does the bank open/What time does it close?	**Når åpner banken/Når stenger den?**	nawr **awp**nerr **bahng**kern/nawr **stehng**err dehn
I'm expecting some money from home. Has it arrived?	**Jeg venter penger hjemmefra. Har de kommet?**	yay **vehn**terr **pehng**err **yehm**merfrar. harr dee **kom**mert
Can you give me some small change, please?	**Kan De gi meg litt vekslepenger?**	kahn dee yee may lit **vehk**slerpehngerr

Shops, stores and services

Where is the nearest chemist's (pharmacy)?	**Hvor er nærmeste apotek?**	voor ær **nær**merster ahpo**tayk**
the nearest hairdresser's	**den nærmeste frisør**	dehn **nær**merster fri**surr**
the photo shop	**fotoforretningen**	**foo**tooforrehtningern
the jeweller's	**gullsmeden**	**gewl**ssmaydern
the department store	**varemagasinet**	**var**rermahgahsseener
the police station	**politistasjonen**	poo**lite**estahshoonern
the garage	**parkeringshuset**	pahr**kay**ringsshewsser
How do I get there?	**Hvordan kommer jeg dit?**	**voor**dahn **kom**merr yay deet
Is it within walking distance?	**Er det for langt å gå dit?**	ær day for lahngt aw gaw deet

Service

Can you help me, please?	**Kan De være så vennlig å hjelpe meg?**	kahn dee **væ**ærer saw **vehn**lee aw **yehl**per may
Can you show me this? And that, too.	**Kan De vise meg den? Og den også.**	kahn dee **vee**ser may dehn. awg dehn **aws**saw
It's too expensive/too big/too small.	**Det er for dyrt/for stort/for lite.**	day ær for dewrt/for stoort/for **lee**ter

NORWEGIAN

Can you show me some more?	**Kan De vise meg flere?**	kahn dee **vee**sser may flayrer
something better	**noe bedre**	nooer baydrer
something cheaper	**noe billigere**	nooer billigerrer
How much is this? And that?	**Hvor mye koster dette? Og det?**	voor **mewer koss**terr dehtter? awg day
It's not quite what I want.	**Det er ikke akkurat hva jeg vil ha.**	day ær **ikker ahk**hewrart var yay vil har
I like it.	**Jeg liker det.**	yay **lee**kerr day

Chemist's (Pharmacy)

| I'd like something for a cold/for a cough/for travel sickness. | **Jeg vil gjerne ha noe for en for-kjølelse/mot hoste/ mot reisesyke.** | yay vil **yææ**ner har nooer for ayn for**khur**lerlser/ moot **hoos**ster/moot **righs**serssewker |
| Can you recommend something for hay-fever/for sunburn? | **Kan De anbefale noe mot høysnue/ mot solbrenthet?** | kahn dee ahn**ber**farler nooer moot **hoys**snewer/ moot **sool**brehnthayt |

Toiletry

May I have some razor blades?	**Kan jeg få noen barberblader?**	kahn yay faw nooern bahr**bayr**blarderr
some shaving cream	**en barberkrem**	ayn bahr**bayr**krehm
some toothpaste	**en tannpasta**	ayn **tahn**pahsstah
I'd like some soap.	**Jeg vil gjerne ha en såpe.**	yay vil **yææ**ner har ayn **saw**per
some suntan oil	**en solbadolje**	ayn **sool**bardolyer

At the barber's

I'd like a haircut, please.	**Jeg vil gjerne ha håret klippet.**	yay vil **yææ**ner har **haw**rer klippert
Short/Leave it long.	**Kort/La det være langt.**	kort/lar day **vææ**rer lahngt
A razor cut, please.	**Skåret med barber-kniv.**	**skaw**rert may(d) bahr**bayr**kneev

At the hairdresser's

| I'd like a shampoo and set, please. | **Jeg vil gjerne ha vask og legg.** | yay vil **yææ**ner har vahsk awg lehg |

I'd like a bleach.	**Jeg vil gjerne ha det bleket.**	yay vil **yææ**ner har day **blay**kert
a permanent	**en permanent**	ayn pehr**mah**nehnt
a colour rinse	**en fargeskylling**	ayn **fahr**gershewlling
a manicure	**en manikyr**	ayn mahnee**kewr**

Photography

| I'd like a film for this camera. | **Jeg ville gjerne ha en film til dette apparatet.** | yay vil **yææ**ner har ayn film til **deht**ter ahppah**rar**ter |
| This camera doesn't work. | **Dette apparatet virker ikke.** | **deht**ter ahppah**rar**ter **veer**ker ikker |

At the post office

| Where's the nearest post office, please? | **Hvor ligger det nærmeste post-kontoret?** | voor **lig**gerr day **nær**merster **post**koontoorer |
| I'd like to send this by express (special delivery)/by air mail. | **Jeg vil gjerne sende dette som ilpost/med luftpost.** | yay vil **yææ**ner **sehn**ner **deht**ter som **eel**post/may(d) **lewft**post |

Service stations

Where is the nearest service station, please?	**Kan De si meg hvor den nærmeste ben-sinstasjonen ligger?**	kahn dee see may voor dehn **nær**merster behn-**seen**stahshoonern **lig**gerr
Fill her up, please.	**Full tank, takk.**	fewl tahnk tahk
Check the oil, please.	**Vil de kontrollere oljen?**	vil dee koontroo**lay**rer **ol**yern
Would you check the tyres?	**Vil De kontrollere dekkene?**	vil dee koontroo**lay**rer **dehk**kerner

Street directions

Can you show me on the map where I am?	**Kan De vise meg på kartet hvor jeg er?**	kahn dee **vees**ser may paw **kah**ter voor yay ær
You're on the wrong road.	**De er på feil vei.**	dee ær paw fayl vay
Go back to...	**Kjør tilbake til ...**	khurr til**bar**ker til
Go straight ahead.	**Kjør rett frem.**	khurr reht frehm
It's on the left/on the right.	**Det er på venstre side/på høyre side.**	day ær paw **vehn**strer seeder/paw **hoy**rer seeder

Accidents

May I use your telephone?	**Kan jeg få låne telefonen Deres?**	kahn yay faw **lawner** taylerfoonern **dayrerss**
Call a doctor quickly.	**Tilkall en lege øyeblikkelig.**	tilkahl ayn **layger** oyerblikkerlee
Call an ambulance.	**Ring etter en sykebil.**	ring **ehtterr** ayn **sew**kerbeel
Please call the police.	**Vennligst ring til politiet.**	**vehn**ligst ring til pooli**teeer**

Numbers

zero	**null**	newl
one	**en**	ayn
two	**to**	too
three	**tre**	tray
four	**fire**	feerer
five	**fem**	fehm
six	**seks**	sehks
seven	**sju**	shew
eight	**åtte**	otter
nine	**ni**	nee
ten	**ti**	tee
eleven	**elleve**	ehlver
twelve	**tolv**	tol
thirteen	**tretten**	trehttern
fourteen	**fjorten**	fyoortern
fifteen	**femten**	fehmtern
sixteen	**seksten**	sighstern
seventeen	**sytten**	sewttern
eighteen	**atten**	ahttern
nineteen	**nitten**	nittern
twenty	**tjue**	khewer
twenty-one	**tjueen**	khewerayn
thirty	**tretti**	trehttee
forty	**førti**	furtee
fifty	**femti**	fehmtee
sixty	**seksti**	sehkstee
seventy	**sytti**	sewttee
eighty	**åtti**	ottee
ninety	**nitti**	nittee
one hundred	**hundre**	hewndrer
one thousand	**tusen**	tewssern
ten thousand	**ti tusen**	tee tewssern

Days

It's Sunday.	**Det er søndag.**	day ær **surn**darg
Monday	**mandag**	**mahn**darg
Tuesday	**tirsdag**	**teerss**darg
Wednesday	**onsdag**	**oonss**darg
Thursday	**torsdag**	**torsh**darg
Friday	**fredag**	**fray**darg
Saturday	**lørdag**	**lur**darg
yesterday	**i går**	ee gawr
today	**i dag**	ee darg
tomorrow	**i morgen**	ee **maw**ern
morning/afternoon	**morgen/ettermiddag**	**maw**ern/**eht**terrmiddarg
evening/night	**aften/natt**	**ahf**tern/naht

Months

January	**januar**	yahne**warr**
February	**februar**	faybre**warr**
March	**mars**	mahsh
April	**april**	ah**preel**
May	**mai**	**migh**
June	**juni**	**yew**nee
July	**juli**	**yew**lee
August	**august**	**ow**gewst
September	**september**	sehp**tehm**berr
October	**oktober**	ok**taw**berr
November	**november**	no**vehm**berr
December	**desember**	days**sehm**berr
Merry Christmas!	**God Jul! Godt**	goo yewl! got newtt awr
Happy New Year!	**Nytt År!**	

NORWEGIAN

POLISH

Guide to Pronunciation

Note that Polish has some diacritical letters—letters with accent marks—which we do not know in English.

Letter	Approximate pronunciation	Symbol	Example	
Consonants				
b, f, k, l, m, p, z	are pronounced as in English			
cz	like **ch** in **ch**urch	ch	**czy**	chi
dż	like **j** in **j**am	j	**dżem**	jehm
g	as in **g**irl	g	**guma**	**gu**mah
j	like **y** in **y**et	y	**jak**	yahk
ł	like **w** in **w**in	w	**ładny**	**wahd**ni
n	as in English but put your tongue against the front teeth and not the teeth ridge	n	**na**	nah
s	as in **s**it	s/ss	**sam**	sahm
sz	like **sh** in **sh**ine	sh	**szal**	shahl
t, d	as in English but put your tongue against the front teeth and not against the teeth ridge	t d	**tak** **dom**	tahk dom
w	like **v** in **v**an	v	**woda**	**vo**dah
ż or rz	like **s** in plea**s**ure	zh	**żelazo** **rzeka**	zheh**lah**zo **zheh**kah

Sounds distinctly different

An often recurring phenomenon in the Slavic languages is "softening", or the "softened" pronunciation of consonants. Examples of this in Polish are ć, dź, ń, ś and ź. A similar effect can be produced by pronouncing y as in yet— but very, very short—after the consonant.

c	like the English sequence ts in tsetse pronounced quickly	ts	co	tso
ć	pronounced like the Polish c but softer	tsh	ciało	tshahwo
dz	like the English sequence ds in beds pronounced quickly	dz	dzwonek	dzvonehk
dź or dzi	pronounced like the Polish dz but softer	dzh	dział	dzhahw
h or ch	similar to English h but with much more friction	h	herbata chudy	hehrbahtah hoodi
ń or ni	pronounced like the English n but softer	ñ	nie	ñeh
r	like the Scottish r (vibration of the tip of the tongue); note that it is also pronounced at the end of words	r	rak	rahk
ś or si	pronounced like the English s but softer	s'	się ktoś	s'eh ktos'
ź or zi	pronounced like the English z but softer	z'	zielony	z'ehloni

Notice that voiced sounds become completely devoiced at the end of a word or in the context of other voiceless sounds, i.e., they are pronounced like their voiceless counterparts (e.g., b of chleb is pronounced like p; w of rów is pronounced like f; rz and z in przez like sz and s, etc.).

POLISH

Vowels

a	like English **u** in c**u**lt or American **o** in c**o**llege	ah	**tak**	tahk
e	like **e** in t**e**n	eh	**lek**	lehk
i	like **ee** in f**ee**t	ee	**ile**	eeleh
y	like **i** in f**i**t	i	**ty**	ti
o	like **o** in c**o**t	o	**kot**	kot
u or ó	a sound between the English **u** in p**u**t and **oo** in b**oo**ts	oo	**drut**	droot
ą	is pronounced **on** before a consonant; when it's the final letter, it is pronounced like French **an** in fiancé	on	**prąd**	pront
		awng	**są**	sawng
ę	is pronounced **en** before a consonant or like **e** in b**e**d when it is the final letter	ehn	**pęd**	pehnt
		eh	**tę**	teh

Some diphthongs

ej	like **a** in t**a**ke	ay	**dobrej**	**dob**ray
aj	like **i** in l**i**ke	igh	**daj**	digh

The stress falls in Polish on the next to the last syllable, e.g., **głodny** (**gwod**ni), **drogeria** (dro**geh**ryah).

POLISH

Some basic expressions

Yes.	**Tak.**	tahk
No.	**Nie.**	ñeh
Please.	**Proszę.**	**pro**sheh
Thank you.	**Dziękuję.**	dzhehn**kooy**eh
Thank you very much.	**Dziękuję bardzo.**	dzhehn**kooy**eh **bahr**dzo
That's all right.	**Proszę bardzo.**	**pro**sheh **bahr**dzo

Greetings

Good morning.	**Dzień dobry.**	dzhehñ **do**bri
Good afternoon.	**Dzień dobry.**	dzhehñ **do**bri
Good evening.	**Dobry wieczór.**	**do**bri **vyeh**choor
Good night.	**Dobranoc.**	do**brah**nots
Good-bye.	**Do widzenia.**	do vee**dzeh**ñah
See you later.	**Do zobaczenia.**	do zobah**cheh**ñah
This is Mr. . . .	**To jest pan . . .**	to yehst pahn
This is Mrs. . . .	**To jest pani . . .**	to yehst **pah**ñee
This is Miss . . .	**To jest pani . . .**	to yehst **pah**ñee
I'm very pleased to meet you.	**Miło mi pana/panią poznać.**	**mee**wo mee **pah**na/**pah**ñawng po**znah**tsh
How are you?	**Jak się pan/pani miewa?**	yahk s'eh pahn/**pah**ñee **myeh**vah
Very well, thank you.	**Bardzo dobrze, dziękuję.**	**bahr**dzo **do**bzheh dzhehn**kooy**eh
And you?	**A pan/pani?**	ah pahn/**pah**ñee
Fine.	**Dobrze.**	**do**bzheh
Excuse me.	**Przepraszam.**	psheh**prah**shahm

Questions

Where?	**Gdzie?**	gdzheh
Where is . . . ?	**Gdzie jest . . . ?**	gdzheh yehst
Where are . . . ?	**Gdzie są . . . ?**	gdzheh sawng
When?	**Kiedy?**	**kyeh**di

What?	**Co?**	tso
How?	**Jak?**	yahk
How much?	**Ile?**	**ee**leh
How many?	**Ile?**	**ee**leh
Who?	**Kto?**	kto
Why?	**Dlaczego?**	dlah**cheh**go
Which?	**Który?**	**ktoo**ri
What do you call this?	**Jak się to nazywa?**	yahk s'eh to nah**zi**vah
What do you call that?	**Jak się tamto nazywa?**	yahk s'eh **tahm**to nah**zi**vah
What does this mean?	**Co to znaczy?**	tso to **znah**chi
What does that mean?	**Co tamto znaczy?**	tso **tahm**to **znah**chi

POLISH

Do you speak . . . ?

Do you speak English?	**Czy pan/pani mówi po angielsku?**	chi pahn/**pah**ñee **moo**vee po ahn**gyehl**skoo
Do you speak German?	**Czy pan/pani mówi po niemiecku?**	chi pahn/**pah**ñee **moo**vee po nyeh**myeht**skoo
Do you speak French?	**Czy pan/pani mówi po francusku?**	chi pahn/**pah**ñee **moo**vee po frahn**tsoo**skoo
Do you speak Spanish?	**Czy pan/pani mówi po hiszpańsku?**	chi pahn/**pah**ñee **moo**vee po heesh**pahñ**skoo
Do you speak Italian?	**Czy pan/pani mówi po włosku?**	chi pahn/**pah**ñee **moo**vee po **vwo**skoo
Could you speak more slowly, please?	**Proszę mówić trochę wolniej.**	**pro**sheh **moo**veetsh **tro**heh **vol**ñay
Please point to the phrase in the book.	**Proszę wskazać odpowiednie zdanie w moich rozmówkach.**	**pro**sheh **fskah**zahtsh odpo**vyehd**ñeh **zdah**ñeh **fmoeeh** rozmoofkahh
Just a minute. I'll see if I can find it in this book.	**Chwileczkę. Zobaczę czy to jest w moich rozmów-kach.**	hfeeleh**chkeh**. zo**bah**cheh chi to yehst fmoeeh rozmoofkahh
I understand.	**Rozumiem.**	ro**zoo**myehm
I don't understand.	**Nie rozumiem.**	ñeh ro**zoo**myehm

Can ... ?

Can I have ... ?	**Czy mogę dostać ...?**	chi **mo**geh **doss**tahtsh
Can we have ... ?	**Czy możemy dostać ...?**	chi mo**zheh**my **doss**tahtsh
Can you show me ... ?	**Czy może mi pan/pani pokazać ...?**	chi **mo**zheh mee pahn/**pah**ñee po**kah**zahtsh
Can you tell me ... ?	**Czy może mi pan/pani powiedzieć ...?**	chi **mo**zheh mee pahn/**pah**ñee po**vyeh**dzhehtsh
Can you help me, please?	**Czy może mi pan/pani pomóc?**	chi **mo**zheh mee pahn/**pah**ñee po**moots**

Wanting

I'd like ...	**Chciałbym ...**	**htshahw**bim
We'd like ...	**Chcielibyśmy ...**	**htsheh**leebis'mi
Please give me ...	**Proszę mi dać ...**	**pro**sheh mee dahsh
Give it to me, please.	**Proszę mi to dać.**	**pro**sheh mee to dahtsh
Please bring me ...	**Proszę przynieść mi ...**	**pro**sheh **pshi**ñehs'tsh mee
Bring it to me, please.	**Proszę mi to przynieść.**	**pro**sheh mee to **pshi**ñehs'tsh
I'm hungry.	**Chce mi się jeść.**	htseh mee s'eh yes'tsh
I'm thirsty.	**Chce mi się pić.**	htseh mee s'eh peetsh
I'm tired.	**Jestem zmęczony.**	**yeh**sstehm zmehn**cho**ni
I'm lost.	**Zgubiłem się.**	zgoo**bee**vehm s'eh
It's important.	**To ważne.**	to **vah**zhneh
It's urgent.	**To pilne.**	to **peel**neh
Hurry up!	**Niech się pan/pani pospieszy!**	ñehh s'eh pahn/**pah**ñee po**spyeh**shi

It is/There is ...

It is/It's ...	**To jest ...**	to yehst
Is it ... ?	**Czy to jest ...?**	chi to yehst
It isn't ...	**To nie jest ...**	to ñeh yehst

There is/There are ...	**Jest/Są ...**	yehst/sawng
Is there/Are there ... ?	**Czy jest/Czy są ... ?**	chi yehst/chi sawng
There isn't/There aren't ...	**Nie ma ...**	ñeh mah
There isn't any/There aren't any.	**Nie ma.**	ñeh mah

A few common words

big/small	**duży/mały**	doozhi/mahwi
quick/slow	**szybki/wolny**	shipkee/volni
early/late	**wczesny/późny**	fchehssni/pooz'ni
cheap/expensive	**tani/drogi**	tahñee/drogee
near/far	**bliski/daleki**	bleesskee/dahlehkee
hot/cold	**gorący/zimny**	gorontsi/z'eemni
full/empty	**pełny/pusty**	pehwni/poossti
easy/difficult	**łatwy/trudny**	wahtfi/troodni
heavy/light	**ciężki/lekki**	tshehnshkee/lehkkee
open/shut	**otwarty/zamknięty**	otfahrti/zahmkñehnti
right/wrong	**słuszny/niesłuszny**	swooshni/ñehswooshni
old/new	**stary/nowy**	stahri/novi
old/young	**stary/młody**	stahri/mwodi
beautiful/ugly	**piękny/brzydki**	pyehnkni/bzhitkee
good/bad	**dobry/zły**	dobri/zwi
better/worse	**lepszy/gorszy**	lehpsi/gorshi

A few prepositions and some more useful words

at	**w**	v
on	**na**	nah
in	**w**	v
to	**do**	do
from	**z, od**	z od
inside	**wewnątrz**	vehvnontsh
outside	**na zewnątrz**	nah zehvnontsh
up	**do góry**	do goori
down	**na dół**	nah doow
before	**przed**	psheht
after	**po**	po
with	**z**	z
without	**bez**	behss
through	**przez**	pshehss
towards	**w kierunku**	fkyehroonkoo
until	**aż do**	ahzh do

POLISH

during	podczas	potchahss
and	i	ee
or	lub	loop
not	nie	ñeh
nothing	nic	ñeets
none	żaden	zhahdehn
very	bardzo	bahrdzo
also	także	tahgzheh
soon	wkrótce	fkroottseh
perhaps	może	mozheh
here	tutaj	tootigh
there	tam	tahm
now	teraz	tehrahss
then	potem	potehm

Arrival

Your passport, please.	Paszport proszę.	pahshport prosheh
Here it is.	Proszę.	prosheh
Have you anything to declare?	Czy ma pan/pani coś do zadeklarowania?	chi mah pahn/pahñee tsos' do zahdehklahrovahñah
No, nothing at all.	Nie, nic.	ñeh ñeets
Porter!	Bagażowy!	bahgahzhovi
Can you help me with my luggage, please?	Proszę pomóc mi nieść te walizki.	prosheh pomoots mee ñehs'tsh teh vahleeskee
That's my suitcase.	To moja walizka.	to moyah vahleeskah
Where's the bus for the centre of town, please?	Gdzie jest autobus do centrum?	gdzheh yehst ahwtobooss do tsehntroom
This way, please.	Proszę tędy.	prosheh tehndi

Changing money

Can you change a traveller's cheque, please?	Czy może pan/pani wymienić mi czek podróżny?	chi mozheh pahn/pahñee vimyehñeetsh mee chehk podroozhni
Where's the nearest bank, please?	Gdzie jest najbliższy bank?	gdzheh yehst nighbleeshshi bahnk

Car rental

I'd like a car.	**Chcę wynająć samochód.**	htseh vinamyontsh sahmohoot
For how long?	**Na jak długo?**	nah yahk dwoogo
A day/Four days/ A week/Two weeks.	**Jeden dzień/Cztery dni/Tydzień/Dwa tygodnie.**	yehdehn dzhehñ/chtehri dñee/tidzhehñ/dvah tigodñeh

Taxi

Where can I get a taxi?	**Gdzie są taksówki?**	gdzheh sawng tahksoofkee
What's the fare to . . . ?	**Ile kosztuje przejazd do . . . ?**	eeleh koshtooyeh pshehyahst do
Take me to this address, please.	**Proszę mnie zawieźć na ten adres.**	prosheh mñeh zahvyehs'tsh nah tehn ahdrehss
I'm in a hurry.	**Spieszy mi się.**	spyehshi mee s'eh
Could you drive more slowly, please?	**Proszę jechać wolniej.**	prosheh vehhahtsh volñay

POLISH

Hotel and other accommodation

My name is . . .	**Nazywam się . . .**	nahzivahm s'eh
Have you a reservation?	**Czy ma pan/pani rezerwację?**	chi mah pahn/pahñee rehzehrvahtsyeh
Yes, here's the confirmation.	**Tak, oto kwit.**	tahk oto kfeet
I'd like . . .	**Proszę . . .**	prosheh
I'd like a single room/a double room.	**Proszę jednoosobowy pokój/dwuosobowy pokój.**	prosheh yehdnoosobovi pokooy/dvoosobovi pokooy
a room with a bath/ with a shower	**pokój z łazienką/ z prysznicem**	pokooy zwahz'ehnkawng/ sprishñeetsehm

How much?

What's the price per night/per week/per month?	**Ile kosztuje doba/ tydzień/miesiąc?**	eeleh koshtooyeh dobah/ tidzhehñ/myehs'onts
May I see the room?	**Czy mogę zobaczyć pokój?**	chi mogeh zobahchitsh pokooy

I'm sorry, I don't like it.	**Niestety nie podoba mi się.**	ñehsstehti ñeh podobah mee s'eh
Yes, that's fine. I'll take it.	**Dobrze. Biorę go.**	dobzheh. byoreh go
What's my room number, please?	**Jaki jest numer mojego pokoju?**	yahkee yehst noomehr moyehgo pokoyoo
Number 123.	**Numer 123.**	noomehr 123

Service, please

Who is it?	**Kto tam?**	kto tahm
Just a minute.	**Chwileczkę.**	hfeelehchkeh
Come in! The door's open.	**Proszę! Drzwi otwarte.**	prosheh! jvee otfahrteh
May we have breakfast in our room?	**Czy możemy zjeść śniadanie w pokoju?**	chi mozhehmi zyehs'tsh s'ñahdahñeh fpokoyoo

Breakfast

I'll have . . .	**Proszę . . .**	prosheh
I'll have some fruit juice.	**Proszę sok.**	prosheh sok
a boiled egg	**jajko gotowane**	yighko gotovahneh
a fried egg	**jajko sadzone**	yighko sahdzoneh
some bacon/some ham	**bekon/szynkę**	behkon/shinkeh
some toast	**grzanki**	gzhahnkee
a pot of tea	**dzbanek herbaty**	dzbahnehk hehrbahti
a cup of tea	**filiżankę herbaty**	feeleezhahnkeh hehrbahti
some coffee	**kawę**	kahveh
some chocolate	**gorącą czekoladę**	gorontsawng chehkolahdeh
more butter	**więcej masła**	vyehntsay mahsswah
some hot water	**trochę gorącej wody**	troheh gorontsay vodi

Difficulties

The central heating doesn't work.	**Centralne ogrze-wanie nie działa.**	tsehntrahlneh ogzheh-vahñeh ñeh dzhahdawah
the light/the socket	**światło/gniazdko**	s'fyahtwo/gñahsstko
the tap/the toilet	**kurek/ubikacja**	koorehk/oobeekahtsyah

| There's no hot water. | **Nie ma ciepłej wody.** | ñeh mah **tsheh**pway **vo**di |
| May I see the manager, please? | **Chcę rozmawiać z kierownikiem.** | htseh rozmahvyahtsh skehrovneekehm |

Telephone—Mail

There's a call for you.	**Telefon do pana/pani.**	teh**leh**fon do **pah**nah/**pah**ñee
Hold the line, please.	**Proszę się nie roz- łączać.**	**pro**sheh s'eh ñeh rozwonchahtsh
Operator, I've been cut off.	**Proszę pana, przer- wano mi.**	**pro**sheh **pah**nah pshehr**vah**no mee
Did anyone telephone me?	**Czy ktoś do mnie dzwonił?**	chi ktos' do mñeh **dzvo**ñeew
Is there any mail for me?	**Czy jest dla mnie poczta?**	chi yehst dlah mñeh **poch**tah
Are there any messages for me?	**Czy jest jakaś wiadomość dla mnie?**	chi yehst **yah**kahs' vyah**do**mos'tsh dlah mñeh

Checking out

May I have my bill, please?	**Proszę rachunek.**	**pro**sheh rah**hoo**nehk
We're in a great hurry.	**Bardzo się spie- szymy.**	**bahr**dzo s'eh spyeh**shi**mi
It's been a very en- joyable stay.	**Bardzo miło spę- dziliśmy tutaj czas.**	**bahr**dzo **mee**wo spehndzhee**lees'**mi **too**tigh chahss

Eating out

Good evening, sir/ Good evening, madam.	**Dobry wieczór panu/Dobry wieczór pani.**	**do**bri **vyeh**choor **pah**noo/**do**bri **vyeh**choor **pah**ñee
Good evening. I'd like a table for two, please.	**Dobry wieczór. Proszę o stolik dla dwóch osób.**	**do**bri **vyeh**choor. **pro**sheh o **sto**leek dlah dyooh **o**soop
Do you have a fixed- price menu?	**Czy są obiady firmowe?**	chi sawng o**byah**di feer**mo**veh
May I see the à la carte menu?	**Proszę kartę.**	**pro**sheh **kahr**teh

POLISH

May we have an ashtray, please?	**Proszę popielniczkę.**	prosheh popyehlнеechkeh
some bread	**pieczywo**	pyehchivo
a fork	**widelec**	veedehlehts
a knife	**nóż**	noosh
a spoon	**łyżkę**	wishkeh
a plate	**talerz**	tahlehsh
a glass	**szklankę**	shklahnkeh
a napkin	**serwetkę**	sehrvehtkeh
another chair	**jeszcze jedno krzesło**	yehshcheh yehdno kshehsswo
Where's the gentlemen's toilet (men's room)?	**Gdzie jest toaleta dla panów?**	gdzheh yehst twahlehtah dlah pahnoof
Where's the ladies' toilet (ladies' room)?	**Gdzie jest toaleta dla pań?**	gdzheh yehst twahlehtah dlah pahñ

Appetizers

I'd like some . . .	**Proszę . . .**	prosheh
I'd like some assorted appetizers.	**Proszę zestaw zakąsek.**	prosheh zehsstahf zahkonsehk
orange juice	**sok pomarańczowy**	sok pomahrahñchovi
ham	**szynkę**	shinkeh
melon	**melona**	mehlonah
pâté	**pasztet**	pahshteht
smoked salmon	**wędzonego łososia**	vehndzonehgo wossos'ah
shrimps (shrimp)	**krewetki**	krehvehtkee

Soup

Have you any . . . ?	**Czy jest . . . ?**	chi yehst
Have you any chicken soup?	**Czy jest rosół z kury?**	chi yehst rossoow skoori
vegetable soup	**zupa jarzynowa**	zoopah yahzhinovah
onion soup	**zupa cebulowa**	zoopah tsehboolovah

Fish

I'd like some . . .	**Proszę . . .**	prosheh
I'd like some fish.	**Proszę rybę.**	prosheh ribeh
sole	**solę**	soleh
trout	**pstrąga**	pstrongah
lobster	**homara**	homahrah
crayfish	**langustę**	lahngoossteh
prawns	**krewetki**	krehvehtkee

POLISH

I'd like it . . .	Proszę rybę . . .	prosheh ribeh
I'd like it steamed.	Proszę rybę duszoną.	prosheh ribeh dooshonawng
grilled	z rusztu	zrooshtoo
boiled	gotowaną	gotovahnawng
baked	zapiekaną	zahpyehkahnawng
fried	smażoną	smahzhonawng

Meat—Poultry—Game

I'd like some . . .	Proszę . . .	prosheh
I'd like some beef.	Proszę wołowinę.	prosheh vowoveeneh
a beef steak	befsztyk	behfshtik
some roast beef	pieczeń wołowa	pyehcheñ vowovawng
a veal cutlet	sznycel cielęcy	shnitsehl tshehlehntsi
mutton	baraninę	bahrahñeeneh
lamb	jagnię	yahgñeh
a pork chop	kotlet schabowy	kotleht shahbovi
roast pork	pieczeń wieprzową	pyehcheñ vyehpshovawng
hare	danie z zająca	dahñeh z zahyontsah
chicken	kurczę	koorcheh
roast chicken	kurczę pieczone	koorcheh pyehchoneh
duck	kaczkę	kahchkeh
How do you like your meat?	Jak ma być podane?	yahk mah bitsh podahneh
rare	po angielsku	po ahngehlskoo
medium	średnio wysmażone	s'rehdño vissmahzhoneh
well done	mocno wysmażone	motsno vissmahzhoneh

Vegetables

What vegetables have you got?	Jakie są jarzyny?	yahkeh sawng yahzhini
I'd like some . . .	Proszę . . .	prosheh
I'd like some asparagus.	Proszę szparagi.	prosheh shpahrahgee
green beans	zieloną fasolkę	z'ehlonawng fahssolkeh
mushrooms	pieczarki	pyehchahrkee
carrots	marchewkę	mahrhehfkeh
onions	cebulę	tsehbooleh
red cabbage	czerwoną kapustę	chehrvonawng kahpoossteh
spinach	szpinak	shpeenahk
rice	ryż	rish

POLISH

peas	**groszek**	**gro**shehk
tomatoes	**pomidory**	pomee**dori**
green salad	**sałatę**	sah**wah**teh
potatoes	**ziemniaki**	z'ehm**ñah**kee

Desserts

Nothing more, thanks.	**To wszystko, dziękuję.**	to **fshiss**tko dzhehn**koo**yeh
Just a small portion, please.	**Małą porcję proszę.**	**mah**wawng **port**syeh **pro**sheh
Have you any ice-cream?	**Czy są lody?**	chi sawng **lo**di
fruit salad	**sałatka owocowa**	sah**waht**kah ovo**tso**vah
fresh fruit	**świeże owoce**	s'**fyeh**zheh o**vot**seh
cheese	**ser**	sehr

Drink

What would you like to drink?	**Co podać do picia?**	tso **po**dahtsh do **peet**shah
I'll have a beer, please.	**Proszę piwo.**	**pro**sheh **pee**vo
I'll have a whisky, please.	**Proszę whisky.**	**pro**sheh **wiss**kee

Wine

I'd like a bottle of wine.	**Proszę butelkę wina.**	**pro**sheh boo**tehl**keh **vee**nah
red wine	**czerwonego wina**	chehrvo**neh**go **vee**nah
rosé wine	**rosé**	,,rosé''
white wine	**białego wina**	byah**weh**go **vee**nah
Cheers!	**Na zdrowie!**	nah **zdro**vyeh

The bill (check)

May I have the bill (check) please?	**Proszę o rachunek.**	**pro**sheh o rah**hoo**nehk
Is service included?	**Czy obejmuje obsługę?**	chi obay**moo**yeh op**swoo**geh
Everything's included.	**Rachunek obejmuje wszystko.**	rah**hoo**nehk obay**moo**yeh **fshiss**tko
Thank you, that was a very good meal.	**Dziękuję, jedzenie było bardzo dobre.**	dzhehn**koo**yeh yeh**dzeh**ñeh **bi**wo **bahr**dzo **do**breh

POLISH

Travelling

Where's the railway station, please?	**Przepraszam, gdzie jest stacja kolejowa?**	psheh**prah**shahm gdzheh yehst **stah**tsyah kolehyovah
Where's the ticket office, please?	**Przepraszam, gdzie jest kasa biletowa?**	psheh**prah**shahm gdzheh yehst **kah**ssah beelehtovah
I'd like a ticket to . . .	**Proszę bilet do . . .**	**prosheh** beeleht do
First or second class?	**Pierwsza czy druga klasa?**	**pyehr**shah chi **droo**gah **klah**ssah
First class, please.	**Proszę pierwszą klasę.**	**prosheh** pyeh**r**shawng **klah**sseh
Single or return (one way or round-trip)?	**W jedną stronę czy powrotny?**	v **yehd**nawng **stroneh** chi po**vrotni**
Do I have to change trains?	**Czy muszę się przesiadać?**	chi **moo**sheh s'eh pshehs'**ay**dahtsh
What platform does the train leave from?	**Z którego peronu odchodzi pociąg?**	s**ktoorehgo** peh**rono**o ot**hodzhee potshonk**
Where's the nearest underground station?	**Gdzie jest najbliższa stacja metro?**	gdzheh yehst nigh**bleesh**shah **stah**tsyah **mehtro**
Where's the bus station, please?	**Gdzie jest dworzec autobusowy?**	gdzheh yehst **dvo**zhehts ahwtoboo**ssovi**
When's the first bus to . . . ?	**Kiedy odjeżdża pierwszy autobus do . . . ?**	**kehdi** odyeh**zhjah pyehr**shi ahwto**booss** do
the last bus the next bus	**ostatni autobus następny autobus**	os**stahtñee** ahwto**booss** nah**sstehmpni** ahwto**booss**
Please let me off at the next stop.	**Proszę się zatrzymać na następnym przystanku.**	**prosheh** s'eh zaht**shimahtsh** nah nah**sstehmpnim** pshiss**tahnkoo**

Relaxing

What's on at the cinema (movies)?	**Co grają w kinie?**	tso **grah**yawng f**kee**ñeñ
What's on at the theatre?	**Co grają w teatrze?**	tso **grah**yawng fteh**ah**chsheh
What time does the film begin? And the play?	**O której zaczyna się film? A sztuka?**	o **ktooray** zah**chinah** s'eh feelm? ah **shtoo**kah
Are there any tickets for tonight?	**Czy są bilety na dzisiaj wieczór?**	chi sawng bee**leh**ti nah **dzhee**ss'igh **vyeh**choor

| Where can we go dancing? | Gdzie można pójść potańczyć? | gdzheh mozhnah pooys'tsh potahñchitsh |
| Would you like to dance? | Czy mogę prosić? | chi mogeh pross'eetsh |

Introductions

How do you do?	Dzień dobry.	dzhehñ dobri
How are you?	Jak się pan/pani miewa?	yahk s'eh pahn/pahñee myehvah
Very well, thank you. And you?	Dobrze, dziękuję. A pan/pani?	dobzheh dzhehnkooyeh. ah pahn/pahñee
May I introduce Miss Philips?	To jest pani Philips.	to yehst pahñee Philips
My name is...	Nazywam się...	nahzivahm s'eh
I'm very pleased to meet you.	Bardzo mi miło.	bahrdzo mee meewo
How long have you been here?	Od jak dawna pan/pani jest tutaj?	od yahk dahvnah pahn/pahñee yehst tootigh
It was nice meeting you.	Miło mi było pana/panią poznać.	meewo mee biwo pahnah/pahñawng poznahtsh

Dating

Would you like a cigarette?	Czy zapali pani?	chi zahpahlee pahñee
May I get you a drink?	Czy napije się pani czegoś?	chi nahpeeyeh s'eh pahñee chehgos'
Do you have a light, please?	Czy mogę prosić o ogień?	chi mogeh pross'eetsh o ogehñ
Are you waiting for someone?	Czy pan/pani na kogoś czeka?	chi pahn/pahñee nah kogos' chehkah
Are you free this evening?	Czy pan/pani ma dzisiaj wolny wieczór?	chi pahn/pahñee mah dzheess'igh volni vyehchoor
Where shall we meet?	Gdzie się spotkamy?	gdzheh s'eh spotkahmi
What time shall I meet you?	O której się spotkamy?	o ktooray s'eh spotkahmi
May I take you home?	Czy mogę panią odwieźć do domu?	chi mogeh pahñawng odvyehs'tsh do domoo

Thank you, it's been a wonderful evening.	**Dziękuję za cudowny wieczór.**	dzhehn**kooyeh** zah tsoo**dovni vyeh**choor
What's your telephone number?	**Jaki jest pana/pani numer telefonu?**	**yah**kee yehst pahnah/**pah**ñee noomehr tehlehfonoo
Do you live alone?	**Czy pani mieszka sama?**	chi **pah**ñee **myehsh**kah sahmah
What time is your last train?	**O której ma pan/pani ostatni pociąg?**	o **kto**tray mah pahn/**pah**ñee os**tahtnee potshonk**
Good-night . . .	**Dobranoc . . .**	do**brah**nots

Banks

Where's the nearest bank, please?	**Przepraszam, gdzie jest najbliższy bank?**	psheh**prah**shahm gdzheh yehst nigh**bleesh**shi bahnk
Where can I cash some traveller's cheques?	**Gdzie mogę wymienić czeki podróżne?**	gdzheh mogeh vimyeh**ñ**eetsh **chehk**kee podroozhneh
What time does the bank open? What time does it close?	**O której otwiera się bank? O której się zamyka?**	o **ktoo**ray otf**yeh**rah s'eh bahnk o **ktoo**ray s'eh zah**mi**kah
I'm expecting some money from home. Has it arrived?	**Oczekuję na przekaz pieniężny z domu. Czy już nadszedł?**	ocheh**kooyeh** nah psheh**kahss** pyeñ**ehn**zhni zdomoo. chi yoosh **nahts**sheht
Can you give me some small change, please?	**Proszę mi dać trochę drobnych.**	**prosheh** mee dahtsh **troheh** drobnih

Shops, stores and services

Where is the nearest chemist's (pharmacy)?	**Gdzie jest najbliższa apteka?**	gdzheh yehst nigh**bleesh**shah ahp**teh**kah
the nearest hairdresser's	**zakład fryzjerski**	**zah**kwaht friz **yehr**skee
the photo shop	**sklep fotograficzny**	sklehp fotograh**feech**ni
the jeweller's	**jubiler**	yoo**beel**ehr
the department store	**dom towarowy**	dom tovah**rovi**
the police station	**posterunek milicji**	posteh**roo**nehk meelee**ets**yee
the garage	**warsztat samochodowy**	**vahr**shtaht sahmoho**do**vi

POLISH

| How do I get there? | Jak się tam dostać? | yahk s'eh tahm **doss**tahtsh |
| Is it within walking distance? | Czy dojdę tam pieszo? | chi **doy**deh tahm **pyeh**sho |

Service

Can you help me, please?	Proszę pana/panią!	**pro**sheh **pah**nah/**pah**ñawng
Can you show me this? And that, too.	Proszę mi to pokazać! I tamto też.	**pro**sheh mee to pokah-zahtsh. ee **tahm**to tehsh
It's too expensive/ too big/too small.	Jest za drogi/za duży/za mały.	yehst zah **dro**gee/zah **doo**zhi/zah **mah**wi
Can you show me some more?	Czy może mi pan/ pani pokazać inne?	chi **mo**zheh mee pahn/ **pah**ñee pokah**zah**tsh **een**neh
something better something cheaper	coś lepszego coś tańszego	tsos'**lehp**shehgo tsos' **tah**ñshehgo
How much is this? And that?	Ile to kosztuje? A tamto?	**ee**leh to kosh**too**yeh? ah **tahm**to
It's not quite what I want.	Nie to chciałem.	ñeh to **htshah**wehm
I like it.	Podoba mi się to.	po**do**bah mee s'eh to

Chemist's (Pharmacy)

| I'd like something for a cold/for a cough/for travel sickness. | Proszę coś na przeziębienie/na kaszel/na mdłości. | **pro**sheh tsos' nah pshehz'ehm**byeh**ñeh/nah **kah**shehl/nah **mdwos**'tshee |
| Can you recommend something for hay-fever/for sunburn? | Czy może mi pan/pani polecić coś na katar sienny/na oparzenie słoneczne? | chi **mo**zheh mee pahn/ **pah**ñee po**leh**tsheetsh tsos' nah **kah**tahr **s'ehn**ni/ nah opah**zheh**ñeh swo**nehch**neh |

Toiletry

May I have some razor blades?	Poproszę żyletki.	po**pro**sheh zhi**leht**kee
some shaving cream some toothpaste	krem do golenia pastę do zębów	krehm do go**leh**ñah **pahs**steh do **zehm**boof
I'd like some soap.	Proszę mydło.	**pro**sheh **mid**wo
some suntan oil	olejek do opalania	o**leh**yehk do opah**lah**ñah

At the barber's

I'd like a haircut, please.	**Proszę mnie ostrzyc.**	prosheh mñeh **oss**tshits
Short/Leave it long.	**Krótko/Proszę zostawić długie.**	**kroot**ko/**pro**sheh zostahveetsh **dwoo**gyeh
A razor cut, please.	**Strzyżenie brzytwą, proszę.**	stshi**zheh**ñeh **bzhit**fawng **pro**sheh

At the hairdresser's

I'd like a shampoo and set, please.	**Proszę mycie i ułożenie.**	**pro**sheh **mit**sheh ee oo**wo**zhehñeh
I'd like a bleach.	**Proszę rozjaśnić.**	**pro**sheh rozyahs'ñeetsh
a permanent	**trwała**	**trfah**wawng
a colour rinse	**płukankę koloryzu- jącą**	pwoo**kahn**keh kolorizoo**yon**tsawng
a manicure	**manicure**	mahñee**kyoor**

Photography

I'd like a film for this camera.	**Proszę film do tego aparatu.**	**pro**sheh feelm do **teh**go ahpah**rah**too
This camera doesn't work.	**Popsuł mi się aparat.**	**pop**soow mee s'eh ah**pah**raht

At the post office

Where's the nearest post office, please?	**Przepraszam, gdzie jest najbliższa poczta?**	psheh**prah**shahm gdzheh yehst nigh**bleesh**shah **poch**tah
I'd like to send this by express (special delivery)/by air mail.	**Chcę to nadać ekspresem/pocztą lotniczą.**	htseh to **nah**dahtsh ehk**spreh**ssehm/**poch**tawng lot**ñee**chawng

Service stations

Where is the nearest service station, please?	**Przepraszam, gdzie jest najbliższa stacja benzynowa?**	psheh**prah**shahm gdzheh yehst nigh**bleesh**shah **stah**tsyah behnzi**no**vah
Fill her up, please.	**Proszę napełnić zbiornik.**	**pro**sheh nah**pehw**ñeetsh **zbyor**ñeek
Check the oil, please.	**Proszę sprawdzić olej.**	**pro**sheh **sprahv**dzheetsh **o**lay
Would you check the tyres?	**Proszę sprawdzić opony.**	**pro**sheh **sprahv**dzheetsh o**po**ni

POLISH

POLISH

Street directions

Can you show me on the map where I am?	Czy może pan/pani pokazać mi na mapie gdzie teraz jestem?	chi mozheh pahn/**pah**ñee pokahzahtsh mee nah **mah**pyeh gdzheh **teh**rahss **yehss**tehm
You're on the wrong road.	Pan/pani jedzie nie tą szosą.	pahn/**pah**ñee **yeh**dzheh ñeh tawng **shos**sawng
Go back to . . .	Proszę zawrócić do . . .	**pro**sheh zah**vroots**heetsh do
Go straight ahead.	Proszę jechać prosto.	**pro**sheh **yeh**hahtsh **pros**sto
It's on the left/on the right.	To jest na lewo/na prawo.	to yehst nah **leh**vo/nah **prah**vo

Accidents

May I use your telephone?	Czy mogę skorzystać z telefonu?	chi **mo**geh sko**zhiss**tahtsh **steh**leh**fo**noo
Call a doctor quickly.	Proszę wezwać lekarza, szybko.	**pro**sheh **vehz**vahtsh leh**kah**zhah **ship**ko
Call an ambulance.	Proszę wezwać pogotowie.	**pro**sheh **vehz**vahtsh pogo**to**vyeh
Please call the police.	Proszę wezwać milicję.	**pro**sheh **vehz**vahtsh mee**leet**syeh

Numbers

one	jeden	**yeh**dehn
two	dwa	dvah
three	trzy	chshi
four	cztery	**chteh**ri
five	pięć	pyehñtsh
six	sześć	shehs'tsh
seven	siedem	s'**eh**dehm
eight	osiem	**os**'ehm
nine	dziewięć	**dzheh**vyehñtsh
ten	dziesięć	**dzhehs**'ehñtsh
eleven	jedenaście	yehdeh**nahs**'tsheh
twelve	dwanaście	dvah**nahs**'tsheh
thirteen	trzynaście	chshi**nahs**'tsheh
fourteen	czternaście	chtehr**nahs**'tsheh
fifteen	piętnaście	pyeht**nahs**'tsheh
sixteen	szesnaście	shehss**nahs**'tsheh
seventeen	siedemnaście	s'ehdehm**nahs**'tsheh
eighteen	osiemnaście	os'ehm**nahs**'tsheh
nineteen	dziewiętnaście	dzhehvyeht**nahs**'tsheh

twenty	dwadzieścia	dvah**dzhehs**'tshah
twenty-one	dwadzieścia jeden	dvah**dzhehs**'tshah **yeh**dehn
thirty	trzydzieści	chshid**zhehs**'tshee
forty	czterdzieści	chtehr**dzhehs**'tshee
fifty	pięćdziesiąt	pyehñ**dzhehs**'ont
sixty	sześćdziesiąt	shehs'**dzhehs**'ont
seventy	siedemdziesiąt	s'ehdehm**dzhehs**'ont
eighty	osiemdziesiąt	os'ehm**dzhehs**'ont
ninety	dziewięćdziesiąt	dzhehvyehñ**dzhehs**'ont
one hundred	sto	sto
one thousand	tysiąc	tis'onts
ten thousand	dziesięć tysięcy	**dzhehs**'ehñtsh tis'**ehn**tsi

Days

It's Sunday.	Dzisiaj jest niedziela.	**dzhees**s'igh yehst ñeh**dzeh**lah
Monday	poniedziałek	poñeh**dzhah**wehk
Tuesday	wtorek	**ftorehk**
Wednesday	środa	**s'rodah**
Thursday	czwartek	**chfahr**tehk
Friday	piątek	**pyon**tehk
Saturday	sobota	sobotah
yesterday	wczoraj	fchorigh
today	dzisiaj	**dzhees**s'igh
tomorrow	jutro	**yoo**tro
morning/afternoon	rano/popołudnie	**rah**no/popo**wood**ñeh
evening/night	wieczór/noc	**vyeh**choor/nots

Months

January	styczeń	**sti**chehñ
February	luty	**loo**ti
March	marzec	**mah**zhehts
April	kwiecień	**kfyeh**tshehñ
May	maj	migh
June	czerwiec	**chehr**vyehts
July	lipiec	**lee**pyehts
August	sierpień	**s'ehr**pyehñ
September	wrzesień	vzhe**hss**'ehñ
October	październik	pahz'**dzhehr**ñeek
November	listopad	leess**to**paht
December	grudzień	**groo**dzhehñ
Merry Christmas!	Wesołych Świąt!	vehsowih s'fyont!
Happy New Year!	Szczęśliwego Nowego Roku!	schehhns'lee**veh**go no**veh**go rokoo

PORTUGUESE

Guide to Pronunciation

Letter	Approximate pronunciation	Symbol	Example	
Consonants				
f, k, l, p, t, v	as in English			
b	as in English, but often less decisive (more like **v**)	b	**boca**	boaker
		bh	**abrir**	erbhreer
c	1) before **e** and **i**, like **s** in **s**it	s	**cedo**	saydhoo
	2) elsewhere, like **k** in **k**ill	k	**casa**	kahzer
ç	like **s** in **s**it	s	**começar**	koomersahr
ch	like **sh** in **sh**ut	sh	**chamar**	shermahr
d	as in English, but often less decisive (more like **th** in **th**is)	d	**dia**	deeer
		dh	**nada**	nahdher
g	1) before **a**, **o** and **u** or a consonant, or after **l**, **n** and **r**, like **g** in **g**o	g	**garfo**	gahrfoo
	2) between vowels, like a soft version of the **ch** in Scottish lo**ch**	ǵ	**rogar**	rooǵahr
	3) before **e** and **i**, like **s** in pleasure	zh	**gelo**	zhayloo

h	always silent		**homem**	omahng^y
j	like **s** in plea**s**ure	zh	**já**	zhah
lh	like **lll** in mi**lli**on	ly	**olho**	olyoo
m	1) between a vowel and a consonant, or at the end of a word ("finally"), it indicates that the vowel is nasalized (see "Nasal vowels")		**embalar** **bom**	ahng^{y}bah**lahr** bawng
	2) elsewhere like **m** in met	m	**mais**	mighsh
n	1) when initial or between vowels, like **n** in **no**	n	**novo**	no**a**voo
	2) in a consonant group and in plural endings it nasalizes the preceding vowel, but is generally silent		**branco** **homens**	brahngkoo omahng^{y}sh
nh	like **ni** in o**ni**on	ny	**vinho**	vee**ny**oo
q	like **k** in kill	k	**quadro**	kwahdh**roo**
r	strongly trilled as in Scottish speech	r	**rua**	roo**er**
s	1) when initial, after a consonant or written **ss**, like **s** in sit	s	**saber**	ser**bhayr**
	2) between vowels (not necessarily in the same word), like **z** in ra**z**or	z	**casa** **as aves**	kah**z**er erz ahver**sh**
	3) when final, or before **c, f, p, q, t**, like **sh** in **sh**ut	sh	**país**	pereesh
	4) elsewhere, like **s** in plea**s**ure	zh	**cisne**	see**zh**ner
x	1) generally like **sh** in **sh**ut	sh	**baixo**	bigh**sh**oo
	2) in **ex-** before a vowel, like **z** in ra**z**or	z	**exacto**	i**z**ahtoo
z	1) when initial or between vowels like **z** in ra**z**or	z	**zero**	**z**ehroo
	2) when final or before **c, f, p, q, s** or **t**, like **sh** in **sh**ut	sh	**feliz**	ferlee**sh**
	3) elsewhere like **s** in plea**s**ure	zh	**luz da**	loo**zh** der

Vowels

a	1) when stressed (see under "Stressing") it is like a mixture of the **u** in **cut** and the **a** in **party**	ah	**nado**	**nah**dhoo
	2) when unstressed or before **m**, **n** or **nh** but not in the same syllable like **a** in **about**	er*	**porta**	**por**ter
e	1) when stressed generally like **e** in **get**	eh	**pertu**	**peh**rtoo
	2) when stressed sometimes like **a** in **late**	ay	**cabelo**	ker**bhay**loo
	3) when unstressed, like **er** in **other**	er*	**pesado**	per**zah**dhoo
	4) at the beginning of a word, and in certain other cases, like **i** in **hit**	i	**antes** **exacto**	**ern**tish i**zah**too
é	like **e** in **get**	eh	**café**	ker**feh**
ê	like **a** in **late**	ay	**mês**	maysh
i	1) when stressed like **ee** in **seed**	ee	**riso**	**ree**zoo
	2) when unstressed, like **i** in **coming**	i	**final**	fi**nahl**
o	1) when stressed, like **o** in **rod**	o	**fora**	**for**er
	2) when unstressed, usually like **oo** in **foot**	oo	**caso**	**kah**zoo
	3) sometimes when stressed or unstressed, like **o** in **note** (most common o-sound)	oa	**voltar** **Lisboa**	voal**tahr** lizh**voa**er
ô, ou	like **o** in **note**	oa	**pôs**	poash
u	1) generally like **oo** in **soon**	oo	**número**	**noo**merroo
	2) silent in **gu** and **qu** before **e** or **i**		**querer**	ker**rayr**

* The **r** should not be pronounced when reading this transcription.

Diphthongs

A diphthong is two vowels pronounced as a single vowel sound, e.g., in English **boy** there is a diphthong consisting of **o** plus a weak **i** sound. In Portuguese diphthongs, **a**, **e** and **o** are strong vowels and **i** and **u** are weak vowels. In diphthongs the strong vowels are pronounced with more stress (louder) than the weak ones, e.g., **ai** is pronounced like **igh** in **sigh**, and **au** like **ow** in **how**. Sometimes the weak vowels can combine to make a diphthong. Apart from these generalizations the exact pronunciation of Portuguese diphthongs is not easy to predict.

PORTUGUESE

Nasal vowels

These are pronounced through the mouth and through the nose at the same time, just as in the French nasal vowels (e.g., in the French **bon**) and quite similar to the nasal twang heard in some areas of America and Britain.

ã, am, an	something like **ung** in **lung**, or like **an** in French **dans**	ahng	**maçã**	mer**sahng**
em, en	something like **ing** in **sing**, but recalling also the **a** in late	ayng	**cento**	**sayng**too
im, in	a nasalized version of the **ea** in learn	eeng	**cinco**	**seeng**koo
õ, om, on	like **orn** in **corncob** or like **on** in French **bon**	awng	**bom**	bawng
um, un	something like a North of England pronunciation of **ung** in **lung** (a nasalized version of **u** in **put**)	oong	**um**	oong

Semi-nasalized diphthongs

In these, the first element is nasalized and combined with a weak **i** (pronounced like **y** in **yet**) or **u** pronounced like **w** in **was**).

ãe, ãi, êm, final en, usually final em			
	pronounced as **ã** followed by **y** in yet	ahng^y	**mãe**	mahng^y
			sêm	sahng^y
ão, final unstressed am			
	pronounced as **ã** followed by **w** in **was**	ahng^w	**mão**	mahng^w
õe, oi	pronounced as **õ** followed by **y** in yet	awng^y	**põe**	pawng^y
ui	like nasal vowel **u** followed by **y** in yet	oong^y	**muito**	**moong**^{y}too

Stressing

1) If a word ends with **a**, **e** or **o**, the stress falls on the next to the last syllable, e.g., **rosa** (pronounced **roa**zer). Plural endings **m** and **s** are generally disregarded.

2) All other words are stressed on the last syllable, e.g., **animal** (pronounced ernee**mahl**).

Words not stressed in accordance with these rules have an accent (´ or `) over the vowel of the stressed syllable.

Some basic expressions

Yes.	**Sim.**	seeng
No.	**Não.**	nahng^w
Please.	**Por favor.**	poor fer**voar**
Thank you.	**Obrigado.**	obree**g**ahdhoo
Thank you very much.	**Muito obrigado.**	moong^ytoo obree**g**ahdhoo
That's all right.	**Não tem de quê.**	nahng^w tayng der kay

Greetings

Good morning.	**Bom dia.**	bawng **dee**er
Good afternoon.	**Boa tarde.**	boaer **tahr**der
Good evening.	**Boa noite.**	boaer **noy**ter
Good night.	**Boa noite.**	boaer **noy**ter
Good-bye.	**Adeus.**	erdheh**oo**sh
See you later.	**Até logo.**	ertay loa**g**oo
This is Mr....	**Apresento-lhe o Senhor...**	erprer**zayn**toolyer oo say**ñoar**
This is Mrs....	**Apresento-lhe a Senhora...**	erprer**zayn**toolyer er say**ñoar**er
This is Miss...	**Apresento-lhe a Menina...**	erprer**zayn**toolyer er mer-**nee**ner
I'm very pleased to meet you.	**Muito prazer em conhecê-lo.**	moong^ytoo prer**thehr** ayng koo**ñer**thayloo
How are you?	**Como está?**	koamoo ish**tah**
Very well, thank you.	**Muito bem, obrigado.**	moong^ytoo bayng obree**g**ahdhoo
And you?	**E você?**	ee vo**say**
Fine.	**Bem.**	bayng
Excuse me.	**Desculpe.**	dehsh**kool**per

Questions

Where?	**Onde?**	onder
Where is...?	**Onde está...?**	onder ish**tah**
Where are...?	**Onde estão...?**	onder ish**tahng**^w

PORTUGUESE

When?	**Quando?**	kwahndoo
What?	**O quê?**	oo kay
How?	**Como?**	koamoo
How much?	**Quanto?**	kwahntoo
How many?	**Quantos?**	kwahntoosh
Who?	**Quem?**	kayng
Why?	**Porquê?**	poorkay
Which?	**Qual?**	kwahl
What do you call this?	**Como se chama isto?**	koamoo ser **sher**mer **ees**htoo
What do you call that?	**Como se chama aquilo?**	koamoo ser **sher**mer er**kee**loo
What does this mean?	**Que significa isto?**	kay seeg**nee**feeker **ees**htoo
What does that mean?	**Que significa aquilo?**	kay seeg**nee**feeker er**kee**loo

Do you speak ... ?

Do you speak English?	**Fala inglês?**	fahler eeng**glaysh**
Do you speak German?	**Fala alemão?**	fahler erler**mahng**ʷ
Do you speak French?	**Fala francês?**	fahler frahng**saysh**
Do you speak Spanish?	**Fala espanhol?**	fahler ishper**ñol**
Do you speak Italian?	**Fala italiano?**	fahler eeter**lyah**noo
Could you speak more slowly, please?	**Pode falar mais devagar, por favor?**	poahdher fer**lahr** mighsh derver**gahr** poor fer**voar**
Please point to the phrase in the book.	**Por favor, indique-me a frase no livro.**	poor fer**voar** een**dee**ker-mer er **frah**zer noo **leev**roo
Just a minute. I'll see if I can find it in this book.	**Um momento por favor, vou ver se posso encontrá-la neste livro.**	oong moo**mayng**too poor fer**voar** voa vayr ser **poss**soo ingkon**trah**rler **nehs**ter **leev**roo
I understand.	**Compreendo.**	kawngpri**ayng**doo
I don't understand.	**Não compreendo.**	nahngʷ kawngpri**ayng**doo

Can...?

Can I have...?	**Pode dar-me?**	poadher **dahr**mer
Can we have...?	**Pode dar-nos...?**	poadher **dahr**noosh
Can you show me...?	**Pode mostrar-me...?**	poadher moosh**trahr**mer
Can you tell me...?	**Pode dizer-me...?**	poadher dee**zehr**mer
Can you help me, please?	**Pode ajudar-me, por favor?**	poadher erzhood**dahr**mer poor fer**voar**

Wanting

I'd like...	**Queria...**	kerree**er**
We'd like...	**Queríamos...**	kerree**er**moosh
Please give me...	**Por favor, dê-me...**	poor fer**voar** daymer
Give it to me, please.	**Dê-mo, por favor.**	daymoo poor fer**voar**
Please bring me...	**Por favor, traga-me...**	poor fer**voar** trah**g**ermer
Bring it to me, please.	**Traga-mo, por favor.**	trah**g**er moo poor fer**voar**
I'm hungry.	**Tenho fome.**	teh**ñ**oo fomer
I'm thirsty.	**Tenho sede.**	teh**ñ**oo sehdher
I'm tired.	**Estou cansado.**	ishtoa kern**sahd**hoo
I'm lost.	**Estou perdido.**	ishtoa perr**dheed**hoo
It's important.	**É importante.**	eh impoor**tahn**ter
It's urgent.	**É urgente.**	eh oor**zhehn**ter
Hurry up!	**Depressa!**	der**preh**ser

It is/There is...

It is/It's...	**É...**	eh
Is it...?	**É...?**	eh
It isn't...	**Não é...**	nahng^w eh
There is/There are...	**Há...**	ah
Is there/Are there...?	**Há...?**	ah

PORTUGUESE

| There isn't/There aren't... | **Não há...** | nawng^w ah |
| There isn't any/There aren't any. | **Não há nenhum/Não há nenhuns** (**Não há nenhuma/Não há nenhumas**). | nawng^w ah niñoong/ nawng^w ah niñoongsh (nawng^w ah niñoongmer/ nawng^w ah niñoong-mersh) |

A few common words

big/small	**grande/pequeno**	grahnder/perkehnoo
quick/slow	**rápido/lento**	rahpeedhoo/lehntoo
early/late	**cedo/tarde**	sehdhoo/tahrder
cheap/expensive	**barato/caro**	berrahtoo/kahroo
near/far	**perto/longe**	pehrtoo/lawngzher
hot/cold	**quente/frio**	kehnter/freeoo
full/empty	**cheio/vazio**	shayoo/verzeeoo
easy/difficult	**fácil/difícil**	fahseel/derfeeseel
heavy/light	**pesado/leve**	perzahdhoo/lehver
open/shut	**aberto/fechado**	erbehrtoo/fershahdhoo
right/wrong	**certo/errado**	sehrtoo/ehrrahdhoo
old/new	**velho/novo**	vehlyoo/noavoo
old/young	**idoso/jovem**	eedhoazoo/zhovayng
beautiful/ugly	**belo/feio**	behloo/fayoo
good/bad	**bom/mau**	bawng/mow
better/worse	**melhor/pior**	milyor/peeor

Some prepositions and a few more useful words

at	**a**	ah
on	**sobre**	soabrer
in	**em**	ayng
to	**para**	perrer
from	**de**	der
inside	**dentro**	dehntroo
outside	**fora**	forer
up	**em cima**	ayng seemer
down	**em baixo**	ayng bighshoo
before	**antes**	erntish
after	**depois**	derpoysh
with	**com**	kawng
without	**sem**	sayng
through	**através**	ertrervehsh
towards	**para**	perrer
until	**até**	erteh
during	**durante**	doorahnter

and	e	ee
or	ou	oa
not	não	nawng^w
nothing	nada	nahdher
none	nenhum	ningñoong
very	muito	moong^ytoo
also	também	tahngbayng
soon	em breve	ayng brehver
perhaps	talvez	tahlvaysh
here	aqui	erkee
there	ali	erlee
now	agora	erġorer
then	depois	derpoysh

Arrival

Your passport, please.	O passaporte, por favor.	oo pahserporter poor fervoar
Here it is.	Aqui está.	erkee ishtah
Have you anything to declare?	Tem alguma coisa declarar?	tayng ahlġoomer koyzer er dherklerrahr
No, nothing at all.	Não, nada.	nawng^w nahdher
Porter!	Bagageiro!	berġerzhayroo
Can you help me with my luggage, please?	Pode levar-me a bagagem, por favor?	poadher lervahrmer er bergahzhayng poor fervoar
That's my suitcase.	Esta é a minha mala.	ehshter eh er meeñer mahler
Where's the bus to the centre of town, please?	Onde posso apanhar o autocarro para o centro da cidade, por favor?	onder posssoo erperñahr oo owtookahrroo perrer oo sehntroo der seedhahdher poor fervoar
This way, please.	Por aqui, por favor.	poor erkee poor fervoar

Changing money

| Can you change a traveller's cheque, please? | Pode cambiar-me um cheque de viagem, por favor? | poadher kermbyahrmer oong shehk der vyahzhayng poor fervoar |
| Where's the nearest bank, please? | Onde fica o banco mais próximo, por favor? | onder feeker oo bahngkoo mighsh proseemoo poor fervoar |

Car rental

I'd like a car.	**Queria alugar um carro.**	kerreeer erloo**g**ahr oong **kah**rroo
For how long?	**Por quanto tempo?**	poor **kwahn**too tayng**poo**
A day/Four days/ A week/Two weeks	**Um dia/Quatro dias/Uma semana/ Duas semanas.**	oong **dee**er/**kwah**troo **dee**ersh/**oo**mer ser**mah**ner/**doo**ersh ser**mah**nersh

Taxi

Where can I get a taxi?	**Onde posso encontrar um táxi?**	**on**der **poss**soo ingkon**trah**r oong **tah**ksee
What's the fare to...?	**Qual é o preço do percurso para...?**	kwahl ay oo **preh**soo doo perr**koor**soo **perr**er
Take me to this address, please.	**Leve-me a esta morada, por favor.**	**leh**vermer er **ehsh**ter **moo**rahdher poor fer**voar**
I'm in a hurry.	**Estou com pressa.**	ish**toa** kawng **preh**ser
Could you drive more slowly, please?	**Pode ir mais devagar, por favor?**	**poa**dher eer mighsh der**veg**ahr poor fer**voar**

Hotel and other accommodation

My name is...	**O meu nome é...**	oo **meh**oo **noa**mer eh
Have you a reservation?	**Reservou?**	rerzerr**voa**
Yes, here's the confirmation.	**Sim, aqui está a confirmação.**	seeng er**kee** ish**tah** er kawng**feer**mer**sahng**ᵂ
I'd like...	**Quero...**	**keh**roo
I'd like a single room/a double room.	**Quero um quarto de uma cama/um quarto de casal.**	**keh**roo oong **kwahr**too der **oo**mer **ker**mer/oong **kwahr**too der ker**zahl**
a room with a bath/with a shower	**um quarto com banho/com chuveiro**	oong **kwahr**too kawng **bah**ñoo/kawng shoo**vay**roo

How much?

What's the price per night/per week/per month?	**Qual é o preço por noite/por semana/ por mês?**	kwahl eh oo **preh**soo poor **noy**ter/poor ser**mah**ner/poor maysh
May I see the room?	**Posso ver o quarto?**	**poss**soo vehr oo **kwahr**too

I'm sorry, I don't like it.	Lamento, mas não gosto.	lermehntoo mersh nahng^wgoshtoo
Yes, that's fine. I'll take it.	Sim, está bem. Fico com ele.	seeng ishtah bayng. fee-koo kawng ehler
What's my room number, please?	Qual é o número do meu quarto, por favor?	kwahl eh oo noomerroo doo mehoo kwahrtoo poor fervoar
Number 123.	Número 123.	noomerroo 123.

Service, please

Who is it?	Quem é?	kayng eh
Just a minute.	Um momento.	oong moomehntoo
Come in! The door's open.	Entre! A porta está aberta.	ehntrer er porter ishtah erbehrter
May we have breakfast in our room?	Podemos ter o pequeno almoço no quarto?	poodhehmoosh tehr oo perkehnoo ahlmosoo nookwahrtoo

Breakfast

I'll have ...	Tomo ...	tomoo
I'll have some fruit juice.	Tomo sumo de fruta.	tomoo soomoo der frooter
a boiled egg	um ovo kozido	oong ovoo koozeedhoo
a fried egg	um ovo estrelado	oong ovoo ishtrerlahdhoo
some bacon/some ham	toucinho/presunto	toaseeñoo/prerzoontoo
some toast	torradas	toorrahdhersh
a pot of tea	um bule de chá	oong booler der shah
a cup of tea	uma chávena de chá	oomer shahverner der shah
some coffee	café	kerfeh
some chocolate	chocolate	shookoolahter
more butter	mais manteiga	mighsh merntayğer
some hot water	água quente	ahgwer kaynter

Difficulties

The central heating doesn't work.	O aquecimento central não funciona.	oo erkehseemehntoo sehntrahl nahng^w foonsyoaner
the light/the socket	a luz/a tomada	er loosh/er toomahdher
the tap/the toilet	a torneira/a casa de banho	er toornayrer/er kahzer der bahñoo

PORTUGUESE

| There's no hot water. | **Não há água quente.** | nahng^w ah ahǧwer kaynter |
| May I see the manager, please? | **Posso falar com o director, por favor?** | posssoo ferlahr kawng oo deerehtoar poor fervoar |

Telephone—Mail

There's a call for you.	**Há uma chamada para si.**	ah oomer shermahdher perrer see
Hold the line, please.	**Aguarde um momento, por favor.**	ergwahrder oong moomehntoo poor fervoar
Operator, I've been cut off.	**Telefonista, cortaram-me a ligação.**	terlerfooneeshter koortahremmer er leegersahng^w
Did anyone telephone me?	**Alguém me chamou?**	ahlgayng mer shermoa
Is there any mail for me?	**Há correio para mim?**	ah koorrayoo perrer meeng
Are there any messages for me?	**Há alguma mensagem para mim.**	ah ahlgoomer mayngsahzhayng perrer meeng

Checking out

May I have my bill, please?	**Pode dar-me a conta, por favor?**	poadher dahrmer er konter poor fervoar
We're in a great hurry.	**Temos muita pressa.**	taymoosh moong^yter prehser
It's been a very enjoyable stay.	**Tivemos uma óptima estadia.**	teevehmoosh oomer oteemer ishterdheeer

Eating out

Good evening, sir/ Good evening, madam.	**Boa noite, Senhor/Boa noite, Senhora.**	boaer noyter sayñoar/boaer noyter sayñoarer
Good evening. I'd like a table for two, please.	**Boa noite. Desejo uma mesa para dois, por favor.**	boaer noyter. derzehzhoo oomer mayzer perrer doysh poor fervoar
Do you have a fixed-price menu?	**Tem um menu de preço fixo?**	tayng oong mehnoo der prehsoo feeksoo
May I see the à la carte menu?	**Pode dar-me o menu?**	poadher dahrmer oo mehnoo

May we have an ashtray, please?	Pode-nos dar um cinzeiro, por favor?	poadhernoosh dahr oong seenzayroo poor fervoar
some bread	pão	pahng^w
a fork	um garfo	oong gahrfoo
a knife	uma faca	oomer fahker
a spoon	uma colher	oomer koolyehr
a plate	um prato	oong prahtoo
a glass	um copo	oong kopoo
a napkin	um guardanapo	oong gwerrdernahpoo
another chair	outra cadeira	oatrer kerdhayrer
Where's the gentle-men's toilet (men's room)?	Onde é a casa de banho dos cavalheiros?	onder eh er kahzer der bahñoo doosh kerver-lyayroosh
Where's the ladies' toilet (ladies' room)?	Onde é a casa de banho das senhoras?	onder eh er kahzer der bahñoo dersh say ñoarersh

Appetizers

I'd like some ...	Queria ...	kerreeer
I'd like some assorted appetizers.	Queria uns acepipes variados.	kerreeer oongsh erser-peepersh verryahdoosh
orange juice	um sumo de laranja	oong soomoo der ler-rahngzher
ham	fiambre	fyahngbrer
melon	melão	merlahng^w
pâté	pâté	pahtay
smoked salmon	salmão fumado	sahlmahng^w foomahdhoo
shrimps (shrimp)	camarões	kermerrawng^ysh

Soup

Have you any ... ?	Tem ... ?	tayng
Have you any chicken soup?	Tem caldo de galinha?	tayng kahldoo der gerlee-ñer
vegetable soup	sopa de legumes	soaper der lergoomersh
onion soup	sopa de cebola	soaper der cerboaler

Fish

I'd like some ...	Queria ...	kerreeer
I'd like some fish.	Queria peixe.	kerreeer paysher
sole	linguado	linggwahdhoo
trout	truta	trooter
lobster	lagosta	lergoashter
crayfish	caranguejo	kerrernggayzhoo
prawns	lagostins	lergooshteengsh

I'd like it . . .	**Quero-o . . .**	kehroooo
I'd like it steamed.	**Quero-o cozido a vapor.**	kehroooo koozeedhoo er verpoar
grilled	**grelhado**	grilyahdhoo
boiled	**cozido**	koozeedhoo
baked	**no forno**	noo foarnoo
fried	**frito**	freetoo

Meat—Poultry—Game

I'd like some . . .	**Queria . . .**	kerreeer
I'd like some beef.	**Queria carne de vaca.**	kerreeer kahrner der vahker
a beef steak	**um bife**	oong beefer
some roast beef	**rósbife**	rozbeefer
a veal cutlet	**uma costeleta de vitela**	oomer kooshterlayter der veetehler
mutton	**carneiro**	kerrnayroo
lamb	**borrego**	boorayġoo
a pork chop	**uma costeleta de porco**	oomer kooshterlayter der poarkoo
roast pork	**porco assado**	poarkoo ersahdhoo
hare	**lebre**	lehbrer
chicken	**frango**	frahnggoo
roast chicken	**frango assado**	frahnggoo ersahdhoo
duck	**pato**	pahtoo
How do you like your meat?	**Como deseja a carne?**	koamoo derzayzher er kahrner
rare	**mal passada**	mahl persahdher
medium	**médio**	mehdyoo
well done	**bem passada**	bayng persahdher

Vegetables

What vegetables have you got?	**Que legumes tem?**	ker lerġoomersh tayng
I'd like some . . .	**Queria . . .**	kerreeer
I'd like some asparagus.	**Queria espargos.**	kerreeer ishpahrgoosh
green beans	**feijão verde**	fayzhahngʷ vehrder
mushrooms	**cogumelos**	kooġoomehloosh
carrots	**cenouras**	sinoarersh
onions	**cebolas**	serboalersh
red cabbage	**repolho**	rerpoalyoo
spinach	**espinafres**	ishpeenahfrersh

PORTUGUESE

rice	arroz	erroash
peas	ervilhas	errveelyersh
tomatoes	tomates	toomahtersh
green salad	salada de alface	serlahdher der ahlfahser
potatoes	batatas	bertahtersh

Desserts

Nothing more, thanks.	Mais nada, obrigado.	mighsh nahdher obreegahdhoo
Just a small portion, please.	Muito pouco, por favor.	moong^{y}too poakoo poor fervoar
Have you any ice-cream?	Tem gelados?	tayng zherlahdoosh
fruit salad	salada de frutas	serlahder dher frootersh
fresh fruit	fruta fresca	frooter frayshker
cheese	queijo	kayzhoo

Drink

What would you like to drink?	Que deseja tomar?	ker derzayzher toomahr
I'll have a beer, please.	Queria uma cerveja, por favor.	kerreeer oomer serrvayzher poor fervoar
I'll have a whisky, please.	Queria um whisky, por favor.	kerreeer oong weeshkee poor fervoar

Wine

I'd like a bottle of wine.	Queria uma garrafa de vinho.	kerreeer oomer gerrahfer der veeñoo
red wine	vinho tinto	veeñoo teentoo
rosé wine	vinho rosé	veeñoo rozay
white wine	vinho branco	veeñoo brahngkoo
Cheers!	Saúde!	seroodher

The bill (check)

| May I have the bill (check) please? | Pode dar-me a conta, por favor? | poadher dahrmer er konter poor fervoar |
| Is service included? | O serviço está incluído? | oo serrveesoo ishtah eengklooeedhoo |

PORTUGUESE

| Everything's included. | **Tudo incluído.** | **too**dhoo eengkloo**ee**dhoo |
| Thank you, that was a very good meal. | **Obrigado, foi uma boa refeição.** | obree**gah**dhoo foy **oo**mer **boa**er rerfay**sahng**ʷ |

Travelling

Where's the railway station, please?	**Onde é a estação de caminho de ferro, por favor?**	**onder** eh er ishter**sahng**ʷ der kermee**ñoo** der **feh**roo poor fer**voar**
Where's the ticket office, please?	**Onde é a bilheteira, por favor?**	**onder** eh er beelyer**tay**rer poor fer**voar**
I'd like a ticket to ...	**Queria um bilhete para ...**	ker**reee**r oong beel**yay**ter **perrer**
First or second class?	**De primeira ou segunda classe?**	der pree**may**rer oa ser**goon**der **klah**ser
First class, please.	**De primeira, por favor.**	der pree**may**rer poor fer**voar**
Single or return (one way or round-trip)?	**Uma ida ou ida e volta?**	**oo**mer **eed**er oa **eed**er ee **volt**er
Do I have to change trains?	**Devo mudar de comboio?**	**day**voo moo**dahr** der koam**boy**oo
What platform does the train leave from?	**De que cais parte o comboio?**	der ker kighsh **pahr**ter oo koam**boy**oo
Where's the nearest underground (subway) station?	**Onde é a estação de metro mais próxima?**	**onder** eh er ishter**sahng**ʷ der **meh**troo mighsh **pro**seemer
Where's the bus station, please?	**Onde é a estação dos autocarros?**	**onder** eh er ishter**sahng**ʷ doosh owtoo**kah**roosh
When's the first bus to ...?	**A que horas parte o primeiro autocarro para ...?**	er ker **orersh pahr**ter oo pree**may**roo owtoo**kah**roo **perrer**
the last bus	**o último autocarro**	oo **ool**timoo owtoo**kah**roo
the next bus	**o próximo autocarro**	oo **pro**seemoo owtoo**kah**roo
Please let me off at the next stop.	**Por favor, deixe-me sair na próxima paragem.**	poor fer**voar day**shermer ser**eer** ner **pro**seemer per**rah**zhayng

Relaxing

| What's on at the cinema (movies)? | **O que há no cinema?** | oo ker ah noo see**nay**mer |

What's on at the theatre?	**O que há no teatro?**	oo ker ah noo tiahtroo
What time does the film begin? And the play?	**A que horas começa o filme? E a peça?**	ah ker orersh koomehser oo feelmer. ee er pehser
Are there any tickets for tonight?	**Há bilhetes para esta noite?**	ah beelyaytersh perrer ehshter noyter
Where can we go dancing?	**Onde podemos ir dançar?**	onder poodhehmoosh eer dahnsahr
Would you like to dance?	**Quer dançar?**	kehr dahnsahr

Introductions

How do you do?	**Bom dia.**	bawng deeer
How are you?	**Como está?**	koamoo ishtah
Very well, thank you. And you?	**Muito bem, obrigado. E você?**	moong^ytoo bayng obreegahdhoo. ee vosay
May I introduce Miss Philips?	**Apresento-lhe a Menina Philips.**	erprerzayntoolyer er merneener Philips
My name is . . .	**O meu nome é . . .**	oo mehoo noamer eh
I'm very pleased to meet you.	**Tenho muito prazer em conhecê-lo.**	tayñoo moong^ytoo prerzehr ayng kooñersayloo
How long have you been here?	**Há quanto tempo está cá?**	ah kwahntoo tayngpoo ishtah kah
It was nice meeting you.	**Tive muito prazer em conhecê-lo.**	teever moong^ytoo prerzehr ayng kooñersayloo

Dating

Would you like a cigarette?	**Quer um cigarro?**	kehr oong seegahroo
May I get you a drink?	**Posso oferecer-lhe uma bebida?**	posssoo oferrersehrlyer oomer berbeedher
Do you have a light, please?	**Tem lume, por favor?**	tayng loomer poor fervoar
Are you waiting for someone?	**Espera alguém?**	ishpayrer ahlgayng
Are you free this evening?	**Está livre esta noite?**	ishtah leevrer ehshter noyter
Where shall we meet?	**Onde nos podemos encontrar?**	onder noosh poodhehmoosh ingkoantrahr

PORTUGUESE

What time shall I meet you?	A que horas posso encontra-la?	er ker orersh posssoo ingkoantrahler
May I take you home?	Posso leva-la a casa?	posssoo lervahler er kahzer
Thank you, it's been a wonderful evening.	Obrigado por esta noite tão agradável.	obreegahdhoo poor ehshter noyter tahng^w ergrerdhahvehl
What's your telephone number?	Qual é o seu número de telefone?	kwahl eh oo sehoo noomerroo de terlerfoner
Do you live alone?	Vive só?	veever so
What time is your last train?	A que horas é o seu último comboio?	er ker orersh eh oo sehoo ooltimoo koamboyoo
Good-night...	Boa noite...	boaer noyter

Banks

Where's the nearest bank, please?	Onde é o Banco mais próximo, por favor?	onder eh oo bahngkoo mighsh proseemoo poor fervoar
Where can I cash some traveller's cheques?	Onde posso trocar alguuns cheques de viagem?	onder posssoo trookahr ahlgoongsh shehks der vyahzhayng
What time does the bank open? What time does it close?	A que horas abre o Banco? A que horas fecha?	er ker orersh ahbrer oo bahngkoo? er ker orersh fehsher
I'm expecting some money from home. Has it arrived?	Aguardo dinheiro da familia. Já chegou?	ergwahrdhoo diñayroo der fermeelyer. zhah shergoa
Can you give me some small change, please?	Pode dar-me alguns trocos, por favor?	poadher dahrmer ahlgoongsh trokoosh poor fervoar

Shops, stores and services

Where is the nearest chemist's (pharmacy)?	Onde é a farmácia mais próxima?	onder eh er ferrmahseeer mighsh proseemer
the nearest hairdresser's	o cabeleireiro mais próximo	o kerberleerayroo mighsh proseemoo
the photo shop	a loja de artigos fotográficos	er lozher der errteegoosh footoograhfeekoosh
the jeweller's	a ourivesaria	er oareevserreeer
the department store	o armazém	oo ahrmerzayng

the police station	o posto de policia	oo **posh**too der poolee-seeer
the garage	a garagem	er gerrahzhayng
How do I get there?	Como vou lá ter?	koamoo voa lah tehr
Is it within walking distance?	Pode-se ir a pé?	poadherser eer ah peh

Service

Can you help me, please?	Pode ajudar-me, por favor?	poadher erzhood**hah**rmer poor fer**voar**
Can you show me this? And that, too.	Pode mostrar-me isto? e aquilo também.	poadher moosht**rah**rmer eeshtoo ee er**kee**loo tahm**bayng**
It's too expensive/ too big/too small.	É muito caro/muito grande/muito pequeno.	eh moong^{y}too kahroo/ moong^{y}too grahnder/ moong^{y}too perkehnoo

Can you show me some more?	Pode mostrar-me mais alguns?	poadher moosht**rah**rmer mighsh ahl**goong**sh
something better	algo melhor	ahlgoo milyoar
something cheaper	algo mais barato	ahlgoo mighsh ber**rah**too
How much is this? And that?	Quanto custa isto? E aquilo?	kwahntoo kooshter eesh-too? ee er**kee**loo
It's not quite what I want.	Não é exatamente o que quero.	nahng^w eh izahter**mehn**ter oo ker **keh**roo
I like it.	Gosto disto.	goshtoo **deesh**too

Chemist's (Pharmacy)

| I'd like something for a cold/for a cough/for travel sickness. | Queria qualquer coisa para a constipação/para a tosse/para o enjôo de viagem. | kerreeer kwahl**kehr** koyzer perrer er kawngshtipersahng^w/perrer er toser/perrer oo ayng-zhoaoo der vyah**zhayng** |
| Can you recommend something for hay-fever/for sunburn? | Pode indicar-me algo para a alergia do polen/para quei-maduras do sol? | poadher eendeekahrmer ahlgoo perrer er erler-zheeer doo polayn/perrer kaymer**dhoo**rersh doo sol |

PORTUGUESE

Toiletry

May I have some razor blades?	**Pode dar-me lâminas de barbear?**	poadher dahrmer lahmeenersh der berrbyahr
some shaving cream	**creme para a barba**	kreaymer perrer er bahrber
some toothpaste	**uma pasta de dentes**	oomer pahshter der dehntish
I'd like some soap.	**Queria um sabonete.**	kerreeer oom serboonehter
some suntan oil	**um óleo para bronzear**	oong olyoo perrer bronzeeahr

At the barber's

I'd like a haircut, please.	**Quero cortar o cabelo, por favor.**	kehroo koortahr oo kerbayloo poor fervoar
Short/Leave it long.	**Curto/Deixe-o comprido.**	koortoo/daysheroo kompreedoo
A razor cut, please.	**A navalha, por favor.**	er nervahlyer poor fervoar

At the hairdresser's

I'd like a shampoo and set, please.	**Queria um champô e mise, por favor.**	kerreeer oong shahmpoa ee meezer poor fervoar
I'd like a bleach.	**Queria aloirar o cabelo.**	kerreeer erloyrahr oo kerbayloo
a permanent	**fazer uma permanente**	ferzehr oomer pehrmernehnter
a colour rinse	**pintar o cabelo**	peentahr oo kerbayloo
a manicure	**uma manicura**	oomer merneekoorer

Photography

I'd like a film for this camera.	**Queria um rolo para esta máquina fotográfica.**	kerreeer oong roaloo perrer ehshter mahkeener footoograhfeeker
This camera doesn't work.	**Esta máquina não funciona bem.**	ehshter mahkeener nahng^w foonsyoaner bayng

At the post office

| Where's the nearest post office, please? | **Qual é o correio mais próximo, por favor?** | kwahl eh oo koorayoo mighsh proseemoo poor fervoar |
| I'd like to send this by express (special delivery)/by air mail. | **Queria enviar isto por expresso/por avião.** | kerreeer ayngveeahr eeshtoo poor ishprehsoo/poor erveeahng^w |

Service stations

Where is the nearest service station, please?	**Qual é a estação de serviço mais próxima, por favor?**	kwahl eh er ishtersahng^w der serrveesoo mighsh proseemer poor fervoar
Fill her up, please.	**Encha o depósito, por favor.**	ayngsher oo derpozeetoo poor fervoar
Check the oil, please.	**Verifique o óleo, por favor.**	verreefeeker oo olyoo poor fervoar
Would you check the tyres?	**Pode verificar os pneus?**	poadher verreefeekahr oosh pnehoosh

Street directions

Can you show me on the map where I am?	**Pode mostrar-me no mapa onde me encontro?**	poadher mooshtrahrmer noo mahper onder mer ayngkontroo
You're on the wrong road.	**Está na estrada errada.**	ishtah ner ishtrahdher errahdher
Go back to...	**Volte atrás até...**	volter ertrahsh erteh
Go straight ahead.	**Sempre em frente.**	saymprer ayng fraynter
It's on the left/on the right.	**É à esquerda/à direita.**	eh ah ishkehrder/ah dirayter

Accidents

May I use your telephone?	**Posso telefonar?**	posssoo terlerfoonahr
Call a doctor quickly.	**Chame um médico depressa.**	shermer oong maydeekoo derprehser
Call an ambulance.	**Chame uma ambulância.**	shermer oomer ermboolahngseeer
Please call the police.	**Chame a polícia, por favor.**	shermer er pooleeseeer poor fervoar

PORTUGUESE

Numbers

one	**um**	oong
two	**dois**	doysh
three	**três**	traysh
four	**quatro**	kwahtro
five	**cinco**	**seeng**koo
six	**seis**	saysh
seven	**sete**	**seh**ter
eight	**oito**	**oy**too
nine	**nove**	**nov**er
ten	**dez**	dehsh
eleven	**onze**	**awng**zer
twelve	**doze**	**doa**zer
thirteen	**treze**	**tray**zer
fourteen	**catorze**	ker**toar**zer
fifteen	**quinze**	**keen**zer
sixteen	**dezasseis**	derzer**saysh**
seventeen	**dezassete**	derzer**seh**ter
eighteen	**dezoito**	der**zoy**too
nineteen	**dezanove**	derzer**nov**er
twenty	**vinte**	**veen**ter
twenty-one	**vinte e um**	**veen**ter ee oong
thirty	**trinta**	**treen**ter
forty	**quarenta**	kwer**rehn**ter
fifty	**cinquenta**	seeng**kwehn**ter
sixty	**sessenta**	ser**sehn**ter
seventy	**setenta**	ser**tehn**ter
eighty	**oitenta**	oy**tehn**ter
ninety	**noventa**	noo**vehn**ter
one hundred	**cem**	sayng
one thousand	**mil**	meel
ten thousand	**dez mil**	dehsh meel

Days

It's Sunday.	**É domingo.**	eh doo**meeng**goo
Monday	**segunda-feira**	ser**goon**der fayrer
Tuesday	**terça-feira**	**teh**rser fayrer
Wednesday	**quarta-feira**	**kwah**rter fayrer
Thursday	**quinta-feira**	**keen**ter fayrer
Friday	**sexta-feira**	**saysh**ter fayrer
Saturday	**sábado**	**sah**berdhoo
yesterday	**ontem**	**awng**tayng
today	**hoje**	**oa**zher
tomorrow	**amanhã**	ahmer**ñahng**
morning/afternoon	**manhã/tarde**	mer**ñahng**/**tah**rder
evening/night	**noite/noite**	**noy**ter/**noy**ter

Months

January	**Janeiro**	zher**nay**roo
February	**Fevereiro**	ferver**ray**roo
March	**Março**	**mahr**soo
April	**Abril**	er**breel**
May	**Maio**	**migh**oo
June	**Junho**	**zhoo**ñoo
July	**Julho**	**zhool**yoo
August	**Agosto**	er**goash**too
September	**Setembro**	ser**tayng**broo
October	**Outubro**	oa**too**broo
November	**Novembro**	noo**vayng**broo
December	**Dezembro**	der**zayng**broo
Merry Christmas!	**Feliz Natal/Feliz**	fer**leesh** ner**tahl**/fer**leesh**
Happy New Year!	**Ano Novo!**	**ah**noo **no**voo

RUSSIAN

Guide to Pronunciation

Letter	Approximate pronunciation	Symbol	Example	
Vowels				
а	between the **a** in cat and the **ar** in cart	ah	как	kahk
е	like **ye** in yet	yeh	где	gdyeh
ё	like **yo** in yonder	yo	мёд	myod
и	like **ee** in see	ee	синий	**see**nyee
й	like **y** in gay or boy	y	бой	boy
о	like **o** in hot	o	стол	stol
у	like **oo** in boot	oo	улица	**oo**leetsah
ы	similar to **i** in hit	i	вы	vi
э	like **e** in met	eh	эта	**eh**tah
ю	like **u** in duke	yoo	юг	yoog
я	like **ya** in yard	yah	мясо	**myah**sah

Consonants

б	like **b** in **b**it	b	был	bil
в	like **v** in **v**ine	v	ваш	vahsh
г	like **g** in **g**o	g	город	**go**rahd
д	like **d** in **d**o	d	да	dah
ж	like **s** in plea**s**ure	zh	жаркий	**zhahr**kee
з	like **z** in **z**oo	z	за	zah
к	like **k** in **k**itten	k	карта	**kahr**tah
л	like **l** in **l**ose	l	лампа	**lahm**pah
м	like **m** in **m**y	m	масло	**mahss**lah
н	like **n** in **n**ot	n	нет	nyeht
п	like **p** in **p**ot	p	парк	pahrk
р	like **r** in **r**un	r	русский	**rooss**kee
с	like **s** in **s**ee	s/ss	слово	**slo**vah
т	like **t** in **t**ip	t	там	tahm
ф	like **f** in **f**ace	f	ферма	**fyehr**mah
х	like **ch** in Scottish lo**ch**	kh	хлеб	kh lyehb
ц	like **ts** in si**ts**	ts	цена	**tsee**nah
ч	like **ch** in **ch**ip	ch	час	chahss
ш	like **sh** in **sh**ut	sh	ваша	**vah**shah
щ	like **sh** followed by **ch**	shch	щётка	**shchyot**kah

Other letters

ь	gives a "soft" pronunciation to the preceding consonant. A similar effect can be produced by pronouncing **y** as in **y**et—but very, very short—after the consonant. In our transcription we shall show this with an apostrophe (') after the soft consonant.
ъ	is sometimes used between two parts of a compound word, when the second part begins with **я**, **ю**, or **е**, to show that the pronunciation of the word should incorporate a clear separation of the two parts.

Diphthongs

ай	like **igh** in s**igh**	igh	чай	chigh
яй	like the previous sound, but preceded by the **y** in **y**es	yigh	негодяй	nyehgo**dyigh**
ой	like **oy** in b**oy**	oy	вой	voy
ей	like **ya** in **Ya**tes	yay	соловей	solov**yay**
ый	like **i** in bit followed by the **y** in **y**es	iy	красивый	krah**see**viy
уй	like **oo** in good followed by the **y** in **y**es	ooy	дуй	dooy
юй	like the previous sound, but preceded by the **y** in **y**es	yooy	плюй	plyooy

RUSSIAN

The effects of non-stress

If a vowel or diphthong is not stressed, it often changes its pronunciation. This could be called a weakening of the sound.

| о | unstressed, is pronounced like Russian **a** | ah | отец | ah**tyehts** |
| е, я, и, ой, ей, ий | unstressed, are pronounced like a short **yee** sound | yee or ee | теперь английский | tyee**pyehr'** ahn**gleeskee** |

The alphabet

The column at the left shows printed capital and small letters while the centre column shows handwritten capital and small letters. The right-hand column will help you to pronounce the names of these letters in Russian.

А а	𝒜 𝒶	ah
Б б	𝐵 б	beh
В в	𝐵 в	veh
Г г	𝒢 г	geh
Д д	𝒟 д	deh
Е е	𝓔 е	yeh
Ё ё	𝓔 ё	yoh
Ж ж	𝒲 ж	zheh
З з	𝒵	zeh
И и	𝒰 и	ee
Й й	𝒰 й	ee **kraht**koyeh
К к	𝒦 к	kah
Л л	𝓛 л	ehl
М м	𝓜 М	ehm
Н н	𝓗 н	ehn
О о	𝒪 о	o
П п	𝒫 п	peh

Р р	𝒫 р	ehr
С с	𝒞 с	ehs
Т т	𝒯 т	teh
У у	𝒰 у	oo
Ф ф	ф ф	ehf
Х х	𝒳 х	khah
Ц ц	𝒰 ц	tseh
Ч ч	𝒰 ч	chah
Ш ш	𝒲 ш	shah
Щ щ	𝒲 щ	shchah
Ъ ъ	ъ	**tvyor**diy znahk
Ы ы	ы	yeh**ree**
Ь ь	ь	**myah**kee znahk
Э э	𝒟 э	eh obo**rot**noyeh
Ю ю	𝒲 ю	yoo
Я я	𝒴 Я	yah

RUSSIAN

RUSSIAN

Some basic expressions

Yes.	Да.	dah
No.	Нет.	nyeht
Please.	Пожалуйста.	pah**zhah**loostah
Thank you.	Спасибо.	spah**see**bah
Thank you very much.	Большое спасибо.	bahl'**sho**yee spah**see**bah
That's all right.	Не за что.	nyee zah **shto**

Greetings

Good morning.	Доброе утро.	dobrahyee **oo**tro
Good afternoon.	Добрый день.	dobri **dyehn'**
Good evening.	Добрый вечер.	dobri **vyeh**chyeer
Good night.	Спокойной ночи.	spah**koy**nigh **no**chee
Good-bye.	До свидания.	dah svee**dah**neeyah
See you later.	До встречи.	dah **vstryeh**chee
This is Mr....	Это господин ...	ehtah gahspah**deen**
This is Mrs....	Это госпожа ...	ehtah gahspah**zhah**
This is Miss ...	Это госпожа ...	ehtah gahspah**zhah**
I'm very pleased to meet you.	Очень приятно.	ochyeen' preey**aht**nah
How are you?	Как дела?	kahk dyeh**lah**
Very well, thank you. And you?	Спасибо, хорошо. Как у Вас?	spah**see**bah khahrah**sho** kahk oo **vahs**
Fine.	Прекрасно.	pryee**krahs**nah
Excuse me.	Простите.	prahs**tee**tyee

Questions

Where?	Где?	gdyeh
Where is...?	Где...?	gdyeh
Where are...?	Где...?	gdyeh
When?	Когда?	kahg**dah**
What?	Что?	shto
How?	Как?	kahk
How much?	Сколько?	**skol**'kah
How many?	Сколько?	**skol**'kah

Who?	Кто?	kto
Why?	Почему?	pahchyee**moo**
Which?	Какой?	kah**koy**
What do you call this?	Как это называется?	kahk **eh**tah nahzi**vah**yeetsah
What do you call that?	Как это называется?	kahk **eh**tah nahzi**vah**yeetsah
What does this mean?	Что это значит?	shto **eh**tah **znah**cheet
What does that mean?	Что это значит?	shto **eh**tah **znah**cheet

Do you speak...?

Do you speak English?	Вы говорите по-английски?	vi gahvah**ree**tyee pah ahn**glee**skee
Do you speak German?	Вы говорите по-немецки?	vi gahvah**ree**tyee pah nyee**myeht**skee
Do you speak French?	Вы говорите по-французски?	vi gahvah**ree**tyee pah frahn**tsoo**skee
Do you speak Spanish?	Вы говорите по-испански?	vi gahvah**ree**tyee pah eespahnskee
Do you speak Italian?	Вы говорите по-итальянски?	vi gahvah**ree**tyee pah eetahl'yahnskee
Could you speak more slowly, please?	Могли-бы вы говорить медленнее?	mah**glee**bi vi gahvah**reet'** **myeh**dlyeenyehyee
Please point to the phrase in the book.	Покажите мне, пожалуйста, фразу в книге.	pahkah**zhee**tyee mnyeh pahzhahloostah **frah**zoo v **knee**gyee
Just a minute. I'll see if I can find it in this book.	Минуточку. Я посмотрю, смогу ли я её найти в книжке.	mee**noo**tahchkoo yah pahsmah**tryoo** smah**goo**lee yah yee**yo** nigh**tee** v **knee**zhkyee
I understand.	Я понимаю.	yah pahnyee**mah**yoo
I don't understand.	Я не понимаю.	yah nyee pahnyee**mah**yoo

Can...?

Can I have...?	Можно...?	**mozh**nah
Can we have...?	Можно...?	**mozh**nah
Can you show me...?	Вы мне можете показать...?	vi mnyeh **mozh**yeetyee pahkah**zaht'**

| Can you tell me . . . ? | Вы мне можете сказать . . . ? | vi mnyeh **mozhyeetyee** skah**zaht'** |
| Can you help me, please? | Пожалуйста помогите мне. | pah**zhah**loostah pahmah**ghee**tyee mnyeh |

Wanting

I'd like . . .	Я хотел бы . . .	yah khah**tyehl** bi
We'd like . . .	Мы хотели бы . . .	mi khah**tyehl**ee bi
Please give me . . .	Дайте мне, пожалуйста, . . .	**digh**tyee mnyeh pah**zhah**loostah
Give it to me, please.	Дайте мне это, пожалуйста.	**digh**tyee mnyeh **eh**tah pah**zhah**loostah
Please bring me . . .	Принесите мне, пожалуйста . . .	preenyee**see**tyee mnyeh pah**zhah**loostah
Bring it to me, please.	Принесите мне это, пожалуйста.	preenyee**see**tyee mnyeh **eh**tah pah**zhah**loostah
I'm hungry.	Я голодный.	yah gahlodni
I'm thirsty.	Мне хочется пить.	mnyeh khochyeetsah **peet'**
I'm tired.	Я устал.	yah oostahl
I'm lost.	Я заблудился.	yah zahbloodeelsah
It's important.	Это важно.	**eh**tah **vahzh**nah
It's urgent.	Это срочно.	**eh**tah **sroch**nah
Hurry up!	Скорее!	skah**ryeh**yee

It is/There is . . .

The words "it is/there is" are often dropped in Russian. For example, the word холодно (**kholahdnah**) alone conveys the idea "It is cold".

It is/It's . . .	Это . . .	**eh**tah
Is it . . . ?	Это . . . ?	**eh**tah
It isn't . . .	Это не . . .	**eh**tah nyeh
There is/There are . . .	Есть . . .	yehst'
Is there/Are there . . . ?	Есть-ли . . . ?	**yehst'** lee
There isn't/There aren't . . .	Нет ли . . .	nyeht lee
There isn't any/There aren't any.	Нет ли.	nyeht lee

A few common words

big/small	большой/ маленький	bahl**shoy**/**mah**lyeen'kee
quick/slow	быстро/медленно	**bi**strah/**myeh**dlyeenah
early/late	рано/поздно	**rah**nah/**poz**nah
cheap/expensive	дёшево/дорого	**dyo**shyeevah/**do**rahgah
near/far	близко/далеко	**blees**kah/dahlyee**eko**
hot/cold	горячо/холодно	gah**ryah**chyo/**kho**lahdnah
full/empty	полный/пустой	**pol**ni/poo**stoy**
easy/difficult	легко/трудно	lyee**khko**/**trood**nah
heavy/light	тяжёлый/легкий	tyee**zho**li/**lyokh**kee
open/shut	открыто/закрыто	ah**tkri**tah/zah**kri**tah
right/wrong	верно/неверно	**vyehr**nah/nyee**vyehr**nah
old/new	старый/новый	**stah**riy/**no**vi
old/young	старый/молодой	**stah**ri/mahlah**doy**
beautiful/ugly	красиво/уродливо	krah**see**vah/oo**rod**leevah
good/bad	хорошо/плохо	khahrah**sho**/**plo**khah
better/worse	лучше/хуже	**loo**chyee/**khoo**zhyee

Some prepositions and a few more useful words

at	в	v
on	на	nah
in	в	v
to	к	k
from	от	ot
inside	внутри	vnoo**tree**
outside	снаружи	snah**roo**zhee
up	вверх	v**vyehr**kh
down	вниз	v**nees**
before	до	do
after	после	**pos**lyee
with	с	s
without	без	byeh**ss**
through	через	**chyeh**ryeess
towards	к	k
until	до	do
during	во время	vah **vryeh**myee
and	и	ee
or	или	**ee**lee
not	не	nyeh
nothing	ничего	neechyee**vo**
none	ни один	nyeh ah**deen**

very	очень	**o**chyeen'
also	тоже	**to**zhyee
soon	скоро	**sko**rah
perhaps	может быть	**mo**zhyeet bit'
here	здесь	zdyehs'
there	там	tahm
now	теперь	tyee**pyehr**'
then	тогда	tahg**dah**

Arrival

Your passport, please.	Ваш паспорт, пожалуйста.	vahsh **pahs**pahrt pah**zhah**loostah
Here it is.	Пожалуйста.	pah**zhah**loostah
Have you anything to declare?	У Вас есть что-либо заявить для таможни?	oo vahs yehst' **shto**leebah zah**yah**veet' dlyah **tah**mahzhnyee
No, nothing at all.	Нет, ничего.	nyeht nyee**chee**voo
Porter!	Носильщик!	nah**seel**'shcheek
Can you help me with my luggage, please?	Пожалуйста возьмите мой багаж?	pah**zhah**loostah vah**zmee**tyeh moy bah**gahzh**
That's my suitcase.	Это мой чемодан.	**eh**tah moy cheemah**dahn**
Where's the tourist office?	Где бюро Интуриста?	gdyeh bjoo**ro** eentoo**ree**stah
This way, please.	Сюда, пожалуйста.	syoo**dah** pah**zhah**loostah

Changing money

| Can you change a traveller's cheque, please? | Можете ли Вы разменять аккредитив? | **mo**zhehtyeh lee vi rahz-myeh**nyaht**' ahkryeh-**dyee**tyeev |
| Where's the nearest bank, please? | Где ближайший банк? | gdyeh blee**zhigh**sheey bahnk |

Car rental

I'd like a car.	Мне нужна машина.	mnyeh noozh**nah** mah-**shee**nah
For how long?	На какое время?	nah kah**ko**yeh **vryeh**myah
A day/Four days/ A week/Two weeks.	На день/на четыре дня/на неделю/на две недели.	nah dyehn'/nah chyeh**tir**yeh dnyah/nah nyeh**dyeh**lyoo/nah dvyeh nyeh**dyeh**lee

RUSSIAN

Taxi

Where can I get a taxi?	Где я могу найти такси?	gdyeh yah mah**goo** night-**yee** tahk**see**
What's the fare to . . . ?	Сколько стоит доехать до . . . ?	**skol**'kah **sto**eet dah**yeh**-khaht' dah
Take me to this address, please.	Довезите меня по этому адресу, пожалуйста.	dahvee**zee**tyeh myeh**nyah** pah **eh**tahmoo **ah**dryehsoo pahzhah**loo**stah
I'm in a hurry.	Я спешу.	yah spee**shoo**
Could you drive more slowly, please?	Могли бы Вы ехать медленнее?	mah**glee** bi vi **yeh**khaht' **myehd**lyehnnyehyeh

Hotel and other accommodation

My name is . . .	Моя фамилия . . .	mah**yah** fah**mee**leeyah . . .
Have you a reservation?	Вы резервировали номер?	vi ryehzyehr**vee**rahvahlee **no**myehr
Yes, here's the confirmation.	Да, вот подтверждение.	dah vot pahdtvyehr**zhdyeh**nyeeyeh
We reserved a single room/ a double room.	Мы забронировали одинарный / двойной номер.	mi zahbran**yee**rahvahlee ahdee**nahr**niy/dvigh**noy no**myehr
a room with a bath/with a shower	номер с ванной/с душем	**no**myehr s **vahn**nigh/ s **doo**shahm
What's my room number, please?	Какой у меня номер комнаты?	kah**koy** oo myeh**nyah no**myehr **kom**nahti
Number 123.	Номер 123.	**no**myehr 123

Service, please

Who is it?	Кто там?	**kto** tahm
Just a minute, please.	Одну минуту, пожалуйста.	ahd**noo** mee**noo**too pahzhah**loo**stah
Come in! The door's open.	Войдите! Дверь открыта.	vigh**dyee**tyeh! dvyehr' aht**kri**tah
May we have breakfast in our room?	Можно получить завтрак в нашей комнате?	**mozh**nah pahloo**cheet' zah**vtrahk v **nah**shay **kom**nahtyeh

RUSSIAN

Breakfast

I'll have . . .	Я хотел бы . . .	yah khah**tyehl** bi
I'll have some fruit juice.	Я хотел бы фруктовый сок.	yah khah**tyehl** bi frook**to**viy sok
a boiled egg	варёное яйцо	vah**ry**onahyeh yight**so**
a fried egg	яичницу	yah**yeech**nyeetsoo
some bacon/some ham	бекон/ветчину	**byeh**kon/veechee**noo**
some toast	тост	tost
a pot of tea	чай в чайничке	chigh v **chigh**nyeechkyeh
a cup of tea	чашку чая	**chahsh**koo **chah**yah
some coffee	кофе	**ko**fyeh
some chocolate	шоколад	shah**kah**lahd
more butter	больше масла	**bol'**sheh **mahs**lah
some hot water	горячей воды	gah**ryah**chyay vah**di**

Difficulties

The central heating doesn't work.	Центральное отопление не работает.	tsehn**trahl'**nahyeh ah**tah**plyeh nyeeyeh nyeh rah**bo**tahyeht
the light/the socket	свет/штепсель	svyeht/**shtehp**sehl'
the tap/the toilet	кран/туалет	krahn/tooah**lyeht**
There's no hot water.	Нет горячей воды.	nyeht gah**ryah**chyay vah**di**
May I see the manager, please?	Можно поговорить с администратором?	**mozh**nah pahgahvah**reet'** s ahdmeenyee**strah**tahrom

Telephone—Mail

There's a call for you.	Вас к телефону.	vahs k tyeh**lyeh**fonoo
Hold the line, please.	Подождите у телефона.	pahdahzh**dyee**tyeh oo tyeh**lyeh**fonah
Operator, I've been cut off.	Девушка, нас прервали.	**dyeh**vooshkah nahs pryeh**rvah**lee
Did anyone telephone me?	Мне кто-нибудь звонил?	mnyeh **kto**nyeebood' zvah**nyeel**
Is there any mail for me?	Есть для меня почта?	yehst' dlyah myeh**nyah** **poch**tah
Are there any messages for me?	Мне никто не оставил записки?	mnyeh nyee**kto** nyeh ah**stah**veel zah**pees**kee

Checking out

May I have my bill, please?	Могу ли я получить счёт?	mah**goo** lee yah pahloo**cheet'** shchyot
We're in a great hurry.	Мы очень спешим.	mi **ochehn'** spee**shim**
It's been a very enjoyable stay.	Пребывание было очень приятным.	preebi**vah**nyeeyeh **bi**lah **ochehn'** preey**aht**nim

Eating out

Good evening, sir/ Good evening, madam.	Добрый вечер, господин/ Добрый вечер госпожа.	**do**briy **vyeh**chehr gahspah**dyeen**/**do**briy **vyeh**chehr gahspah**zhah**
Good evening, I'd like a table for two, please.	Добрый вечер. Я хотел бы столик на двоих.	**do**briy **vyeh**chehr. yah khah**tyehl** bi **sto**leek nah dvah**yeekh**
Do you have a fixed-price menu?	У Вас есть меню?	oo vahs yehst' meh**nyoo**
May I see the à la carte menu?	У Вас есть обеденное меню?	oo vahs yehst' ah**byeh**-dyehn**nah**yeh meh**nyoo**
May we have an ashtray, please?	Можно попросить пепельницу?	**mozh**nah pahprah**seet'** **pyeh**pyehl'nyee tsoo
some bread	хлеб	**khl**yehb
a fork	вилку	**veel**koo
a knife	нож	nozh
a spoon	ложку	**lozh**koo
a plate	тарелку	tah**ryehl**koo
a glass	стакан	stah**kahn**
a napkin	салфетку	sahl**fyeht**koo
another chair	другой стул	droo**goy** stool
Where's the gentlemen's toilet (men's room)?	Где мужской туалет?	gdyeh moozh**skoy** tooah**lyeht**
Where's the ladies' toilet (ladies' room)?	Где женский туалет?	gdyeh **zhehn**skeey tooah**lyeht**

Appetizers

I'd like some . . .	Я хотел бы . . .	yah khah**tyehl** bi
I'd like some assorted appetizers.	Я хотел бы ассорти.	yah khah**tyehl** bi ahsor-**tyee**

orange juice	апельсиновый сок	ahpyehl'**see**nahviy sok
ham	ветчину	veecheenoo
melon	дыню	dinyoo
pâté	паштет	pah**shtyeht**
smoked salmon	сёмгу	**syom**goo
shrimps (shrimp)	креветок	kryeh**vyeh**tahk

Soup

Have you any . . . ?	Есть у Вас . . . ?	yehst' oo vahs
Have you any chicken soup?	Есть у Вас суп с курицей?	yehst' oo vahs soop s **koo**reetsay
vegetable soup	овощной суп	ovahshch**noy** soop
onion soup	луковый суп	**loo**kahviy soop

Fish

I'd like some . . .	Я хотел бы . . .	yah khah**tyehl** bi
I'd like some fish.	Я хотел бы рыбу.	yah khah**tyehl** bi **ri**boo
sole	морской язык	mahr**skoy** yah**zik**
trout	форель	fah**rehl'**
lobster	омаров	o**mah**rahv
crayfish	лангуст	lahn**goost**
prawns	креветок	kryeh**vyeh**tahk
I'd like it . . .	Я бы хотел это . . .	yah bi khah**tyehl** **eh**tah
I'd like it steamed.	Я бы хотел это паровое.	yah bi khah**tyehl** **eh**tah pahrah**voy**eh
grilled	жареное на рашпере.	**zhah**ryehnahyeh nah rahsh**pyeh**ryeh
boiled	отварное	ahtvahr**noy**eh
baked	печёное	pyehch**yo**nahyeh
fried	жареное	**zhah**ryehnahyeh

Meat—Poultry—Game

I'd like some . . .	Я бы хотел . . .	yah bi khah**tyehl**
I'd like some beef.	Я бы хотел говядину.	yahbi khah**tyehl** gah**vyah**dyeenoo
a beef steak	бифштекс	beef**shtehks**
some roast beef	ростбиф	rost**beef**
a veal cutlet	телячью котлету	tyeh**lyah**chyoo kaht-**lyeh**too

mutton	баранину	bahrahnyeenoo
lamb	мясо барашка	myahsah bahrahshkah
a pork chop	свиную котлету	sveenooyoo kahtlyehtoo
roast pork	жареную свинину	zhahryehnooyoo sveenyeenoo
hare	зайца	zightsah
chicken	цыплёнка	tsiplyonkah
roast chicken	жареного цыплёнка	zhahryehnahvah tsiplyonkah
duck	утку	ootkoo

Vegetables

What vegetables have you got?	Какие овощи у Вас есть?	kahkeeyeh ovahshchee oo vahs yehst'
I'd like some . . .	Я бы хотел . . .	yah bi khahtyehl
I'd like some asparagus.	Я бы хотел спаржу.	yah bi khahtyehl spahrzhoo
green beans	бобы	bobi
mushrooms	грибы	greebi
carrots	морковь	mahrkov'
onions	лук	look
red cabbage	красную капусту	krahsnooyoo kahpoostoo
spinach	шпинат	shpeenaht
rice	рис	rees
peas	горох	gahrokh
tomatoes	помидоры	pahmeedori
green salad	зелёный салат	zyehlyoniy sahlaht
potatoes	картофель	kahrtofyehl'

RUSSIAN

Desserts

Nothing more, thanks.	Больше ничего, спасибо.	bol'sheh nyeechyehvo spahseebah
Just a small portion, please.	Маленькую порцию, пожалуйста.	mahlyehn'kooyoo portsiyoo pahzhahloostah
Have you any ice-cream?	У Вас есть мороженое?	oo vahs yehst' mahrozhehnahyeh
fruit salad	салат из фруктов	sahlaht eez frooktahv
fresh fruit	свежие фрукты	svyehzhiyeh frookti
cheese	сыр	sir

Drink

What would you like to drink?	Что бы вы хотели выпить?	shto bi vi khah**tyeh**lee **vi**peet'
I'll have a beer, please.	Пиво, пожалуйста.	**pee**vah pah**zhah**loostah
I'll have a whisky, please.	Виски, пожалуйста.	**vee**skee pah**zhah**loostah

Wine

I'd like a bottle of wine.	Я бы хотел бутылку вина.	yah bi khah**tyehl** bootil-koo **vee**nah
red wine	красного вина	**krahs**nahvah **vee**nah
rosé wine	розового вина	**ro**zahvahvah **vee**nah
white wine	белого вина	**byeh**lahvah **vee**nah
Cheers!	На здоровье!	nah zdah**rov**yeh

The bill (check)

May I have the bill (check) please?	Пожалуйста счёт!	pah**zhah**loostahs-chyot
Is service included?	Обслуживание включено?	ahb**sloo**zhivahnyeeyeh vklyoochehno
Everything's included.	Всё включено.	vsyo vklyoochehno
Thank you, that was a very good meal.	Спасибо, всё было очень вкусно.	spah**see**bah, vsyo **bi**lah **ochehn' vkoos**nah

Travelling

Where's the railway station, please?	Пожалуйста, где вокзал?	pah**zhah**loostah gdyeh vahk**zahl**
Where's the ticket office, please?	Пожалуйста, где касса?	pah**zhah**loostah gdyeh **kah**sah
I'd like a ticket to ...	Мне нужен билет до ...	mnyeh **noo**zhehn bee**lyeht** dah
First or second class?	Первый или второй класс?	**pyehr**viy **ee**lee vtah**roy** klahss
First class, please.	Первый класс, пожалуйста.	**pyehr**viy klahss pah**zhah**loostah
Single or return (one way or round-trip)?	В один или оба конца?	v ah**dyeen ee**lee **o**bah kahn**tsah**

Do I have to change trains?	Мне надо будет делать пересадку.	mnyeh **nah**dah **boo**dyeht **dyeh**laht' peereesahdkoo
What platform does the train leave from?	С какой платформы отправляется поезд?	s kah**koy** plahtformi ahtprahvlyahyehtsah poyehzd
Where's the nearest underground station?	Где ближайшая станция метро?	gdyeh bleezhighshahyah **stahn**tsiyah myeh**tro**
Where's the bus station, please?	Где автобусная остановка?	gdyeh ahv**to**boosnahyah ahstahnovkah
When's the first bus to . . . ?	Когда идёт первый автобус в . . . ?	kahg**dah** eed**yot** pyeh**r**viy ahv**to**boos v
the last bus	последний автобус	pah**slyehd**nyeey ahv**to**boos
the next bus	следующий автобус	**slyeh**doosshcheey ahv**to**boos
Please let me off at the next stop.	Дайте мне выйти на следующей остановке, пожалуйста.	**digh**tyeh mnyeh **viy**tee nah **slyeh**dooshchay ahstahnovkee pah**zhah**loostah

Relaxing

What's on at the cinema (movies)?	Что идёт в кино?	shto eed**yot** v kee**no**
What's on at the theatre?	Что идёт в театре?	shto eed**yot** v tyeh**ah**tryeh
What time does the film begin?	Когда начинается фильм?	kahg**dah** nahchee**nah**yehtsah feel'm
And the play?	А пьеса?	ah **pyeh**sah
Are there any tickets for tonight?	Есть билеты на вечер?	yehst' beel**yeh**ti nah **vyeh**chehr
Where can we go dancing?	Куда можно пойти танцевать?	koo**dah mozh**nah pight**yee** tahntsi**vaht'**
Would you like to dance?	Хотите ли вы потанцевать?	khat**yee**tyeh lee vi pahtahntsi**vaht'**

Introductions

How do you do?	Добрый день?	**dob**riy dyehn'
How are you?	Как поживаете?	kahk pahzhi**vah**yehtyeh
Very well, thank you. And you?	Спасибо, очень хорошо. А Вы?	spah**see**bah **o**chehn' khahrah**sho**. ah vi
May I introduce Miss Philips?	Разрешите представить мисс филипс?	rahzree**shi**tyeh pryehd**stah**veet' Miss Philips
My name is . . .	Меня зовут . . .	myeh**nyah** zah**voot**
I'm very pleased to meet you.	Очень приятно.	**o**chehn' preey**aht**nah
How long have you been here?	Вы давно уже здесь?	vi dah**vno** oo**zheh** zdyehs'
It was nice meeting you.	Было очень приятно с Вами встретиться.	**bi**lah **o**chehn' preey**aht**nah s **vah**mee **vstryeh**teetsah

RUSSIAN

Dating

Would you like a cigarette?	Хотите сигарету?	khah**tyee**tyeh seegah**ryeh**too
May I get you a drink?	Хотите что-нибудь выпить?	khah**tyee**tyeh **shto**nyeebood' **vi**peet'
Do you have a light, please?	У Вас есть спички?	vahs yehst' **speech**kee
Are you free this evening?	Вы свободны сегодня вечером?	vi svah**bo**dni seevo**dn**yah **vyeh**chehrahm
Where shall we meet?	Где мы встретимся?	gdyeh mi **vstryeh**tyeem**syah**
What time shall I meet you?	Когда я Вас встречу?	kahg**dah** yah vahs **vstryeh**choo
Thank you, it's been a wonderful evening.	Спасибо, это был чудесный вечер.	spah**see**bah, **eh**tah bil choo**dyehs**niy **vyeh**chehr
What time is your last train?	Когда уходит Ваш последний поезд?	kahg**dah** oo**kho**dyeet vahsh pah**slyehd**nyeey **poy**ehzd
Good-night . . .	Доброй ночи . . .	**dob**righ **no**chee

Banks

Where's the nearest bank, please?	Где ближайший банк?	gdyeh blee**zhigh**shiy bahnk
Where can I cash some traveller's cheques?	Где я могу обменять аккредитивы?	gdyeh yah mah**goo** ahb-myeh**nyaht'** ahkryeh-dee**tyee**vi
What time does the bank open/What time does it close?	Когда открывается банк/когда он закрывается?	kahg**dah** ahtkrivah**yehtsah** bahnk/kahg**dah** on zah-krivah**yehtsah**
I'm expecting some money from home. Has it arrived?	Я жду деньги из дому. Они прибыли?	yah zhdoo **dyehn**'ghee **eez**dahmoo. ah**nyee** **pree**bilee
Can you give me some small change, please?	Дайте мне, пожалуйста, мелочью?	**dight**yeh mnyeh pah-**zhah**loostah **myeh**lahchyo

Shops, stores and services

Where is the nearest chemist (pharmacy)?	Где ближайшая аптека?	gdyeh blee**zhigh**shahyah ahp**tyeh**kah
the nearest hair-dresser's	ближайшая парикмахерская	blee**zhigh**shahyah pah-reek**mahk**hehrskahyah
the photo shop	фотомагазин	fotomahgah**zeen**
the jeweller's	ювелирный магазин	yooveel**eer**niy mahgah**zeen**
the department store	универмаг	oonyeevyehr**mahg**
the police station	отделение милиции	ahtdyeh**lyeh**nyeeyeh mee**lee**tsiee
the garage	гараж	gah**rahzh**
How do I get there?	Как мне туда проехать?	kahk mnyeh too**dah** prah**yehk**haht'
Is it within walking distance?	Можно дойти пешком?	**mozh**nah dight**yee** peesh**kom**

Service

Can you help me, please?	Помогите мне, пожалуйста?	pahmah**ghee**tyeh mnyeh pah**zhah**loostah
Can you show me this? And that, too.	Покажите мне, пожалуйста, это. И то тоже.	pahkah**zhi**tyeh mnyeh pah**zhah**loostah ehtah. ee to to**zheh**
It's too expensive/too big/too small.	Это слишком дорого/слишком велико/слишком мало.	ehtah sleesh**kahm** dorah-gah/**sleesh**kahm vyehlee-ko/sleesn̦kahm mahlo.

Can you show me some more?	Вы мне можете показать еще?	vi mnyeh **mo**zhehtyeh pahkah**zaht'** yehsh**shchyo**
something better	Что-нибудь получше	**shto**nyeebood' pah**looch**sheh
something cheaper	Что-нибудь подешевле	**shto**nyeebood' pahdyee**shehv**lee
How much is this? And that?	Сколько стоит это? И то?	**skol**'kah **sto**eet **eh**tah? ee to?
It's not quite what I want.	Это не совсем то, что я хочу.	**eh**tah nyeh sahv**syehm** to shto yah khah**choo**
I like it.	Это мне нравится.	**eh**tah mnyeh **nrah**veetsah.

Chemist's (Pharmacy)

| I'd like something for a cold/for a cough/for travel sickness. | Я хотел бы что-нибудь от простуды/от кашля/от морской болезни. | yah khah**tyehl** bi **shto**nyeebood' aht prah**stoo**di/aht **kahsh**lyah/ aht mar**skoy** bal'**yehz**ni |
| Can you recommend something for hay-fever/for sunburn? | Что Вы мне можете рекомендовать от сенной лихорадки/ от ожогов? | shto vi mnyeh **mo**zhehtyeh ryehkah-myehndah**vaht'** aht **syehn**nigh leekhah**rahd**kee/ aht a**zho**gav |

Toiletry

May I have some razor blades?	У Вас есть лезвия для бритья?	oo vahs yehst' **lyehz**-veeyah dlyah bree**tyah**
some shaving cream	крем для бритья	kryehm dlyah bree**tyah**
some toothpaste	зубная паста	zoob**nah**yah **pah**stah
I'd like some soap.	Мне нужно мыло.	mnyeh **nooz**hnah **mi**lah
some suntan oil	крем для загара	kryehm dlyah zah**gah**rah

At the barber's

I'd like a haircut, please.	Я хотел бы постричься.	yah khah**tyehl** bi pah**streech**syah
Short/Leave it long.	Коротко/оставьте длинные.	**ko**rahtkah/ah**stahv**'tyeh **dleen**niyeh
A razor cut, please.	Бритвой, пожалуйста.	**breet**vigh pah**zhah**loostah

At the hairdresser's

I'd like a shampoo and set, please.	Помойте голову и сделайте укладку, пожалуйста.	pah**moy**tyeh **go**lahvoo ee **sdyeh**lightyeh oo**klahd**koo pah**zhah**loostah
I'd like a bleach.	Мне нужно обесцвечивание.	mnyeh **noozh**nah ahbyeh-**stsvyeh**cheevahnyeeyeh.
a permanent	перманент	pyehrmah**nyehnt**
a colour rinse	оттеночное полоскание	aht**tyeh**nahchnahyeh **pah**lahs**kah**nyeeyeh
a manicure	маникюр	mahnyee**kyoor**

Photography

I'd like a film for this camera.	Мне нужна плёнка для зтого аппарата.	mnyeh noozh**nah plyon**kah dlyah **eh**tahvah ahpah**rah**tah.
This camera doesn't work.	Этот аппарат не работает.	**eh**taht ahpah**raht** nyeh rah**bo**tahyeht.

At the post office

Where's the nearest post office, please?	Где ближайшая почта?	gdyeh blee**zhigh**shahyah **poch**tah
I'd like to send this by express (special delivery)/by air mail.	Я хотел бы послать зто срочно/авиапочтой.	yah khah**tyehl** bi pahs**laht'** ehtah **sroch**nah/ahveeah**poch**tigh

Service stations

Where is the nearest service station, please?	Где ближайшая станция обслуживания?	gdyeh blee**zhigh**shahyah **stahn**tsiyah ahbs**loozh**i-vahnyeeyah
Fill her up, please.	Полный, пожалуйста.	**pol**niy pah**zhah**loostah
Check the oil, please.	Проверьте масло, пожалуйста.	prah**vyehr**'tyeh **mahs**lah pah**zhah**loostah
Would you check the tyres?	Проверьте шины, пожалуйста?	prah**vyehr**'tyeh **shi**ni pah**zhah**loostah

RUSSIAN

Street directions

Can you show me on the map where I am?	Вы мне можете показать на карте, где я?	vi mnyeh **mo**zhehtyeh pahkah**zaht**' nah **kahr**tyeh gdyeh yah
You're on the wrong road.	Вы едете неверно.	vi **yeh**dyehtyeh nyeh**vyehr**nah
Go back to . . .	Вернитесь назад к . . .	vyehr**nyee**tyehs' nah**zahd** k
Go straight ahead.	Вам надо прямо.	vahm **nah**dah **pryah**mah
It's on the left/on the right.	Это слева/справа.	**eh**tah **slyeh**vah/**sprah**vah

Accidents

May I use your telephone?	Можно позвонить по Вашему телефону?	**mozh**nah pahz**vahn**yeet' pah **vahs**hehmoo tyehlyeh**fo**noo
Call a doctor quickly.	Быстро вызовите доктора.	**bist**rah **vi**zahveetyeh **dok**tahrah
Call an ambulance.	Вызовите санитарную машину.	**vi**zahveetyeh sahnyee-**tahr**nooyoo mah**shi**noo
Please call the police.	Вызовите милицию.	**vi**zhaveetyeh meelee**ets**iyoo

Numbers

one	один	ah**dyeen**
two	два	dvah
three	три	tree
four	четыре	chee**tir**yeh
five	пять	pyaht'
six	шесть	shehst'
seven	семь	syehm'
eight	восемь	**vo**syehm'
nine	девять	**dyeh**vyaht'
ten	десять	**dyeh**syaht'
eleven	одиннадцать	ah**dyee**nahtsaht'
twelve	двенадцать	dvee**nah**tsaht'
thirteen	тринадцать	tree**nah**tsaht'
fourteen	четырнадцать	chyeh**tir**nahtsaht'
fifteen	пятнадцать	pyaht**nah**tsaht'
sixteen	шестнадцать	shehst'**nah**tsaht'
seventeen	семнадцать	syehm**nah**tsaht'
eighteen	восемнадцать	vahseem**nah**tsaht'

RUSSIAN

nineteen	девятнадцать	dyehvyaht**nah**tsaht'
twenty	двадцать	**dvah**tsaht'
twenty-one	двадцать один	**dvah**tsaht' ah**dyeen**
thirty	тридцать	**treet**saht'
forty	сорок	**so**rahk
fifty	пятьдесят	peedyee**syaht**
sixty	шестьдесят	shehs'dyeh**syaht**
seventy	семьдесят	**syehm'**dyehsyaht
eighty	восемьдесят	**vo**syehm'dyehsyaht
ninety	девяносто	dyehvyah**no**stah
one hundred	сто	sto
one thousand	тысяча	**ti**syahchah
ten thousand	десять тысяч	**dyeh**syaht' **ti**syahch

Days

It's Sunday.	Воскресенье	vahskryeh**syehn'**yeh
Monday	Понедельник	pahnyee**dyehl'**nyeek
Tuesday	Вторник	**vtor**nyeek
Wednesday	Среда	sryeh**dah**
Thursday	Четверг	chyeht**vyehrg**
Friday	Пятница	**pyaht**nyeetsah
Saturday	Суббота	soo**bo**tah
yesterday	вчера	vchyeh**rah**
today	сегодня	syeh**vod**nyah
tomorrow	завтра	**zahv**trah
morning/afternoon	утро/после обеда	**oo**trah/**pos**lyeh ah**byeh**dah
evening/night	вечер/ночь	**vyeh**chyehr/noch'

Months

January	январь	yahn**vahr'**
February	февраль	fyeh**vrahl'**
March	март	mahrt
April	апрель	ah**pryehl'**
May	май	migh
June	июнь	eey**oon'**
July	июль	eey**ool'**
August	август	**ahv**goost
September	сентябрь	syehn**tyahbr'**
October	октябрь	ahk**tyahbr'**
November	ноябрь	nah**yahbr'**
December	декабрь	dyeh**kahbr'**
Happy New Year!	Счастливого Нового Года!	schah**stlee**vahvah **no**vahvah **go**dah

RUSSIAN

SERBO-CROATIAN

Guide to Pronunciation

Note that Serbo-Croatian has some diacritical letters—with accent marks—which we do not know in English. On the other hand, **q, w, x** and **y** do not exist in Serbo-Croatian. A basic rule for handling Serbo-Croatian might be: pronounce it as it's written—every letter is pronounced, and its pronunciation is always the same, regardless of its position in a word.

Letter	Approximate pronunciation	Symbol	Example	
Consonants				
b	like **b** in **b**rother	b	**brat**	braht
c	like **ts** in **ts**e-**ts**e	ts	**cesta**	tsehsstah
č	like **ch** in **ch**urch	ch	**čuti**	chootee
ć	like **ch** in **ch**eap (a little further forward in the mouth than **č**; called a "soft" **č**)	ch	**ćerka**	chehrkah
d	like **d** in **d**own	d	**dole**	doleh

SERBO-CROATIAN

dž	like **j** in June	j	**džem**	jehm
dj	like **j** in jeep (a "soft" **dž**); also written **đ**	j	**djak**	jahk
f	like **f** in father	f	**figura**	feegoorah
g	like **g** in go	g	**gde**	gdeh
h	like **h** in house	h	**hleb**	hlehb
j	like **y** in yoke	y	**ja**	yah
k	like **k** in key	k	**kuća**	koochah
l	like **l** in lip	l	**lep**	lehp
lj	like **l** in failure	lʸ	**ljubav**	lʸoobahv
m	like **m** in mouth	m	**most**	most
n	like **n** in not	n	**ne**	neh
nj	like **ni** in onion	ñ	**njegov**	ñehgov
p	like **p** in put	p	**policija**	poleetseeyah
r	like **r** in rope	r	**reka**	rehkah
s	like **s** in sister	s/ss	**sestra**	sehsstrah
š	like **sh** in ship	sh	**šta**	shtah
t	like **t** in top	t	**tamo**	tahmo
v	like **v** in very	v	**vrlo**	verlo
z	like **z** in zip	z	**zvezda**	zvehzdah
ž	like **s** in pleasure	zh	**želim**	zhehleem

Note: The letter **r** can also act as a vowel, as for example, in the word **vrlo** or in the name of the island **Krk**; in this case, it should be pronounced rather like a Scottish **r**, e.g., **Krk** is pronounced kerk.

Vowels

a	like **a** in car	ah	**sat**	saht
e	like **e** in get	eh	**svet**	sveht
i	like **i** in it	ee	**iz**	eez
o	like **o** in hot	o	**ovde**	ovdeh
u	like **oo** in boom	oo	**put**	poot

The alphabet

Two different alphabets are used in Yugoslavia. Our Roman alphabet is in use in Slovenia and Croatia; elsewhere the Cyrillic alphabet (more or less like the Russian one) is dominant. Given below are the characters which the Cyrillic alphabet, as used in Yugoslavia, comprises. The column at left shows the printed capital and small letters while written letters are shown in the center column. At right the corresponding letters are shown in the Roman alphabet which we're using in this book.

Printed		Written		Roman
А	а	*A*	*a*	**a**
Б	б	*Б*	*б*	**b**
Ц	ц	*Ц*	*ц*	**c**
Ч	ч	*Ч*	*ч*	**č**
Ћ	ћ	*Ћ*	*ћ*	**ć**
Д	д	*Д*	*д*	**d**
Џ	џ	*Џ*	*џ*	**dž** (cap. **Dž**)
Ђ	ђ	*Ђ*	*ђ*	**dj** or **đ** (cap. **Dj** or **Đ**)
Е	е	*Е*	*е*	**e**
Ф	ф	*Ф*	*ф*	**f**
Г	г	*Г*	*г*	**g**
Х	х	*Х*	*х*	**h**
И	и	*И*	*и*	**i**
Ј	ј	*Ј*	*ј*	**j**
К	к	*К*	*к*	**k**
Л	л	*Л*	*л*	**l**
Љ	љ	*Љ*	*љ*	**lj** (cap. **Lj**)
М	м	*М*	*м*	**m**
Н	н	*Н*	*н*	**n**
Њ	њ	*Њ*	*њ*	**nj** (cap. **Nj**)
О	о	*О*	*о*	**o**
П	п	*П*	*п*	**p**
Р	р	*Р*	*р*	**r**
С	с	*С*	*с*	**s**
Ш	ш	*Ш*	*ш*	**š**
Т	т	*Т*	*т*	**t**
У	у	*У*	*у*	**u**
В	в	*В*	*в*	**v**
З	з	*З*	*з*	**z**
Ж	ж	*Ж*	*ж*	**ž**

SERBO-CROATIAN

Some basic expressions

Yes.	**Da.**	dah
No.	**Ne.**	neh
Please.	**Molim.**	moleem
Thank you.	**Hvala.**	hvahlah
Thank you very much.	**Hvala Vam mnogo.**	hvahlah vahm mnogo
That's all right.	**Molim.**	moleem

Greetings

Good morning.	**Dobro jutro.**	dobro yootro
Good afternoon.	**Dobar dan.**	dobahr dahn
Good evening.	**Dobro veče.**	dobro vehcheh
Good night.	**Laku noć.**	lahkoo noch
Good-bye.	**Zbogom.**	zbogom
See you later.	**Doviđenja.**	doveejehnyah
This is Mr....	**Ovo je Gospodin...**	ovo yeh gospodeen
This is Mrs....	**Ovo je Gospodja...**	ovo yeh gospojah
This is Miss...	**Ovo je Gospod-jica...**	ovo yeh gospojeetsa
I'm very pleased to meet you.	**Milo mi je da sam Vas upoznao.**	meelo mee yeh dah sahm vahss oopoznaho
How are you?	**Kako ste?**	kahko steh
Very well, thank you.	**Hvala, vrlo dobro.**	hvahlah verlo dobro
And you?	**A Vi?**	ah vee
Fine.	**Dobro.**	dobro
Excuse me.	**Izvinite.**	eezveehneehteh

Questions

Where?	**Gde?**	gdeh
Where is...?	**Gde je...?**	gdeh yeh
Where are...?	**Gde su...?**	gdeh soo
When?	**Kad?**	kahd
What?	**Šta?**	shtah

How?	**Kako?**	kahko
How much?	**Koliko?**	koleeko
How many?	**Koliko?**	koleeko
Who?	**Ko?..**	ko
Why?	**Zašto?**	zahshto
Which?	**Koji/Koja/Koje?**	koyee/koyah/koyeh
What do you call this?	**Kako se ovo zove?**	kahko seh ovo zoveh
What do you call that?	**Kako se zove ono?**	kahko seh zoveh ono
What does this mean?	**Šta ovo znači?**	shtah ovo znahchee
What does that mean?	**Šta ono znači?**	shtah ono znahchee

Do you speak . . . ?

Do you speak English?	**Govorite li engleski?**	govoreeteh lee ehnglehskee
Do you speak German?	**Govorite li nemački?**	govoreeteh lee nehmahchkee
Do you speak French?	**Govorite li francuski?**	govoreeteh lee frahntsooskee
Do you speak Spanish?	**Govorite li španski?**	govoreeteh lee shpahnskee
Do you speak Italian?	**Govorite li italijanski?**	govoreeteh lee eetahleeyahnskee
Could you speak more slowly, please?	**Možete li govoriti sporije molim Vas?**	mozhehteh lee govoreeteh sporeeyeh moleem vahss
Please point to the phrase in the book.	**Pokažite mi molim Vas tu frazu u knjizi.**	pokahzheeteh mee moleem vahss too frahzoo oo kñeezee
Just a minute. I'll see if I can find it in this book.	**Samo trenutak. Videću da li mogu da je nadjem u knjizi.**	sahmo trehnootahk. veedehchoo dah lee mogoo dah yeh nahjehm oo kñeezee
I understand.	**Razumem.**	rahzoomehm
I don't understand.	**Ne razumem.**	neh rahzoomehm

SERBO-CROATIAN

Can...?

Can I have...?	**Mogu li dobiti...?**	**mo**goo lee **do**beetee
Can we have...?	**Možemo li dobiti...?**	**mozheh**mo lee **do**beetee
Can you show me...?	**Možete li mi pokazati...?**	**mozheh**teh lee mee po**kah**zahtee
Can you tell me...?	**Možete li mi reći...?**	**mozheh**teh lee mee **reh**chee
Can you help me, please?	**Možete li mi pomoći molim Vas?**	**mozheh**teh lee mee po**mo**chee **mo**leem vahss

Wanting

I'd like...	**Želeo bih...**	**zheh**leho beeh
We'd like...	**Željeli bismo...**	**zheh**lehlee **beess**mo
Please give me...	**Molim Vas dajte mi...**	**mo**leem vahss **dah**yteh mee
Give it to me, please.	**Dajte mi to molim Vas.**	**dah**yteh mee to **mo**leem vahss
Please bring me...	**Molim Vas donesite mi...**	**mo**leem vahss do**neh**seeteh mee
Bring it to me, please.	**Donesite mi to molim Vas.**	do**neh**seeteh mee to **mo**leem vahss
I'm hungry.	**Gladan sam.**	**glah**dahn sahm
I'm thirsty.	**Žedan sam.**	**zheh**dahn sahm
I'm tired.	**Umoran sam.**	**oo**morahn sahm
I'm lost.	**Zalutao sam.**	zah**loo**taho sahm
It's important.	**Važno je.**	**vahzh**no yeh
It's urgent.	**Hitno je.**	**heet**no yeh
Hurry up!	**Požurite!**	po**zhoo**reeteh

It is/There is...

It is/It's...	**To je...**	to yeh
Is it...?	**Da li je to...?**	dah lee yeh to
It isn't...	**To nije...**	to **nee**yeh
There is/There are...	**Ima...**	**ee**mah
Is there/Are there...?	**Ima li...?**	**ee**mah lee

| There isn't/There aren't... | **Nema...** | **neh**mah |
| There isn't any/ There aren't any. | **Nema.** | **neh**mah |

A few common words

big/small	**veliko/malo**	**veh**leeko/**mah**lo
quick/slow	**brzo/sporo**	**berzo/sporo**
early/late	**rano/kasno**	**rah**no/**kahs**no
cheap/expensive	**jeftino/skupo**	**yehf**teeno/**skoo**po
near/far	**blizu/daleko**	**blee**zoo/**dah**lehko
hot/cold	**vruće/hladno**	**vroo**cheh/**hlahd**no
full/empty	**puno/prazno**	**poo**no/**prahz**noh
easy/difficult	**lako/teško**	**lahko/tehshko**
heavy/light	**teško/lako**	**tehshko/lahko**
open/shut	**otvoreno/zatvoreno**	**ot**vorehno/**zaht**vorehno
right/wrong	**tačno/pogrešno**	**tahch**no/**pogresh**no
old/new	**staro/novo**	**stah**ro/**novo**
old/young	**star/mlad**	**stahr/mlahd**
beautiful/ugly	**lepo/ružno**	**lehpo/roozhno**
good/bad	**dobro/loše**	**dobro/losheh**
better/worse	**bolje/lošije**	**bol**^yeh/**losheeyeh**

Some prepositions and a few more useful words

at	**kod**	kod
on	**na**	nah
in	**u**	oo
to	**ka**	kah
from	**od**	od
inside	**unutra**	oo**noo**trah
outside	**napolju**	nah**pol**^yoo
up	**gore**	**goreh**
down	**dole**	**doleh**
before	**pre**	preh
after	**posle**	**posleh**
with	**sa**	sah
without	**bez**	behz
through	**kroz**	kroz
towards	**prema**	**preh**mah
until	**do**	do
during	**za vreme**	zah **vreh**meh
and	**i**	ee
or	**ili**	**ee**lee
not	**ne**	neh
nothing	**ništa**	**neesh**tah

SERBO-CROATIAN

none	**ni jedan**	nee **yeh**dahn
very	**vrlo**	verlo
also	**takodje**	tahkojeh
soon	**uskoro**	oosskoro
perhaps	**možda**	mozhdah
here	**ovde**	ovdeh
there	**tamo**	tahmo
now	**sada**	sahdah
then	**tada**	tahdah

SERBO-CROATIAN

Arrival

Your passport, please.	**Vaš pasoš, molim Vas.**	vahsh **pah**sosh **mo**leem vahss
Here it is.	**Izvolite.**	eez**vo**leeteh
Have you anything to declare?	**Imate li nešto za carinu?**	ee**mah**teh lee **neh**shto zah **tsah**reenoo
No, nothing at all.	**Ne, nemam ništa.**	neh **neh**mahm **nee**shtah
Porter!	**Nosač!**	**no**sahch
Can you help me with my luggage, please?	**Možete li mi poneti prtljag, molim Vas?**	**mo**zhehteh lee mee po**neh**tee pert**l**^yahg **mo**leem vahss
That's my suitcase.	**To je moj kofer.**	to yeh moy **ko**fehr
Where's the bus to the centre of town, please?	**Gde je autobus za centar grada, molim Vas?**	gdeh yeh ahoo**to**booss zah **tsehn**tar **grah**dah **mo**leem vahss
This way, please.	**Ovuda, izvolite.**	**o**voodah eez**vo**leeteh

Changing money

| Can you change a traveller's cheque, please? | **Možete li promeniti putni ček, molim Vas?** | **mo**zhehteh lee pro**meh**neetee **poot**nee chehk **mo**leem vahss |
| Where's the nearest bank, please? | **Gde je najbliža banka, molim Vas?** | gdeh yeh **nahy**bleezhah **bahn**kah **mo**leem vahss |

Car rental

I'd like a car.	**Želeo bih kola.**	**zheh**leho beeh **ko**lah
For how long?	**Za koliko dugo?**	zah ko**lee**ko **doo**go
A day/Four days/ A week/Two weeks.	**Jedan dan/Četiri dana/Nedelju dana/Dve nedelje.**	**yeh**dahn dahn/**cheh**teeree **dah**nah/**neh**dehl^yoo **dah**nah/dveh **neh**dehl^yeh

Taxi

Where can I get a taxi?	**Gde mogu da dobijem taksi?**	gdeh **mo**goo dah **do**beeyehm **tah**ksee
What's the fare to ... ?	**Koliko staje do ... ?**	ko**lee**ko **sta**hyeh do
Take me to this address, please.	**Odvezite me na ovu adresu, molim Vas.**	od**veh**zeeteh meh nah **o**voo ah**dreh**ssoo **mo**leem vahss
I'm in a hurry.	**Žurim se.**	**zhoo**reem seh
Could you drive more slowly, please?	**Da li biste mogli da vozite malo sporije, molim Vas?**	dah lee **bee**steh **mo**glee dah **vo**zeeteh **mah**lo **spo**reeyeh **mo**leem vahss

Hotel and other accommodation

My name is ...	**Ja se zovem ...**	yah seh **zo**vehm
Have you a reservation?	**Imate li rezervaciju?**	**ee**mahteh lee reh-zehr**vah**tseeyoo
Yes, here's the confirmation.	**Da, izvolite potvrdu.**	dah **eez**voleeteh pot**ver**doo
I'd like ...	**Želeo bih ...**	**zheh**leho beeh
I'd like a single room/a double room.	**Želeo bih sobu sa jednim krevetom/sa dva kreveta.**	**zheh**leho beeh **so**boo sah **yehd**neem **kreh**vehtom/sah dvah **kreh**vehtah
a room with a bath/ with a shower	**sobu sa kupatilom/ sa tušem**	**so**boo sah koo**pah**teelom/sah **too**shehm

How much?

What's the price per night/per week/per month?	**Koliko staje za jednu noć/jednu nedelju/mesec?**	ko**lee**ko **sta**hyeh zah **yehd**noo noch/**yehd**noo **neh**dehl^yoo/**meh**ssehts
May I see the room?	**Mogu li da vidim sobu?**	**mo**goo lee dah **vee**deem **so**boo
I'm sorry, I don't like it.	**Nažalost ne dopada mi se.**	**nah**zhahlost neh **do**pahdah mee seh
Yes, that's fine. I'll take it.	**Da, dobra je, uzeću je.**	dah **do**brah yeh **oo**zehchoo yeh
What's my room number, please?	**Koji je broj moje sobe?**	**ko**yee yeh broy **mo**yeh **so**beh
Number 123.	**Broj 123.**	broy 123

Service, please

Who is it?	**Ko je?**	ko yeh
Just a minute.	**Samo jedan trenutak.**	sahmo yehdahn trehnootahk
Come in! The door's open.	**Udjite! Vrata su otvorena.**	oojeeteh. **vrah**tah soo otvorehnah
May we have breakfast in our room?	**Možemo li dobiti doručak u sobi?**	mozhehmo lee dobeetee doroochahk oo sobee

Breakfast

I'll have . . .	**Želeo bih . . .**	zhehleho beeh
I'll have some fruit juice.	**Želeo bih voćni sok.**	zhehleho beeh vochnee sok
a boiled egg	**jedno kuvano jaje**	yehdno koovahno yahyeh
a fried egg	**jedno prženo jaje**	yehdno perzhehno yahyeh
some bacon/some ham	**slaninu/šunku**	slahneenoo/shoonkoo
some toast	**tost**	tost
a pot of tea	**lonče čaja**	loncheh chahyah
a cup of tea	**šoljicu čaja**	shol'eetsoo chahyah
some coffee	**hafu**	kahfoo
some chocolate	**čokoladu**	chokolahdoo
more butter	**još malo putera**	yosh mahlo pootehrah
some hot water	**vruće vode**	vroocheh vodeh

Difficulties

The central heating doesn't work.	**Centralno grejanje ne radi.**	tsentrahlno grehyahñeh neh rahdee
the light/the socket the tap/the toilet	**svetlo/utikač slavina (pipa)/toalet**	svehtlo/ooteekahch slahveenah (peepah)/ toahleht
There's no hot water.	**Nema tople vode.**	nehmah topleh vodeh
May I see the manager, please?	**Želeo bih da govorim sa šefom, molim Vas.**	zhehleho beeh dah govoreem sah shehfom moleem vahss

Telephone—Mail

There's a call for you.	**Imate telefonski poziv.**	eemahteh tehlehfonskee pozeev
Hold the line, please.	**Ostanite na telefonu, molim Vas.**	ostahneeteh nah tehlehfonoo moleem vahss

Operator, I've been cut off.	Gospodjice, veza se prekinula.	gosspojeetseh vehzah seh prehkeenoolah
Did anyone telephone me?	Da li me neko tražio telefonom?	dah lee meh nehko trahzheeo tehlehfonom
Is there any mail for me?	Ima li pošte za mene?	eemah lee poshteh zah mehneh
Are there any messages for me?	Ima li neka poruka za mene?	eemah lee nehkah porookah zah mehneh

Checking out

May I have my bill, please?	Molim Vas račun.	moleem vahss rahchoon
We're in a great hurry.	Jako se žurimo.	yahko seh zhooreemo
It's been a very enjoyable stay.	Boravak je bio vrlo prijatan.	borahvahk yeh beeo verlo preeyahtahn

Eating out

Good evening, sir/ Good evening, madam.	Dobro veče Gospodine/Dobro veče Gospodjo.	dobro vehcheh gospodeeneh/dobro vehcheh gospojo
Good evening. I'd like a table for two, please.	Dobro veče. Hteo bih sto za dvoje molim Vas.	dobro vehcheh. hteho beeh sto zah dvoyeh moleem vahss
Do you have a fixed-price menu?	Imate li meni?	eemahteh lee mehnee
May I see the à la carte menu?	Mogu li da dobijem jelovnik?	mogoo lee dah dobeeyehm yehlovneek
May we have an ashtray, please?	Molim Vas pepeljaru.	moleem vahss pehpehlʲahroo
some bread	hleb	hlehb
a fork	viljušku	veelʲooshkoo
a knife	nož	nozh
a spoon	kašiku	kahsheekoo
a plate	tanjir	tahñeer
a glass	čašu	chahshoo
a napkin	salvetu	sahlvehtoo
another chair	još jednu stolicu	yosh yehdnoo stoleetsoo
Where's the gentlemen's toilet (men's room)?	Gde je toalet za muškarce?	gdeh yeh toahleht zah mooshkahrtseh
Where's the ladies' toilet (ladies' room)?	Gde je toalet za žene?	gdeh yeh toahleht zah zhehneh

Appetizers

I'd like some...	**Hteo bih...**	hteho beeh
I'd like some assorted appetizers.	**Hteo bih mešano predjelo.**	hteho beeh mehshahno prehdyehlo
orange juice	**sok od pomorandže**	sok od pomorahnjeh
ham	**šunku**	shoonkoo
melon	**dinju**	deeñoo
pâté	**paštetu**	pahshtehtoo
smoked salmon	**dimljenog lososa**	deeml'ehnog lossossah
shrimps (shrimp)	**račiće**	rahcheecheh

Soup

Have you any...?	**Imate li...?**	eemahteh lee
Have you any chicken soup?	**Imate li pileću čorbu?**	eemahteh lee peelehchoo chorboo
vegetable soup	**čorbu od povrća**	chorboo od poverchah
onion soup	**čorbu od luka**	chorboo od lookah

Fish

I'd like some...	**Hteo bih...**	hteho beeh
I'd like some fish.	**Hteo bih ribu.**	hteho beeh reeboo
sole	**tabinju**	tahbeeñoo
trout	**pastrmku**	pahstermkoo
lobster	**jastoga**	yahstogah
crayfish	**rak**	rahk
prawns	**kozice**	kozeetseh
I'd like it...	**Želeo bih...**	zhehleho beeh
I'd like it steamed.	**Spremljenu na pari.**	sprehml'ehnoo nah pahree
grilled	**na roštilju**	nah roshteel'oo
boiled	**kuvanu**	koovahnoo
baked	**pečenu**	pehchehnoo
fried	**prženu**	perzhehnoo

Meat—Poultry—Game

I'd like some...	**Želeo bih...**	zhehleho beeh
I'd like some beef.	**Želeo bih govedinu.**	zhehleho beeh govehdeenoo
a beef steak	**govedju šniclu**	govehjoo shneetsloo
some roast beef	**govedje pečenje**	govehjeh pehchehñeh

a veal cutlet	teleći kotlet	tehlehchee kotleht
mutton	ovčetinu	ovchehteenoo
lamb	jagnjetinu	yahgñehteenoo
a pork chop	svinjski kotlet	sveeñskee kotleht
roast pork	svinjsko pečenje	sveeñsko pehchehñeh
hare	zečetinu	zehchehteenoo
chicken	piletinu	peelehteenoo
roast chicken	pečenu piletinu	pehchehnoo peelehteenoo
duck	patku	pahtkoo
How do you like your meat?	Kako pečeno želite meso?	kahko pehchehno zhehleeteh mehsso
rare	polu-pečeno	poloo pehchehno
medium	srednje pečeno	srehdñeh pehchehno
well done	dobro pečeno	dobro pehchehno

Vegetables

What vegetables have you got?	Kakvo povrće imate?	kahkvo povercheh eemahteh
I'd like some...	Želeo bih...	zhehleho beeh
I'd like some asparagus.	Želeo bih špargle.	zhehleho beeh shpahrgleh
green beans	boraniju (mahune)	borahneeyoo (mahhooneh)
mushrooms	pečurke	pehchoorkeh
carrots	šargarepu	shahrgahrehpoo
onions	luk	look
red cabbage	crveni kupus	tservehnee koopooss
spinach	spanać (špinat)	spahnahch (shpeenaht)
rice	pirinač (rižu)	peereenahch (reezhoo)
peas	grašak	grahshahk
tomatoes	paradajz	pahrahdahyz
green salad	zelenu salatu	zehlehnoo sahlahtoo
potatoes	krompir	krompeer

Desserts

Nothing more, thanks.	Ništa više, hvala lepo.	neeshtah veesheh hvahlah lehpo
Just a small portion, please.	Jednu malu porciju, molim.	vehdnoo mahloo portseeyoo moleem
Have you any ice-cream?	Imate li sladoleda?	eemahteh lee slahdolehdah
fruit salad	voćnu salatu	vochnoo sahlahtoo
fresh fruit	sveže voće	svehzheh vocheh
cheese	sir	seer

Drink

What would you like to drink?	**Šta biste željeli da pijete?**	shtah **bee**steh **zheh**lehlee dah **pee**yehteh
I'll have a beer, please.	**Ja bih pivo, molim.**	yah beeh **pee**vo **mo**leem
I'll have a whisky, please.	**Ja bih viski, molim.**	yah beeh **vee**skee **mo**leem

Wine

I'd like a bottle of wine.	**Hteo bih jednu flašu vina.**	hteho beeh **yeh**dnoo **flah**shoo **vee**nah
red wine	**crvenog vina**	**tser**vehnog **vee**nah
rosé wine	**ružice**	**roo**zheetseh
white wine	**belog vina**	**beh**log **vee**nah
Cheers!	**Živeli.**	**zhee**vehlee

The bill (check)

May I have the bill (check) please?	**Molim Vas račun.**	**mo**leem vahss **rah**choon
Is service included?	**Da li je servis uračunat?**	dah lee yeh **sehr**veess **oo**rahchoonaht
Everything's included.	**Sve je uračunato.**	sveh yeh **oo**rahchoonahto
Thank you, that was a very good meal.	**Hvala lepo, jelo je bilo vrlo dobro.**	**hvah**lah **leh**po **yeh**lo yeh **bee**lo **ver**lo **do**bro

Travelling

Where's the railway station, please?	**Gde je železnička stanica (kolodvor), molim Vas?**	gdeh yeh **zheh**lehzneech-kah **stah**neetsah (kolod-vor) **mo**leem vahss
Where's the ticket office, please?	**Gde je šalter za karte, molim Vas?**	gdeh yeh **shahl**tehr zah **kahr**teh **mo**leem vahss
I'd like a ticket to . . .	**Želeo bih kartu do . . .**	**zheh**leho beeh **kahr**too do
First or second class?	**Prvu ili drugu klasu?**	**per**voo **ee**lee **droo**goo **klah**ssoo
First class, please.	**Prvu klasu molim.**	**per**voo **klah**ssoo **mo**leem
Single or return (one way or round-trip)?	**U jednom pravcu ili povratnu?**	oo **yeh**dnom **prah**vtsoo **ee**lee **po**vrahtnoo

Do I have to change trains?	**Moram li presedati?**	morahm lee prehsehdahtee
What platform does the train leave from?	**Sa koga perona polazi voz (vlak)?**	sah kogah pehronah polahzee voz (vlahk)
Where's the nearest underground (subway) station?	**Gde je najbliža stanica podzemne železnice?**	gdeh yeh nahybleezhah stahneetsah podzehmneh zhehlehzneetseh
Where's the bus station, please?	**Gde je autobuska stanica, molim Vas?**	gdeh yeh ahootobooskah stahneetsah moleem vahss
When's the first bus to . . . ?	**Kad polazi prvi autobus za . . . ?**	kahd polahzee pervee ahootobooss zah
the last bus	**poslednji autobus**	poslehdňee ahootobooss
the next bus	**sledeći autobus**	slehdehchee ahootobooss
Please let me off at the next stop.	**Sišao bih na sledećoj stanici.**	seeshaho beeh nah slehdehchoy stahneetsee

Relaxing

What's on at the cinema (movies)?	**Šta se daje u bioskopu (kinu)?**	shtah seh dahyeh oo beeoskopoo (keenoo)
What's on at the theatre?	**Šta se daje u pozorištu (kazalištu)?**	shtah seh dahyeh oo pozoreeshtoo (kazahleeshtoo)
What time does the film begin?	**U koliko sati počinje film?**	oo koleeko sahtee pocheeňeh feelm
And the play?	**A komad?**	ah komahd
Are there any tickets for tonight?	**Ima li karata za večeras?**	eemah lee kahrahtah zah vehchehrahss
Where can we go dancing?	**Gde možemo da idemo na ples?**	gdeh mozhehmo dah eedehmo nah plehss
Would you like to dance?	**Želite li da igrate (plešete)?**	zhehleeteh lee dah eegrahteh (plehshehteh)

Introductions

How do you do?	**Dobar dan.**	dobahr dahn
How are you?	**Kako ste?**	kahko steh
Very well, thank you. And you?	**Hvala, vrlo dobro. A Vi?**	hvahlah verlo dobro. ah vee
May I introduce Miss Philips?	**Mogu li da Vam predstavim Gospodjicu Filips.**	mogoo lee dah vahm prehdstahveem gospojeetsoo Philips

My name is . . .	Ja se zovem . . .	yah seh zovehm
I'm very pleased to meet you.	Drago mi je da sam Vas upoznao.	drahgo mee yeh dah sahm vahss **oo**poznaho
How long have you been here?	Od kad ste ovde?	od **kah**dah steh **ov**deh
It was nice meeting you.	Bilo mi je zadovoljstvo.	**bee**lo mee yeh zahdovol'stvo

Dating

Would you like a cigarette?	Želite li cigaretu?	**zheh**leeteh lee tseegah**reh**too
May I get you a drink?	Da li Vam mogu doneti jedno piće?	dah lee vahm **mo**goo do**neh**tee **yehd**no **pee**cheh
Do you have a light, please?	Imate li šibicu, molim Vas?	ee**mah**teh lee shee**beet**soo **mo**leem vahss
Are you waiting for someone?	Da li čekate nekoga?	dah lee **cheh**kahteh **neh**kogah
Are you free this evening?	Da li ste slobodni večeras?	dah lee steh **slo**bodnee veh**cheh**rahss
Where shall we meet?	Gde ćemo se sastati?	gdeh **cheh**mo seh **sah**stahtee
What time shall I meet you?	Kad ćemo se videti?	kahd **cheh**mo seh **vee**dehtee
May I take you home?	Smem li Vas otpratiti kući?	smehm lee vahss ot**prah**teetee **koo**chee
Thank you, it's been a wonderful evening.	Hvala Vam, bilo je divno veče.	**hvah**lah vahm **bee**lo yeh **deev**no **veh**cheh
What's your telephone number?	Koji je broj Vašeg telefona?	**ko**yee yeh broy **vah**shehg tehleh**fo**nah
Do you live alone?	Da li živite sami?	dah lee **zhee**veeteh **sah**mee
What time is your last train?	Kad ide Vaš poslednji voz (vlak)?	kahd **ee**deh vahsh po**sleh**dnee voz (vlahk)
Good-night . . .	Laku noć . . .	**lah**koo noch

Banks

| Where's the nearest bank, please? | Gde je najbliža banka, molim Vas? | gdeh yeh **nahy**bleezhah **bah**nkah **mo**leem vahss |
| Where can I cash some traveller's cheques? | Gde mogu da unovčim putne čekove? | gdeh **mo**goo dah **oo**nov-cheem **poot**neh **cheh**koveh |

What time does the bank open/What time does it close?	Kad se banka otvara/Kad se zatvara?	kahd seh bahnkah otvahrah/kahd seh zahtvahrah
I'm expecting some money from home. Has it arrived?	Očekujem novac od kuće. Da li je stigao?	ochehkooyehm novahtss od koocheh. dah lee yeh steegaho
Can you give me some small change, please?	Možete li mi dati malo sitnine, molim Vas?	mozhehteh lee mee dahtee mahlo seetneeneh moleem vahss

Shops, stores and services

Where is the nearest chemist's (pharmacy)?	Gde je najbliža apoteka?	gdeh yeh nahybleezhah ahpotehkah
the nearest hairdresser's	najbliži frizer	nahybleezhee freezehr
the photo shop	radnja sa foto materijalom	rahdñah sah foto mahtehreeyahlom
the jeweller's	juvelir	yoovehleer
the department store	robna kuća	robnah koochah
the police station	policijska stanica	poleetseeyskah stahneetsah
the garage	garaža	gahrahzhah
How do I get there?	Kako mogu da dodjem do tamo?	kahko mogoo dah dojehm do tahmo
Is it within walking distance?	Da li se tamo može stići pešice?	dah lee seh tahmo mozheh steechee pehsheetseh

Service

Can you help me, please?	Možete li mi pomoći, molim Vas?	mozhehteh lee mee pomochee moleem vahss
Can you show me this? And that, too.	Možete li mi pokazati ovo? I ono takodje.	mozhehteh lee mee pokahzahtee ovo? ee ono tahkojeh
It's too expensive/too big/too small.	To je suviše skupo/suviše veliko/suviše malo.	to yeh sooveesheh skoopo/sooveesheh vehleeko/sooveesheh mahlo
Can you show me some more?	Možete li mi pokazati još nekoliko?	mozhehteh lee mee pokahzahtee yosh nehkoleeko
something better	nešto bolje	nehshto bol'eh
something cheaper	nešto jevtinije	nehshto yehvteeneeyeh

SERBO-CROATIAN

How much is this? And that?	**Koliko staje ovo? A ono?**	koleeko stahyeh ovo? ah ono
It's not quite what I want.	**To baš nije ono što ja želim.**	to bahsh neeyeh ono shto yah zhehleem
I like it.	**Dopada mi se.**	dopahdah mee seh

Chemist's (Pharmacy)

| I'd like something for a cold/for a cough/for travel sickness. | **Imate li nešto za nazeb/kašalj/putnu bolest?** | eemahteh lee nehshto zah nahzehb/kahshahl^y/pootnoo bolehst |
| Can you recommend something for hay-fever/for sunburn? | **Možete li pre-poručiti nešto za polensku groznicu/ za opekotine od sunca?** | mozhehteh lee prehporoocheetee nehshto zah polehnskoo grozneetsoo/ zah opehkoteeneh od soontsah |

Toiletry

May I have some razor blades?	**Molim Vas žilete.**	moleem vahss zheelehteh
some shaving cream	**pastu za brijanje**	pahstoo zah breeyahñeh
some toothpaste	**pastu za zube**	pahstoo zah zoobeh
I'd like some soap.	**Molim Vas sapun.**	moleem vahss sapoon
some suntan oil	**ulje za sunčanje**	ool^{y}eh zah soonchahñeh

At the barber's

I'd like a haircut, please.	**Šišanje, molim Vas.**	sheeshahñeh moleem vahss
Short/Leave it long.	**Kratko/Ostavite malo duže.**	krahtko/ostahveeteh mahlo doozheh
A razor cut, please.	**Šišanje, molim, brijačem.**	sheeshahñeh moleem breeyahchehm

At the hairdresser's

| I'd like a shampoo and set, please. | **Operite mi kosu i počešljajte me, molim Vas.** | opehreeteh mee kosoo ee pochehshl^{y}ahyteh meh moleem vahss |

I'd like a bleach.	Molim Vas blaj-hanje.	moleem vahss blahyhahñeh
a permanent	trajnu ondulaciju	trahynoo ondoolahtseeyoo
a colour rinse	preliv	prehleev
a manicure	manikir	mahneekeer

Photography

| I'd like a film for this camera. | Hteo bih film za ovaj aparat. | hteho beeh feelm zah ovahy ahpahraht |
| This camera doesn't work. | Ovaj aparat je pokvaren. | ovahy ahpahraht yeh pokvahrehn |

At the post office

| Where's the nearest post office, please? | Gde je najbliža pošta, molim Vas? | gdeh yeh nahybleezhah poshtah moleem vahss |
| I'd like to send this by express (special delivery)/by air mail. | Želeo bih da pošaljem ovo ekspres/avionom. | zhehleo beeh dah poshahl'ehm ovo ehksprehss/ahveeonom |

Service stations

Where is the nearest service station, please?	Gde je najbliža servisna stanica?	gdeh yeh nahybleezhah sehrveessnah stahneetsah
Fill her up, please.	Napunite rezervoar, molim Vas.	nahpooneeteh rehzehrvoahr moleem vahss
Check the oil, please.	Proverite ulje, molim Vas.	provehreeteh ool'eh moleem vahss
Would you check the tyres?	Da li biste hteli da proverite gume?	dah lee beesteh htehlee dah provehreeteh goomeh

Street directions

Can you show me on the map where I am?	Možete li mi pokazati na karti gde se nalazim?	mozhehteh lee mee pokahzahteh nah kahrtee gdeh seh nahlahzeem
You're on the wrong road.	Vi ste na pogrešnom putu.	vee steh nah pogrehshnom pootoo
Go back to...	Vratite se do...	vrahteeteh seh do
Go straight ahead.	Idite pravo napred.	eedeeteh prahvoo nahprehd
It's on the left/on the right.	Na levoj je strani/na desnoj.	nah lehvoy yeh strahnee/nah dehsnoy

Accidents

May I use your telephone?	**Mogu li se poslužiti Vašim telefonom?**	mogoo lee seh posloozheetee vahsheem tehlehfonom
Call a doctor quickly.	**Pozovite brzo doktora.**	pozoveeteh berzo doktorah
Call an ambulance.	**Pozovite kola za hitnu pomoć.**	pozoveeteh kolah zah heetnoo pomoch
Please call the police.	**Pozovite, molim Vas, policiju.**	pozoveeteh moleem vahss poleetseeyoo

Numbers

zero	**nula**	noolah
one	**jedan**	yehdahn
two	**dva**	dvah
three	**tri**	tree
four	**četiri**	chehteeree
five	**pet**	peht
six	**šest**	shehst
seven	**sedam**	sehdahm
eight	**osam**	ossahm
nine	**devet**	dehveht
ten	**deset**	dehseht
eleven	**jedanaest**	yehdahnahehst
twelve	**dvanaest**	dvahnahehst
thirteen	**trinaest**	treenahehst
fourteen	**četrnaest**	chehternahehst
fifteen	**petnaest**	pehtnahehst
sixteen	**šesnaest**	shehssnahehst
seventeen	**sedamnaest**	sehdahmnahehst
eighteen	**osamnaest**	osahmnahehst
nineteen	**devetnaest**	dehvehtnahehst
twenty	**dvadeset**	dvahdehseht
twenty-one	**dvadeset jedan**	dvahdehseht yehdahn
thirty	**trideset**	treedehseht
forty	**četrdeset**	chehterdehseht
fifty	**pedeset**	pehdehseht
sixty	**šezdeset**	shehzdehseht
seventy	**sedamdeset**	sehdahmdehseht
eighty	**osamdeset**	osahmdehseht
ninety	**devedeset**	dehvehdehseht
one hundred	**sto**	sto
one thousand	**hiljadu**	heelʸahdoo
ten thousand	**deset hiljada**	dehseht heelʸahdah

Days

It's Sunday.	Nedelja' je.	nehdehl^yah yeh
Monday	ponedeljak	ponehdehl^yahk
Tuesday	utorak	ootorahk
Wednesday	sreda	srehdah
Thursday	četvrtak	chehtvertahk
Friday	petak	pehtahk
Saturday	subota	soobotah
yesterday	juče	yoocheh
today	danas	dahnahss
tomorrow	sutra	sootrah
morning/afternoon	jutro/posle podne	yootro/posleh podneh
evening/night	veče/noć	vehcheh/noch

Months

January	januar	yahnooahr
February	februar	fehbrooahr
March	mart	mahrt
April	april	ahpreel
May	maj	mahy
June	jun	yoon
July	juli	yoolee
August	avgust	ahvgoost
September	septembar	sehptehmbahr
October	oktobar	oktobahr
November	novembar	novehmbahr
December	decembar	dehtsehmbahr

Merry Christmas!	Srećan Božić!	srehchahn bozheech!
Happy New Year!	Srećna Nova godina!	srehchnah novah godeenah

SERBO-CROATIAN

SPANISH

Guide to Pronunciation

Letter	Approximate pronunciation	Symbol	Example	

Consonants

f, k, l, m, n, p, t, x, y	as in English			
b	1) generally as in English	b	**bueno**	**bway**noa
	2) between vowels, a sound between **b** and **v**	bh	**bebida**	bay**bhee**dhah
c	1) before **e** and **i** like **th** in **th**in	th	**centro**	**thayn**troa
	2) otherwise, like **k** in **k**it	k	**como**	**koa**moa
ch	as in English	ch	**mucho**	**moo**choa
d	1) generally as in **d**og, although less decisive	d	**donde**	**don**day
	2) between vowels and at the end of a word, like **th** in **th**is	dh	**edad**	ay**dhahdh**

g	1) before **e** and **i**, like **ch** in Scottish lo**ch**	kh	**urgente**	oor**kh**ayntay
	2) between vowels and sometimes inside a word, a weak, voiced version of the **ch** in lo**ch**	ĝ	**agua**	ah**ĝ**wah
	3) otherwise, like **g** in **g**o	g	nin**g**uno	neen**g**goonoa
h	always silent		**h**ombre	ombray
j	like **ch** in Scottish lo**ch**	kh	**b**ajo	bah**kh**oa
ll	like **lli** in mi**lli**on	ly	**ll**eno	**ly**aynoa
ñ	like **ni** in o**ni**on	ñ	se**ñ**or	say**ñ**or
qu	like **k** in **k**it	k	**qu**ince	**k**eenthay
r	more strongly trilled (like a Scottish **r**), especially at the beginning of a word	r	**r**ío	**r**eeoa
rr	strongly trilled	rr	a**rr**iba	ah**rr**eebhah
s	always like the **s** in **s**it, often with a slight lisp	s/ss	vi**s**ta	bee**s**tah
			cuanto**s**	kwahntoa**ss**
v	1) tends to be like **b** in **b**ad, but less tense	b	**v**iejo	**b**yaykhoa
	2) between vowels, more like English **v**	bh	ri**v**al	ree**bh**ahl
z	like **th** in **th**in	th	bra**z**o	bra**th**oa

Vowels

a	like **a** in c**a**r, but fairly short	ah	gr**a**cias	gr**ah**thyahss
e	1) sometimes like **a** in l**a**te	ay	d**e**	d**ay**
	2) less often, like **e** in g**e**t	eh	llov**e**r	lyoabh**eh**r
i	like **ee** in f**ee**t	ee	s**i**	s**ee**
o	1) sometimes fairly like **o** in r**o**pe	oa	s**o**pa	s**oa**pah
	2) sometimes like **o** in g**o**t	o	d**o**s	d**o**ss
u	like **oo** in l**oo**t	oo	**u**na	**oo**nah
y	only a vowel when alone or at the end of a word; like **ee** in f**ee**t	ee	**y**	**ee**

N.B. 1) In forming diphthongs, **a**, **e**, and **o** are strong vowels, and **i** and **u** are weak vowels. This means that in diphthongs the strong vowels are pronounced more strongly than the weak ones. If two weak vowels form a diphthong, the second one is pronounced more strongly.
2) The acute accent (´) is used to indicate a syllable that is stressed, e.g., *río* = **ree**oa.
3) In words ending with a consonant, the last syllable is stressed, e.g., *señor* = say**nor**.
4) In words ending with a vowel, the next to the last syllable is stressed, e.g., *mañana* = mah**ñah**nah.

Some basic expressions

Yes.	**Sí.**	see
No.	**No.**	noa
Please.	**Por favor.**	por fah**bhor**
Thank you.	**Gracias.**	**grah**thyahss
Thank you very much.	**Muchas gracias.**	moochahss **grah**thyahss
That's all right.	**No hay de qué.**	noa igh day kay

Greetings

Good morning.	**Buenos días.**	**bway**noass **dee**ahss
Good afternoon.	**Buenas tardes.**	**bway**nahss **tahr**dhayss
Good evening.	**Buenas tardes.**	**bway**nahss **tahr**dhayss
Good night.	**Buenas noches.**	**bway**nahss **noa**chayss
Good-bye.	**Adiós.**	ah**dhyoss**
See you later.	**Hasta luego.**	**ahss**tah **lway**goa
This is Mr....	**Este es el Señor** ...	**ayss**tay ayss ehl say**ñor**
This is Mrs....	**Esta es la Señora** ...	**ayss**tah ayss lah say**ñoa**rah
This is Miss ...	**Esta es la Señorita** ...	**ayss**tah ayss lah say**ñoa**-**ree**tah
I'm very pleased to meet you.	**Encantado de conocerle.**	ayngkahn**tah**dhoa day koanoa**thayr**lay
How are you?	**¿Cómo está usted?**	**koa**moa ayss**tah** ooss**taydh**
Very well, thank you. And you?	**Muy bien, gracias. ¿Y usted?**	mwee byayn **grah**thyahss. ee ooss**taydh**
Fine. Thank you.	**Bien. Gracias.**	byayn **grah**thyahss
Excuse me.	**Dispénseme.**	deess**payn**saymay

Questions

Where?	**¿Dónde?**	**don**day
Where is ...?	**¿Dónde está ...?**	**don**day ayss**tah**
Where are ...?	**¿Dónde están ...?**	**don**day ayss**tahn**
When?	**¿Cuándo?**	**kwahn**doa

SPANISH

What?	¿Qué?	kay
How?	¿Cómo?	**koa**moa
How much?	¿Cuánto?	**kwahn**toa
How many?	¿Cuántos?	**kwahn**toass
Who?	¿Quién?	kyayn
Why?	¿Por qué?	por kay
Which?	¿Cuál?	kwahl
What do you call this?	¿Cómo se llama esto?	**koa**moa say **lyah**mah **ayss**toa
What do you call that?	¿Cómo se llama eso?	**koa**moa say **lyah**mah **ay**soa
What does this mean?	¿Qué quiere decir esto?	kay **kyay**ray day**theer** **ayss**toa
What does that mean?	¿Qué quiere decir eso?	kay **kyay**ray day**theer** **ay**soa

Do you speak . . . ?

Do you speak English?	¿Habla usted inglés?	**ahb**hlah oos**staydh** eeng**glayss**
Do you speak German?	¿Habla usted alemán?	**ahb**hlah oos**staydh** ahlay**mahn**
Do you speak French?	¿Habla usted francés?	**ahb**hlah oos**staydh** frahn**thayss**
Do you speak Spanish?	¿Habla usted español?	**ahb**hlah oos**staydh** aysspah**ñol**
Do you speak Italian?	¿Habla usted italiano?	**ahb**hlah oos**staydh** eetahl**yah**noa
Could you speak more slowly, please?	¿Puede usted hablar más despacio, por favor?	**pway**dhay oos**staydh** ah-**bhlahr** mahss day**spah**-thyoa por fah**bhor**
Please point to the phrase in the book.	Por favor, señale la frase en el libro.	por fah**bhor** say**ñah**lay lah **frah**say ayn ehl **lee**bhroa
Just a minute. I'll see if I can find it in this book.	Un momento. Veré si lo puedo encontrar en este libro.	oon moa**mayn**toa. bay**ray** see loa **pway**dhoa ayngkon**trahr** ayn **ayss**tay **lee**broa
I understand.	Comprendo.	kom**prayn**doa
I don't understand.	No comprendo.	noa kom**prayn**doa

Can...?

Can I have ...?	¿Puede darme ...?	pwaydhay dahrmay
Can we have ...?	¿Puede darnos ...?	pwaydhay dahrnoss
Can you show me ...?	¿Puede usted enseñarme ...?	pwaydhay oosstaydh aynsayñahrmay
Can you tell me ...?	¿Puede usted decirme ...?	pwaydhay oosstaydh daytheermay
Can you help me, please?	¿Puede usted ayudarme, por favor?	pwaydhay oosstaydh ahyoodahrmay por fahbhor

Wanting

I'd like ...	Quisiera ...	keesyayrah
We'd like ...	Quisiéramos ...	keesyayrahmoss
Please give me ...	Por favor, déme ...	por fahbhor daymay
Give it to me, please.	Démelo, por favor.	daymayloa por fahbhor
Please bring me ...	Por favor, tráigame ...	por fahbhor trighgahmay
Bring it to me, please.	Tráigamelo, por favor.	trighgahmayloa por fahbhor
I'm hungry.	Tengo hambre.	taynggoa ahmbray
I'm thirsty.	Tengo sed.	taynggoa saydh
I'm tired.	Estoy cansado.	aysstoy kahnsahdhoa
I'm lost.	Me he perdido.	may ay pehrdheedhoa
It's important.	Es importante.	ayss eempoartahntay
It's urgent.	Es urgente.	ayss oorkhayntay
Hurry up!	¡Dése prisa!	daysay preesah

It is/There is ...

It is/It's ...	Es ...	ayss
Is it ...?	¿Es ...?	ayss
It isn't ...	No es ...	noa ayss
There is/There are ...	Hay ...	igh
Is there/Are there ...?	¿Hay ...?	igh

SPANISH

| There isn't/There aren't... | **No hay ...** | noa igh |
| There isn't any/ There aren't any. | **No hay ninguno/No hay ningunos (No hay ninguna/No hay ningunas).** | noa igh neenggoonoa/noa igh neenggoonoss (noa igh neenggoonah/noa igh neenggoonahss) |

A few common words

big/small	**grande/pequeño**	grahnday/paykaynoa
quick/slow	**rápido/lento**	rahpeedhoa/layntoa
early/late	**temprano/tarde**	taymprahnoa/tahrdhay
cheap/expensive	**barato/caro**	bahrahtoa/kahroa
near/far	**cerca/lejos**	thehrkah/laykhoass
hot/cold	**caliente/frío**	kahlyayntay/freeoa
full/empty	**lleno/vacío**	lyaynoa/bahtheeoa
easy/difficult	**fácil/difícil**	fahtheel/deefeetheel
heavy/light	**pesado/ligero**	paysahdhoa/leekhayroa
open/shut	**abierto/cerrado**	ahbhyehrtoa/thayrrahdhoa
right/wrong	**correcto/incorrecto**	korrehktoa/eengkorrehktoa
old/new	**viejo/nuevo**	byaykhoa/nwaybhoa
old/young	**anciano/joven**	annthyanoa/khoabhayn
beautiful/ugly	**bonito/feo**	boaneetoa/fayoa
good/bad	**bueno/malo**	bwaynoa/mahloa
better/worse	**mejor/peor**	mehkhor/payor

Some prepositions and a few more useful words

at	**a**	ah
on	**sobre**	soabhray
in	**en**	ayn
to	**para**	pahrah
from	**desde**	dayzday
inside	**dentro**	dayntroa
outside	**fuera**	fwayrah
up	**arriba**	ahrreebhah
down	**abajo**	ahbhahkhoa
before	**antes**	ahntayss
after	**después**	daysspwayss
with	**con**	kon
without	**sin**	seen
through	**a través**	ah trahbhayss
towards	**hacia**	ahthyah
until	**hasta**	ahsstah
during	**durante**	doorahntay
and	**y**	ee
or	**o**	oa

SPANISH

not	**no**	noa
nothing	**nada**	**nah**dhah
none	**ninguno**	neeng**goo**noa
very	**muy**	mwee
also	**también**	tahm**bhyayn**
soon	**pronto**	**pront**oa
perhaps	**tal vez**	tal bayth
here	**aquí**	ah**kee**
there	**allí**	ah**lyee**
now	**ahora**	a**horah**
then	**entonces**	ayn**ton**thayss

Arrival

Your passport, please.	**Su pasaporte, por favor.**	soo pahsah**portay** por fah**bhor**
Here it is.	**Aquí está.**	ah**kee** ays**stah**
Have you anything to declare?	**¿Tiene usted algo que declarar?**	**tyay**nay ooss**taydh ahl**goa kay dayklah**rahr**
No, nothing at all.	**No, nada en ab-soluto.**	noa **nah**dhah ayn ahb-soa**loo**toa
Porter!	**¡Mozo!**	**moa**thoa
Can you help me with my luggage, please?	**¿Puede usted ayudarme con mi equipaje, por favor?**	**pway**dhay ooss**taydh** ahyoo**dahr**may kon mee aykee**pah**khay por fah**bhor**
That's my suitcase.	**Esa es mi maleta.**	**ays**sah ayss mee mah**lay**tah
Where's the bus to the centre of town, please?	**¿Dónde está el autobús que va al centro, por favor?**	**don**day ays**stah** ehl ow-toa**booss** kay bah ahl **thayn**troa por fah**bhor**
This way, please.	**Por aquí, por favor.**	por ah**kee** por fah**bhor**

Changing money

| Can you change a traveller's cheque, please? | **¿Puede usted cambiarme un traveller's cheque, por favor?** | **pway**dhay ooss**taydh** kahm**byahr**may oon "traveller's cheque" por fah**bhor** |
| Where's the nearest bank, please? | **¿Dónde está el banco más cercano, por favor?** | **don**day ays**stah** ehl **bahng**koa mahss thehr**kah**noa por fah**bhor** |

SPANISH

Car rental

I'd like a car.	Quisiera un coche.	keesyayrah oon koachay
For how long?	¿Para cuánto tiempo?	pahrah kwahntoa tyaympoa
A day/Four days/ A week/Two weeks.	Un día/Cuatro días/Una semana/Dos semanas.	oon deeah/kwahtroa deeahss/oonah saymahnah/doss saymahnahss

Taxi

Where can I get a taxi?	¿Dónde puedo coger (conseguir) un taxi?	donday pwaydhoa kokhehr (koansaygeer) oon tahksee
What's the fare to...?	¿Cuál es la tarifa a...?	kwahl ayss lah tahreefah ah
Take me to this address, please.	Lléveme a esta dirección, por favor.	lyaybhaymay ah aysstah deerehgthyon por fahbhor
I'm in a hurry.	Tengo mucha prisa.	taynggoa moochah preesah
Could you drive more slowly, please?	¿Puede usted ir más despacio, por favor?	pwaydhay oosstaydh eer mahss daysspahthyoa por fahbhor

Hotel and other accommodation

My name is...	Me llamo...	may lyahmoa
Have you a reservation?	¿Ha hecho usted una reserva?	ah aychoa oosstaydh oonah rrehsehrbhah
Yes, here's the confirmation.	Sí, aquí está la confirmación.	see ahkee aysstah lah konfeermahthyon
I'd like...	Quisiera...	keesyayrah
I'd like a single room/a double room.	Quisiera una habitación sencilla/una habitación doble.	keesyayrah oonah ahbheetahthyon sayntheelyah/oonah ahbheetahthyon doablay
a room with a bath/ with a shower	una habitación con baño/con ducha	oonah ahbheetahthyon kon bahñoa/kon doochah

How much?

| What's the price per night/per week/per month? | ¿Cuánto cuesta por noche/por semana/por mes? | kwahntoa kwaysstah por noachay/por saymahnah/por mayss |

May I see the room?	¿Puedo ver la habitación?	pwaydhoa bayr lah ahbheetahthyon
I'm sorry, I don't like it.	Lo siento, no me gusta.	loa syayntoa noa may goosstah
Yes, that's fine. I'll take it.	Muy bien, la tomaré.	mwee byayn lah toamahray
What's my room number, please?	¿Cuál es el número de mi habitación, por favor?	kwahl ayss ehl noomayroa day mee ahbheetahthyon por fahbhor
Number 123.	Número 123.	noomayroa 123.

Service, please

Who is it?	¿Quién es?	kyayn ayss
Just a minute.	Un momento, por favor.	oon moamayntoa por fahbhor
Come in! The door's open.	¡Adelante! la puerta está abierta.	ahdhaylahntay! lah pwehrtah aysstah ahbhyehrtah
May we have breakfast in our room?	¿Podemos desayunar en nuestra habitación?	poadhaymoass daysahyoonahr ayn nwaysstrah ahbheetahthyon

Breakfast

I'll have . . .	Quisiera . . .	keesyayrah
I'll have some fruit juice.	Quisiera un zumo de fruta.	keesyayrah oon thoomoa day frootah
a boiled egg	un huevo cocido	oon waybhoa koatheedhoa
a fried egg	un huevo frito	oon waybhoa freetoa
some bacon/some ham	un poco de tocino/un poco de jamón	oon poakoa day toatheenoa/oon poakoa day khahmon
some toast	un poco de pan tostado	oon poakoa day pahn toasstahdhoa
a pot of tea	una tetera de té	oonah taytayrah day tay
a cup of tea	una taza de té	oonah tahthah day tay
some coffee	un poco de café	oon poakoa day kahfay
some chocolate	un poco de chocolate	oon poakoa day choakoalahtay
more butter	más mantequilla	mahss mahntaykeelyah
some hot water	un poco de agua caliente	oon poakoa day ahgwah kahlyayntay

Difficulties

The central heating doesn't work.	**La calefacción central no funciona.**	lah kahlayfahk**thyon thayntrahl** noa foon**thyoanah**
the light/the socket the tap/the toilet	**la luz/el enchufe el grifo/el water**	lah looth/ehl ayn**choo**fay ehl **gree**foa/ehl **vah**tehr
There's no hot water.	**No hay agua caliente.**	noa igh ah**ğ**wah kahl**yayn**tay
May I see the manager, please?	**¿Puedo ver al director, por favor?**	**pway**dhoa behr ahl deerehk**tor** por fah**bhor**

Telephone—Mail

There's a call for you.	**Hay una llamada para usted.**	igh **oo**nah lyah**mah**dhah **pah**rah oos**staydh**
Hold the line, please.	**Espere un momento, por favor.**	ayss**pay**ray oon moa**mayn**toa por fah**bhor**
Operator, I've been cut off.	**Telefonista, me han cortado.**	taylayfoa**nees**tah may ahn kortah**dhoa**
Did anyone telephone me?	**¿Me ha llamado alguien?**	may ah lyah**mah**dhoa ahl**gyayn**
Is there any mail for me?	**¿Hay correo para mí?**	igh kor**ray**oa **pah**rah mee
Are there any messages for me?	**¿Hay algún recado para mí?**	igh ahl**goon** raykah**dhoa pah**rah mee

Checking out

May I have my bill, please?	**¿Puede darme mi cuenta, por favor?**	**pway**dhay **dahr**may mee **kwayn**tah por fah**bhor**
We're in a great hurry.	**Tenemos mucha prisa.**	tay**nay**moss **moo**chah **pree**sah
It's been a very enjoyable stay.	**Ha sido una estancia muy agradable.**	ah **see**dhoa **oo**nah ayss**tahn**thyah mwee ahgrah**dhah**bhlay

Eating out

Good evening, sir/ Good evening, madam.	**Buenas noches, señor/Buenas noches, señora.**	**bway**nahss **noa**chayss say**ñor bway**nahss **noa**chayss say**ñoa**rah
Good evening. I'd like a table for two, please.	**Buenas noches. Quisiera una mesa para dos, por favor.**	**bway**nahss **noa**chayss. kee**syay**rah **oo**nah **may**sah **pah**rah doss por fah**bhor**

Do you have a fixed-price menu?	¿Tiene usted un menú de precio fijo?	**tyay**nay ooss**taydh** oon may**noo** day **pray**thyoa **fee**khoa
May I see the à la carte menu?	¿Puedo ver la carta?	**pway**dhoa behr lah **kahr**tah
May we have an ashtray, please?	¿Nos puede traer un cenicero, por favor?	noss **pway**dhay tra**hehr** oon thaynee**thay**roa por fah**bhor**
some bread	un poco de pan	oon **poa**koa day pan
a fork	un tenedor	oon taynay**dhor**
a knife	un cuchillo	oon koo**chee**lyoa
a spoon	una cuchara	**oo**nah koo**chah**rah
a plate	un plato	oon **plah**toa
a glass	un vaso	oon **bah**soa
a napkin	una servilleta	**oo**nah sehrbhee**lyay**tah
another chair	otra silla	**oa**tra **see**lyah
Where's the gentlemen's toilet (men's room)?	¿Dónde está el lavabo de caballeros?	**don**day ayss**tah** ehl lah-**bhah**bhoa day kahbhah**lyay**ross
Where's the ladies' toilet (ladies' room)?	¿Dónde está el lavabo de señoras?	**don**day ayss**tah** ehl lah-**bhah**bhoa day say**ñoa**rahss

Appetizers

I'd like some . . .	Quisiera . . .	kees**yay**rah
I'd like some assorted appetizers.	Quisiera unos entremeses variados.	kees**yay**rah **oo**noss ayntray**may**sayss bahree**ah**dhoss
orange juice	un jugo de naranja	oon **khoo**ǧoa day nah**rahn**khah
ham	jamón	khah**mon**
melon	melón	may**lon**
pâté	pastel de carne	pahss**tehl** day **kahr**nay
smoked salmon	salmón ahumado	sahl**mon** ahoo**mah**dhoa
shrimps (shrimp)	quisquillas	keess**kee**lyahss

Soup

Have you any . . . ?	¿Tiene usted . . . ?	**tyay**nay ooss**taydh**
Have you any chicken soup?	¿Tiene usted sopa de pollo?	**tyay**nay ooss**taydh** **soa**pah day **poal**yoa
vegetable soup	sopa de verduras	**soa**pah day behr**dhoo**rahss
onion soup	sopa de cebollas	**soa**pah day thay**bhoa**lyahss

SPANISH

Fish

I'd like some...	**Quisiera...**	keesyayrah
I'd like some fish.	**Quisiera pescado.**	keesyayrah paysskahdhoa
sole	**lenguado**	laynggwahdhoa
trout	**trucha**	troochah
lobster	**langosta**	langgosstah
crayfish	**cangrejos**	kahngggraykhoss
prawns	**gambas**	gahmbahss
I'd like it...	**Me gustaría...**	may goosstahreeah
I'd like it steamed.	**Me gustaría al vapor.**	may goosstahreeah ahl bahpor
grilled	**a la parrilla**	ah lah pahreelyah
boiled	**cocido**	koatheedhoa
baked	**asado**	ahsahdhoa
fried	**frito**	freetoa

Meat—Poultry—Game

I'd like some...	**Quisiera...**	keesyayrah
I'd like some beef.	**Quisiera carne de vaca.**	keesyayrah **kahr**nay day **bah**kah
a beef steak	**un bistec**	oon beess**tehk**
some roast beef	**rosbif**	rroz**bheef**
a veal cutlet	**una chuleta de ternera**	oonah choolaytah day tehr**nay**rah
mutton	**carnero**	kahr**nay**roa
lamb	**cordero**	kor**dhay**roa
a pork chop	**una chuleta de cerdo**	oonah choolaytah day **thehr**dhoa
roast pork	**cerdo asado**	**thehr**dhoa ah**sah**dhoa
hare	**liebre**	**lyay**bhray
chicken	**pollo**	**poa**lyoa
roast chicken	**pollo asado**	**poa**lyoa ah**sah**dhoa
duck	**pato**	**pah**toa
How do you like your meat?	**¿Cómo le gusta la carne?**	**koa**moa lay **goos**stah lah **kahr**nay
rare	**poco asada**	**poa**koa ah**sah**dhah
medium	**medio asada**	**may**dhyoa ah**sah**dhah
well done	**bien hecha**	byayn **ay**chah

Vegetables

| What vegetables have you got? | **¿Qué verduras tiene usted?** | kay behr**dhoo**rahss **tyay**nah oos**staydh** |
| I'd like some... | **Quisiera...** | keesyayrah |

I'd like some asparagus.	Quisiera unos espárragos.	keesyayrah oonoss ayss-pahrrahğoss
green beans	unas judías verdes	oonahss khoodhyahss behrdhayss
mushrooms	unas setas	oonahss saytahss
carrots	unas zanahorias	oonahss thahnahoryahss
onions	unas cebollas	oonahss thaybhoalyahss
red cabbage	lombarda	loambahrdhah
spinach	unas espinacas	oonahss aysspeenahkahss
rice	un poco de arroz	oon poakoa day ahrroth
peas	unos guisantes	oonos geesahntayss
tomatoes	unos tomates	oonos toamahtayss
green salad	ensalada de lechuga	aynsahlahdhah day lay-chooğah
potatoes	unas patatas	oonahss pahtahtahss

Desserts

Nothing more, thanks.	Nada más, gracias.	nahdhah mahss grah-thyahss
Just a small portion, please.	Una pequeña porción, por favor.	oonah paykayñah por-thyon por fahbhor
Have you any ice-cream?	¿Tiene usted helado?	tyaynay oosstaydh aylah-dhoa
fruit salad	ensalada de fruta	aynsahlahdhah day frootah
fresh fruit	fruta fresca	frootah fraysskah
cheese	queso	kaysoa

Drink

What would you like to drink?	¿Qué le gustaría beber?	kay lay goosstahreeah baybhayr
I'll have a beer, please.	Tomaré una cerveza, por favor.	toamahray oonah thehr-bhaythah por fahbhor
I'll have a whisky, please.	Tomaré un whisky, por favor.	toamahray oon weeskee por fahbhor

SPANISH

Wine

I'd like a bottle of wine.	**Quisiera una botella de vino.**	keesyayrah oonah boatay-lyah day beenoa
red wine	**vino tinto**	beenoa teentoa
rosé wine	**vino clarete**	beenoa klahraytay
white wine	**vino blanco**	beenoa blahngkoa
Cheers!	**¡A su salud!**	ah soo sahloodh

The bill (check)

May I have the bill (check) please?	**¿Podría darme la cuenta, por favor?**	poadhreeah dahrmay lah kwayntah por fahbhor
Is service included?	**¿Está incluido el servicio?**	aysstah eengklooeedhoa ehl sehrbheethyoa
Everything's included.	**Todo está incluido.**	toadhoa aysstah eeng-klooeedhoa
Thank you, that was a very good meal.	**Gracias. Ha sido una comida muy buena.**	grahthyahss. ah seedhoa oonah koameedhah mwee bwaynah

Travelling

Where's the railway station, please?	**¿Dónde está la estación de ferrocarril, por favor?**	donday aysstah lah aysstahthyon day fehrrokahr-reel por fahbhor
Where's the ticket office, please?	**¿Dónde está la taquilla, por favor?**	donday aysstah lah tah-keelyah por fahbhor
I'd like a ticket to ...	**Quisiera un billete para ...**	keesyayrah oon beelyay-tay pahrah
First or second class?	**¿Primera o segunda clase?**	preemayrah o saygoon-dah klahsay
First class, please.	**Primera clase, por favor.**	preemayrah klahsay por fahbhor
Single or return (one way or round-trip)?	**¿Ida, o ida y vuelta?**	eedhah o eedhah ee bwehltah
Do I have to change trains?	**¿Tengo que hacer transbordo?**	taynggoa kay ahthehr trahnzbhoardhoa
What platform does the train leave from?	**¿De qué andén sale el tren?**	day kay ahndayn sahlay ehl trayn
Where's the nearest underground (subway) station?	**¿Dónde está la próxima estación de metro?**	donday aysstah lah prog-seemah aysstahthyon day maytroa

Where's the bus station, please?	**¿Dónde está la estación de auto-buses, por favor?**	don day aysstah lah aysstah**thyon** day owtoa-**booss**ayss por fah**bhor**
When's the first bus to . . . ?	**¿Cuándo sale el primer autobús para . . . ?**	**kwahn**doa **sah**lay ehl pree**mehr** owtoa**booss** pah**rah**
the last bus	**el último autobús**	ehl **oolt**eemoa owtoa-**booss**
the next bus	**el próximo autobús**	ehl pro**ģ**seemoa owtoa-**booss**
Please let me off at the next stop.	**Por favor, pare en la próxima parada.**	por fah**bhor** pah**ray** ayn lah pro**ģ**seemah pah**rah**-dhah

Relaxing

What's on at the cinema (movies)?	**¿Qué dan en el cine?**	kay dahn ayn ehl **thee**nay
What's on at the. theatre?	**¿Qué dan en el teatro?**	kay dahn ayn ehl tay**ah**-troa
What time does the film begin? And the play?	**¿A qué hora em-pieza la película? ¿Y la obra?**	ah kay **oa**rah aym**pyay**-thah lah pay**lee**koolah? ee lah o**ah**brah
Are there any tickets for tonight?	**¿Quedan entradas para esta noche?**	kay**dhahn** ayn**trahd**hahss pah**rah** ayss**tah** noachay
Where can we go dancing?	**¿Dónde se puede ir a bailar?**	don day say **pway**dhay eer ah bigh**lahr**
Would you like to dance?	**¿Quiere usted ballar?**	**kyay**ray ooss**taydh** bigh**lahr**

Introductions

How do you do?	**Buenos días.**	**bway**noss dee**ahss**
How are you?	**¿Cómo está usted?**	**koa**moa ayss**tah** ooss-**taydh**
Very well, thank you. And you?	**Muy bien, gracias. ¿Y usted?**	mwee byayn **grah**thyahss. ee ooss**taydh**
May I introduce Miss Philips?	**¿Me permite pre-sentarle la Señorita Philips?**	may pehr**mee**tay pray-sayn**tahr**lay lah say**ñoa**-**ree**tah Philips
My name is . . .	**Me llamo . . .**	may **lyah**moa
I'm very pleased to meet you.	**Tanto gusto (en conocerle).**	**tahn**toa **gooss**toa (ayn koanoa**thehr**lay)

How long have you been here?	¿Cuánto tiempo lleva usted aquí?	kwahntoa tyaympoa lyaybhah oosstaydh ahkee
It was nice meeting you.	Ha sido un placer conocerle.	ah seedhoa oon plahthehr koanoathehrlay

Dating

Would you like a cigarette?	¿Quiere usted un cigarrillo?	kyayray oosstaydh oon theegahreelyoa
May I get you a drink?	¿Me permite invitarlo a una bebida?	may pehrmeetay eenbheetahrloa ah oonah baybheedhah
Do you have a light, please?	¿Tiene usted fuego, por favor?	tyaynay oosstaydh fwaygoa por fahbhor
Are you waiting for someone?	¿Está usted esperando a alguien?	aysstah oosstaydh aysspayrahndoa ah ahlgyayn
Are you free this evening?	¿Está usted libre esta noche?	aysstah oosstaydh leebhray aysstah noachay
Where shall we meet?	¿Dónde quedamos citados?	donday kaydhahmoss theetahdhoss
What time shall I meet you?	¿A qué hora puedo verla?	ah kay oarah pwaydhoa behrlah
May I take you home?	¿Puedo acompañarla a su casa?	pwaydhoa ahkoampahñahrlah ah soo kahsah
Thank you, it's been a wonderful evening.	Gracias, he pasado una velada maravillosa.	grahthyahss ay pahsahdhoa oona bay lahdhah mahrahbheelyoasah
What's your telephone number?	¿Cuál es su número de teléfono?	kwahl ayss soo noomayroa day taylayfoanoa
Do you live alone?	¿Vive usted sola?	beebhay oosstaydh soalah
What time is your last train?	¿A qué hora sale su último tren?	ah kay oarah sahlay soo oolteemoa trayn
Good-night...	Buenas noches...	bwaynahss noachayss

Banks

Where's the nearest bank, please?	¿Dónde está el banco más cercano, por favor?	donday aysstah ehl bahngkoa mahss thehrkahnoa por fahbhor
Where can I cash some traveller's cheques?	¿Dónde puedo cambiar unos traveller's cheques?	donday pwaydhoa kahmbyahr oonoss "traveller's cheques"

What time does the bank open/What time does it close?	¿A qué hora abren el banco/A qué hora lo cierran?	ah kay oarah ahbrayn ehl bahngkoa/ah kay oarah loa thyehrrahn
I'm expecting some money from home. Has it arrived?	Estoy esperando dinero de casa. ¿Ha llegado?	aysstoy aysspayrahndoa deenayroa day kahsah. ah yaygahdoa
Can you give me some small change, please?	¿Puede usted darme algún dinero suelto, por favor?	pwaydhay oosstaydh dahrmay ahlgoon deenayroa swehltoa por fahbhor

Shops, stores and services

Where is the nearest chemist (pharmacy)?	¿Dónde está la farmacia más cercana?	donday aysstah lah fahrmahtheeah mahss thehrkahnah
the nearest hairdresser's	la peluquería más cercana	lah paylookayreeah mahss thehrkahnah
the photo shop	la tienda fotográfica	lah tyayndha foatoagrahfeekah
the jeweller's	la joyería	lah khoayayreeah
the department store	los grandes almacenes	loss grahndayss ahlmahthaynayss
the police station	la comisaría	lah koameesahreeah
the garage	el garaje	ehl gahrahkhay
How do I get there?	¿Cómo podría ir allí?	koamoa poadhreeah eer ahlyee
Is it within walking distance?	¿Se puede ir andando?	say pwaydhay eer ahndahndoa

Service

Can you help me, please?	¿Puede usted atenderme, por favor?	pwaydhay oosstaydh ahtayndehrmay por fahbhor
Can you show me this? And that, too.	¿Puede usted enseñarme esto? ¿Y aquello también?	pwaydhay oosstaydh aynsayñahrmay aysstoa? ee ahkwaylyoa tahmbyyayn
It's too expensive/too big/too small.	Es demasiado caro/demasiado grande/demasiado pequeño.	ayss daymahsyahdhoa kahroa/daymahsyahdhoa grahnday/daymahsyahdhoa paykayñoa
Can you show me some more?	¿Puede usted enseñarme algo más?	pwaydhay oosstaydh aynsayñahrmay ahlgoa mahss
something better	algo mejor	ahlgoa maykhor
something cheaper	algo más barato	ahlgoa mahss bahrahtoa

SPANISH

How much is this? And that?	¿Cuánto cuesta éste? ¿Y ése?	kwahntoa kwaysstah aysstay? ee aysay
It's not quite what I want.	No es exactamente lo que quiero.	noa ayss ehġsahktah-mayntay loa kay kyayroa
I like it.	Me gusta.	may goosstah

Chemist's (Pharmacy)

| I'd like something for a cold/for a cough/for travel sickness. | Desearía algo para el catarro/para la tos/contra el mareo. | daysayahreeah ahlgoa pahrah ehl kahtahrroa/pahrah lah toss/kontrah ehl mahrayoa |
| Can you recommend something for hay-fever/for sunburn? | ¿Podría recomen-darme algo para la fiebre del heno/para las quema-duras del sol? | poadhreeah raykoamayn-dahrmay ahlgoa pahrah lah fyaybhray dehl ay-noa/pahrah lahss kaymah-dhoorahss dehl sol |

Toiletry

May I have some razor blades?	¿Puede darme unas cuchillas para afeitar?	pwaydhay dahrmay oo-nahss koocheelyahss pah-rah ahfaytahr
some shaving cream	una crema para afeitar	oonah kraymah pahrah ahfaytahr
some toothpaste	una pasta de dientes	oonah pahsstah day dyayntayss
I'd like some soap.	Quisiera jabón.	keesyayrah khahbhon
some suntan oil	aceite bronceador	ahthaytay bronthayahdhor

At the barber's

I'd like a haircut, please.	Quisiera cortarme el pelo, por favor.	keesyayrah kortahrmay ehl payloa por fahbhor
Short/Leave it long.	Corto/Déjemelo largo.	kortoa/daykhaymayloa lahrgoa
A razor cut, please.	Un corte a navaja, por favor.	oon kortay ah nahbhah-khah por fahbhor

At the hairdresser's

| I'd like a shampoo and set, please. | Quiero un lavado y marcado por favor. | kyayroa oon lahbhahdhoa ee mahrkahdhoa por fahbhor |

I'd like a bleach.	**Desearía un aclarado.**	daysayah**ree**ah oon ahklah**rah**dhoa
a permanent	**una permanente**	**oo**nah pehrmah**nayn**tay
a colour rinse	**un reflejo**	oon ray**flay**khoa
a manicure	**una manicura**	**oo**nah mahnee**koo**rah

Photography

| I'd like a film for this camera. | **Desearía un carrete para esta máquina.** | daysayah**ree**ah oon kahr-**ray**tay pahrah ayss**tah mah**keenah |
| This camera doesn't work. | **Esta cámera no funciona.** | ayss**tah kah**mayrah noa foon**thyoa**nah |

At the post office

| Where's the nearest post office, please? | **¿Dónde está la oficina de correos más cercana, por favor?** | **don**day ayss**tah** lah oafee**thee**nah day korre**hoss** mahss thehr**kah**nah por fah**bhor** |
| I'd like to send this by express (special delivery)/by air mail. | **Quisiera enviar esto por correo urgente/por avión.** | kee**syay**rah ay**bhyahr** aysstoa por korre**hoa** oor**khayn**tay/ por ah**bhyon** |

Service stations

Where is the nearest service station, please?	**¿Dónde está la estación de servicio más cercana?**	**don**day ayss**tah** lah ayss-tah**thyon** day sehr**bhee**thyoa mahss thehr**kah**nah
Fill her up, please.	**Llénemelo por favor.**	**lyay**naymayloa por fah**bhor**
Check the oil, please.	**Compruebe el aceite, por favor.**	kom**pr way**bhay ehl ah-**thay**tay por fah**bhor**
Would you check the tyres?	**¿Quiere comprobar los neumáticos?**	**kyay**ray kom pro**ah bhahr** loss nehw**mah**teekoss

Street directions

| Can you show me on the map where I am? | **¿Puede enseñarme en el mapa dónde estoy?** | **pway**dhay aynsay**ñahr**may ayn ehl **mah**pah **don**day ayss**toy** |
| You're on the wrong road. | **Está usted equivocado de camino.** | ayss**tah** oos**taydh** aykee-bhoa**kah**dhoa day kah-**mee**noa |

Go back to ...	Vuelva a ...	bwehlbha a
Go straight ahead.	Siga todo derecho.	seegah toadhoa dayray-choa
It's on the left/on the right.	Está a la izquierda/ a la derecha.	aysstah ah lah eethkyehr-dhah/ah lah dayraychah

Accidents

May I use your telephone?	¿Puedo utilizar su teléfono?	pwaydhoa ooteeleethar soo taylayfoanoa
Call a doctor quickly.	Llame a un médico rápidamente.	lyahmay ah oon maydee-koa rahpeedhamayntay
Call an ambulance.	Llame a una ambulancia.	lyahmay ah oonah ahm-boolahnthyah
Please call the police.	Llame a la policía, por favor.	lyahmay ah lah polee-theeah por fahbhor

Numbers

zero	cero	thayroa
one	uno	oonoa
two	dos	doss
three	tres	trayss
four	cuatro	kwahtroa
five	cinco	theengkoa
six	seis	seheess
seven	siete	syaytay
eight	ocho	oachoa
nine	nueve	nwaybhay
ten	diez	dyayth
eleven	once	onthay
twelve	doce	doathay
thirteen	trece	traythay
fourteen	catorce	kahtorthay
fifteen	quince	keenthay
sixteen	dieciséis	dyehtheeseheess
seventeen	diecisiete	dyehtheesyaytay
eighteen	dieciocho	dyehtheeoachoa
nineteen	diecinueve	dyehtheenwaybhay
twenty	veinte	bayntay
twenty-one	veintiuno	bayntioonoa
thirty	treinta	trayntah
forty	cuarenta	kwahrayntah
fifty	cincuenta	theengkwayntah
sixty	sesenta	saysayntah
seventy	setenta	saytayntah

eighty	**ochenta**	oa**chayn**tah
ninety	**noventa**	noa**bhayn**tah
one hundred	**cien**	thyayn
one thousand	**mil**	meel
ten thousand	**diez mil**	dyayth meel

Days

It's Sunday.	**Es domingo.**	ayss doa**meeng**goa
Monday	**lunes**	**loo**nayss
Tuesday	**martes**	**mahr**tayss
Wednesday	**miércoles**	**myehr**koalayss
Thursday	**jueves**	khway**bhayss**
Friday	**viernes**	**byehr**nayss
Saturday	**sábado**	**sah**bhahdhoa
yesterday	**ayer**	ah**yehr**
today	**hoy**	oy
tomorrow	**mañana**	mah**ñah**nah
morning/afternoon	**mañana/media tarde**	mah**ñah**nah/**may**dhyah **tahr**dhay
evening/night	**tarde/noche**	**tahr**dhay/**noa**chay

Months

January	**enero**	ay**nay**roa
February	**febrero**	fay**bhray**roa
March	**marzo**	**mahr**thoa
April	**abril**	ah**bhreel**
May	**mayo**	**mah**yoa
June	**junio**	**khoon**yoa
July	**julio**	**khool**yoa
August	**agosto**	ah**goss**toa
September	**septiembre**	sayp**tyaym**bray
October	**octubre**	ok**toobh**ray
November	**noviembre**	noa**bhyaym**bray
December	**diciembre**	deeth**yaym**bray
Merry Christmas!	**¡Felices Pascuas!**	fay**lee**thayss **pahss**kwahss!
Happy New Year!	**¡Feliz Año Nuevo!**	fay**leeth** ah**ño** **nway**bhoa

SPANISH

SWEDISH

Guide to Pronunciation

Letter	Approximate pronunciation	Symbol	Example	
Consonants				
b, c, d, f, h, l, m, n, p, v, w, x	as in English			
ch	at the beginning of words borrowed from French, like **sh** in **sh**ut	sh	**chef**	shayf
g	1) before stressed **i, e, y, ä, ö** and sometimes after **l** or **r**, like **y** in **y**et	y	**genast**	**yay**nahst
	2) before **e** and **i** in many words of French origin, like **sh** in **sh**ut	sh	**generös**	shayner**rurss**
	3) elsewhere, generally like **g** in **g**o	g	**gammal**	**gah**mahl
j, dj, gj, lj	like **y** in **y**et	y	**ja**	yar
k	1) before stressed **i, e, y, ä, ö**, generally like **ch** in Scottish lo**ch**, but pronounced in the front of the mouth	kh	**köpa**	**khur**pah
	2) elsewhere, like **k** in **k**it	k	**kål**	koal

kj	like **ch** in Scottish lo**ch**, but pronounced in the front of the mouth	kh	**kjol**	**kh**ool
qu	like **k** in **k**it followed by **v** in **v**at	kv	**Lindquist**	**lind**kvist
r	slightly rolled near the front of the mouth	r	**råd**	road
s	1) in the ending **-sion** like **sh** in **sh**ut	sh	**mission**	mi**sh**oon
	2) elsewhere, like **s** in **s**o	s/ss	**smak**	smark
	3) the groups **sch**, **skj**, **stj** are pronounced like **sh** in **sh**ut	sh	**schema**	**shay**mah
sk	1) before stressed **e**, **i**, **y**, **ä**, **ö**, like **sh** in **sh**ut	sh	**skepp**	**sh**ehp
	2) elsewhere, like **sk** in **sk**ip	sk	**handske**	hahnd**sker**
t	1) in the ending **-tion**, is pronounced like **sh** in **sh**ut or like **ch** in **ch**at	sh	**station**	stah**shoon**
	2) elsewhere, like **t** in **t**op	tsh	**nation**	nah**tschoon**
		t	**talk**	tahlk
tj	like **ch** in Scottish lo**ch**, but pronounced in the front of the mouth; sometimes with a t-sound at the beginning	kh	**tjäna**	**kh**ainah
z	like **s** in **s**o	s	**zon**	soon

N.B. In the groups **rd**, **rl**, **rn**, **rs** and **rt**, the letter **r** is generally not pronounced but influences the pronunciation of the **d**, **l**, **n**, **s** or **t**, which is then pronounced with the end of the tongue *not* on the upper front teeth, but behind the gums of the upper teeth.

Vowels

Vowels in stressed syllables are long if followed at most by one consonant, but are short if followed by two or more consonants. Vowels in unstressed syllables are short.

a	1) when long, like **a** in c**a**r	ar*	**dag**	darg
	2) when short, something like the **u** in c**u**t or **o** in American c**o**llege	ah	**tack**	tahk
e	1) when long, like **ay** in s**ay**, but a *pure* vowel, not a diphthong	ay	**blek**	blayk
	2) in the stressed prefix **er-**, like **a** in m**a**n, but longer	ææ	**erfara**	**æær**farrah
	3) when short, like **e** in g**e**t	eh	**penna**	**peh**na
	4) when unstressed, like **a** in **a**bout	er*	**betala**	ber**tar**lah

---

* The r should not be pronounced when reading this transcription.

ej	like **a** in m**a**te	ay	**nej**	nay
i	1) when long, like **ee** in b**ee**	ee	**vit**	veet
	2) when short, between **ee** in m**ee**t and **i** in h**i**t	i	**bild**	bild
o	1) when long, often like **oo** in s**oo**n, but with the lips more tightly rounded, and with a puff of breath at the end	oo	**sko**	skoo
	2) the same sound can be short	oo	**ost**	oost
	3) when long, it is also sometimes pronounced like **oa** in m**oa**n	oa	**son**	soan
	4) when short, sometimes like **o** in h**o**t	o	**socker**	**so**kkerr
u	1) when long, like Swedish **y**, but with the tongue a little lower in the mouth, and with a puff of breath at the end	ew	**hus**	hewss
	2) when short, a little more like the **u** of put; a very difficult sound	ew	**ung**	ewng
y	pronounce the **ee** of b**ee** and then round your lips without moving your tongue; the sound can be long or short	ew	**vy** **syster**	vew **sew**sterr
å	1) when long, like **aw** in r**aw**, but with the tongue a little higher in the mouth	oa	**gå**	goa
	2) when short, like **o** in h**o**t	o	**sång**	song
ä	1) when followed by **r**, like **a** in m**a**n, long or short	ææ æ	**ära** **värka**	**ææ**rah **vær**kah
	2) elsewhere, like **e** in g**e**t; long or short	ai eh	**läsa** **bäst**	**lai**sah behst
ö	like **u** in f**u**r, long or short; when followed by **r**, it is pronounced with the mouth a little more open	ur*	**röd** **höst** **öra**	rurd hurst **ur**rah

N.B. The principal stress is generally on the *first* syllable of a word, unless it comes from Latin or French.

Throughout the pronunciation section you will notice that some letters are placed in parentheses [e.g. **mew**ker(t)]. In absolutely correct Swedish you should pronounce all the sounds indicated. However, in current usage most Swedes omit the sounds that are shown in parentheses.

---

* The **r** should not be pronounced when reading this transcription.

SWEDISH

SWEDISH

Some basic expressions

Yes.	**Ja.**	yar
No.	**Nej.**	nay
Please.	**Varsågod.**	vahrsoagood
Thank you.	**Tack.**	tahk
Thank you very much.	**Tack så mycket.**	tahk soa **mew**ker(t)
That's all right.	**Ingen orsak.**	ingern oorshark

Greetings

Good morning.	**God morgon.**	goo **mo**ron
Good afternoon.	**God middag.**	goo **mid**dah(g)
Good evening.	**God afton.**	goo **ahf**ton
Good night.	**God natt.**	goo naht
Good-bye.	**Adjö.**	ahyur
See you later.	**Vi ses.**	vee sayss
This is Mr....	**Det här är herr...**	day hæær æær hær
This is Mrs....	**Det här är fru...**	day hæær æær frew
This is Miss...	**Det här är fröken...**	day hæær æær **fru**rkern
I'm very pleased to meet you.	**Angenämt.**	ahnyer**nehmt**
How are you?	**Hur står det till?**	hewr stoar deht til
Very well, thank you. And you?	**Tack bara bra.** **Och Ni själv?**	tahk **bar**rah brar. o(k) nee shehlv
Fine.	**Fint.**	fint
Excuse me.	**Förlåt.**	furr**loat**

Questions

Where?	**Var?**	varr
Where is...?	**Var är...?**	varr ai
Where are...?	**Var är...?**	varr ai
When?	**När?**	næær
What?	**Vad?**	vard
How?	**Hur?**	hewr
How much?	**Hur mycket?**	hewr **mew**ker(t)
How many?	**Hur många?**	hewr **mong**ah

Who?	**Vem?**	vaym
Why?	**Varför?**	**vahr**furr
Which?	**Vilken?**	**vilk**ern
What do you call this?	**Vad heter det här?**	vard **hay**terr day hæær
What do you call that?	**Vad heter det där?**	vard **hay**terr day dæær
What does this mean?	**Vad betyder det här?**	vard ber**tew**derr day hæær
What does that mean?	**Vad betyder det där?**	vard ber**tew**derr day dæær

Do you speak...?

Do you speak English?	**Talar Ni engelska?**	**tar**lahr nee **ehng**erlskah
Do you speak German?	**Talar Ni tyska?**	**tar**lahr nee **tew**skah
Do you speak French?	**Talar Ni franska?**	**tar**lahr nee **frahn**skah
Do you speak Spanish?	**Talar Ni spanska?**	**tar**lahr nee **spahn**skah
Do you speak Italian?	**Talar Ni italienska?**	**tar**lahr nee itah**lieh**nskah
Could you speak more slowly, please?	**Kan Ni vara snäll och tala lite långsammare?**	kahn nee **var**rah snehl o **tar**lah **lee**ter **long**sahmahrer
Please point to the phrase in the book.	**Var snäll och peka på meningen i boken.**	varr snehl o **pay**kah poa **may**ningern ee **book**ern
Just a minute. I'll see if I can find it in this book.	**Ett ögonblick, så ska jag se om jag hittar det i den här boken.**	eht **ur**gonblik soa skar jar(g) say om yar(g) **hit**ahr day ee dehn hæær **book**ern
I understand.	**Jag förstår.**	yar(g) furr**shtoar**
I don't understand.	**Jag förstår inte.**	yar(g) furr**shtoar** inter

Can...?

Can I have...?	**Kan jag få...?**	kahn yar(g) foa
Can we have...?	**Kan vi få...?**	kahn vee foa

SWEDISH

Can you show me...?	**Kan Ni visa mig...?**	kahn nee **vee**sah may
Can you tell me...?	**Kan Ni säga mig...?**	kahn nee **sai**gah may
Can you help me, please?	**Kan Ni vara snäll och hjälpa mig?**	kahn nee **var**rah snehl o **yehl**pah may

Wanting

I'd like...	**Jag skulle vilja ha...**	yar(g) **skewl**ler **vil**yah har
We'd like...	**Vi skulle vilja ha...**	vee **skewl**ler **vil**yah har
Please give me...	**Var snäll och ge mig...**	varr snehl o yay may
Give it to me, please.	**Var snäll och ge mig den.**	varr snehl o yay may dehn
Please bring me...	**Var snäll och hämta...**	varr snehl o **hehm**tah
Bring it to me, please.	**Var snäll och hämta den.**	varr snehl o **hehm**tah dehn
I'm hungry.	**Jag är hungrig.**	yar(g) æær **hewn**gri(g)
I'm thirsty.	**Jag är törstig.**	yar(g) æær **turr**shti(g)
I'm tired.	**Jag är trött.**	yar(g) æær trurt
I'm lost.	**Jag har gått vilse.**	yar(g) harr got **vil**ser
It's important.	**Det är viktigt.**	day æær **vik**tikt
It's urgent.	**Det är brådskande.**	day æær **bros**kahnder
Hurry up!	**Skynda på!**	**shewn**dah poa

It is/There is...

It is/It's...	**Det är...**	day ai
Is it...?	**Är det...?**	ai day
It isn't...	**Det är inte...**	day ai **in**ter
There is/There are...	**Det finns...**	day finss
Is there/Are there...?	**Finns det...**	finss day
There isn't/There aren't...	**Det finns inte...**	day finss **in**ter
There isn't any/There aren't any.	**Det finns ingen/Det finns inga.**	day finss **ing**ern/day finss **ing**ah

A few common words

big/small	**stor/liten**	stoor/**leetern**
quick/slow	**snabb/långsam**	snahb/**long**sahm
early/late	**tidig/sen**	teedi(g)/sayn
cheap/expensive	**billig/dyr**	billi(g)/dewr
near/far	**nära/avlägsen**	nairah/**ahv**lehgsern
hot/cold	**varm/kall**	vahrm/kahl
full/empty	**full/tom**	fewl/toom
easy/difficult	**lätt/svår**	leht/svoar
light/heavy	**lätt/tung**	leht/tewng
open/shut	**öppen/stängd**	urpern/stehngd
right/wrong	**rätt/fel**	reht/fayl
old/new	**gammal/ny**	gahmahl/new
old/young	**gammal/ung**	gahmahl/ewng
beautiful/ugly	**vacker/ful**	vahkerr/fewl
good/bad	**god/dålig**	good/**doa**li(g)
better/worse	**bättre/sämre**	behtrer/**sehm**rer

Some prepositions and a few more useful words

at	**vid**	veed
on	**på**	poa
in	**i**	ee
to	**till**	till
from	**från**	froan
inside	**inne**	inner
outside	**ute**	ewter
up	**upp**	ewp
down	**ner**	nayr
before	**före**	furrer
after	**efter**	ehfterr
with	**med**	mayd
without	**utan**	ewtahn
through	**genom**	yaynom
towards	**mot**	moot
until	**till dess**	til dehss
during	**under**	ewnderr
and	**och**	ok
or	**eller**	ehllerr
not	**inte**	inter
nothing	**ingenting**	ingernting
none	**ingen**	ingern
very	**mycket**	mewker(t)
also	**också**	oksoa
soon	**snart**	snahrt

perhaps	**kanske**	**kahn**sher
here	**här**	hæær
there	**där**	dæær
now	**nu**	new
then	**då**	doa

Arrival

Your passport, please.	**Passet, tack.**	**pah**sert tahk
Here it is.	**Varsågod.**	**vahr**soagood
Have you anything to declare?	**Har Ni någonting att förtulla?**	harr nee **noa**gonting aht **furr**tewlah
No, nothing at all.	**Nej, ingenting alls.**	nay **ing**ernting ahlss
Porter!	**Bärare!**	**bæær**ahrer
Can you help me with my luggage, please?	**Kan Ni vara snäll och hjälpa mig med mitt bagage?**	kahn nee **var**rah snehl o **yehl**pah may mayd mit bah**garsh**
That's my suitcase.	**Det där är min väska.**	day dæær ai meen **vehss**kah
Where's the bus to the centre of town, please?	**Var är bussen som går till centrum?**	varr ai **bewss**ern soam goar til **sehn**troom
This way, please.	**Den här vägen.**	dehn hæær **vai**gern

Changing money

| Can you change a traveller's cheque, please? | **Kan Ni växla in en resecheck?** | kahn nee **vehks**lah in ayn **rays**sershehk |
| Where's the nearest bank, please? | **Var ligger närmaste bank?** | varr **lig**gerr **næær**mahsster bahnk |

Car rental

I'd like a car.	**Jag skulle vilja hyra en bil.**	yar(g) **skew**ller **vil**yah **hew**rah ayn beel
For how long?	**Hur länge?**	hewr **lehng**er
A day/Four days/ A week/Two weeks.	**En dag/Fyra dagar/ En vecka/Två veckor.**	ayn darg/**few**rah **dar**gahr/ayn **veh**kah/tvoa **veh**kor

Taxi

Where can I get a taxi?	**Var kan jag få tag på en taxi?**	varr kahn yar(g) foa targ poa ayn **tahk**si
What's the fare to . . . ?	**Vad kostar det till . . . ?**	vard **koss**tahr day til
Take me to this address, please.	**Var snäll och kör mig till den här adressen.**	varr snehl o khurr may til dehn hæær ah**drehss**sern
I'm in a hurry.	**Jag har bråttom.**	yar(g) harr **brott**tom
Could you drive more slowly, please?	**Skulle Ni kunna köra litet långsammare?**	**skew**ller nee **kewn**nah khurrah **lee**tert long**sah**mahrer

Hotel and other accommodation

My name is . . .	**Mitt namn är . . .**	mit nahmn ai
Have you a reservation?	**Har Ni reserverat?**	harr nee raysæær**vay**raht
Yes, here's the confirmation.	**Ja, här är bekräftelsen.**	yar hæær ai ber**krehf**terl-sern
I'd like . . .	**Jag skulle vilja ha . . .**	yar(g) **skew**ller **vil**yah har
I'd like a single room/a double room.	**Jag skulle vilja ha ett enkelrum/ett dubbelrum.**	yar(g) **skew**ller **vil**yah har eht **ehng**kerlrewm/eht **dewb**berlrewm
a room with a bath/with a shower	**ett rum med bad/med dusch**	eht rewm mayd bard/med dewsh

How much?

What's the price per night/per week/per month?	**Hur mycket kostar det per natt/per vecka/per månad?**	hewr **mewk**er(t) **koss**tahr day pær naht/pær **vehk**ah/pær **moa**nahd
May I see the room?	**Kan jag få se på rummet?**	kahn yar(g) foa say poa **rew**mert
I'm sorry, I don't like it.	**Tyvärr, men jag tycker inte om det.**	tew**vær** mayn yar(g) **tewk**kerr **in**ter om day
Yes, that's fine. I'll take it.	**Ja, det här var bra. Jag tar det.**	yar day hæær varr brar. yar(g) tarr day
What's my room number, please?	**Vilket rumsnummer har jag?**	**vil**kert **rewms**newmerr har yar
Number 123.	**Nummer 123.**	**new**merr 123.

Service, please

Who is it?	**Vem är det?**	vaym ai day
Just a minute.	**Ett ögonblick.**	eht urgonblik
Come in! The door's open.	**Kom in. Dörren är öppen.**	kom in durrern ai urppern
May we have breakfast in our room?	**Kan vi få frukost på rummet?**	kahn vee foa frewkost poa rewmert

Breakfast

I'll have . . .	**Jag ska be att få . . .**	yar(g) skar bay aht foa
I'll have some fruit juice.	**Jag ska be att få juice.**	yar(g) skar bay aht foa yooss
a boiled egg	**ett kokt ägg**	eht kookt ehg
a fried egg	**ett stekt ägg**	eht staykt egh
some bacon/some ham	**bacon/skinka**	baykon/shingkah
some toast	**rostat bröd**	rosstaht brurd
a pot of tea	**en kanna te**	ayn kahnah tay
a cup of tea	**en kopp te**	ayn kop tay
some coffee	**kaffe**	kahffer
some chocolate	**choklad**	shooklard
more butter	**mera smör**	mayrah smurr
some hot water	**lite hett vatten**	leeter heht vahtern

Difficulties

The central heating doesn't work.	**Centralvärmen fungerar inte.**	sehntrarlværmern fewnggayrahr inter
the light/the socket	**ljuset/kontakten**	yewsert/kontahktern
the tap/the toilet	**vattenkranen/toaletten**	vahternkrarnern/twahlehtern
There's no hot water.	**Det finns inget varmvatten.**	day finss ingert vahrmvahtern
May I see the manager, please?	**Kan jag få tala med direktören, tack?**	kan yar(g) foa tarlah mayd direhkturrern tahk

Telephone—Mail

There's a call for you.	**Det är telefon till Er.**	day ai taylayfoan til ayr
Hold the line, please.	**Var god dröj.**	varr good drury

Operator, I've been cut off.	**Fröken, linjen är bruten.**	frurkern linyern ai brewtern
Did anyone telephone me?	**Har någon ringt mig?**	harr noagon ringt may
Is there any mail for me?	**Finns det post till mig?**	finss day post til may
Are there any messages for me?	**Finns det några meddelanden till mig.**	finss day noagra mehdaylahndern til may

Checking out

May I have my bill, please?	**Kan jag få räkningen, tack?**	kahn yar(g) foa rehkningern tahk
We're in a great hurry.	**Vi har mycket bråttom.**	vee harr mewker(t) brottom
It's been a very enjoyable stay.	**Det har varit mycket trevligt att bo här.**	day har varrit mewker(t) trayvligt aht boo hæær

Eating out

Good evening. I'd like a table for two, please.	**God afton. Jag skulle vilja ha ett bord för två.**	goo ahfton. yar(g) skewleh vilyah har eht boord furr tvoa
Do you have a fixed-price menu?	**Har Ni en meny?**	harr nee ayn maynew
May I see the à la carte menu?	**Kan jag få se på à la carte matsedeln?**	kahn yar(g) foa say poa ah lah kahrt martserderln
May we have an ashtray, please?	**Kan vi få en askkopp, tack?**	kahn vee foa ayn ahskkop tahk
some bread	**litet bröd**	leeter(t) brurd
a fork	**en gaffel**	ayn gahferl
a knife	**en kniv**	ayn kneev
a spoon	**en sked**	ayn shayd
a plate	**en tallrik**	ayn tahlrik
a glass	**ett glas**	eht glarss
a napkin	**en servett**	ayn særveht
another chair	**en stol till**	ayn stool til
Where's the gentlemen's toilet (men's room)?	**Var är herrtoaletten?**	varr ai hærtwahlehtern

SWEDISH

| Where's the ladies' toilet (ladies' room)? | **Var är dam-toaletten?** | varr ai **darm**twahlehtern |

Appetizers

I'd like some...	**Jag ska be att få ...**	yar(g) skar bay aht foa
I'd like some assorted appetizers.	**Jag ska be att få några smårätter.**	yar(g) skar bay aht foa noagrah **smoa**rehterr
orange juice	**apelsinjuice**	ahperlseenyooss
ham	**skinka**	shingkah
melon	**melon**	mayloon
pâté	**pastej**	passtayy
smoked salmon	**rökt lax**	rurkt lahks
shrimps (shrimp)	**räkor**	raikoor

Soup

Have you any...?	**Har Ni...?**	harr nee
Have you any chicken soup?	**Har Ni kyckling-soppa?**	harr nee **khewk**lingsopah
vegetable soup	**grönsakssoppa**	**grurn**sahkssopah
onion soup	**löksoppa**	**lurk**sopah

Fish

I'd like some...	**Jag ska be att få ...**	yar(g) skar bay aht foa
I'd like some fish.	**Jag ska be att få en fiskrätt.**	yar(g) skar bay aht foa ayn **fisk**reht
sole	**sjötunga**	**shur**tewngah
trout	**forell**	fo**rehl**
lobster	**hummer**	**hew**merr
crayfish	**kräftor**	**krehf**toor
prawns	**räkor**	**rai**koor
I'd like it...	**Jag skulle vilja ha den...**	yar(g) **skew**ler **vil**yah har dehn
I'd like it steamed.	**Jag skulle vilja ha den ångkokt.**	yar(g) **skew**ler **vil**yah har dehn **ong**kookt
grilled	**grillad**	**gri**lahd
boiled	**kokt**	kookt
baked	**ugnsstekt**	**ewngns**staykt
fried	**stekt**	staykt

SWEDISH

Meat—Poultry—Game

I'd like some...	**Jag ska be att få ...**	yar(g) skar bay aht foa
I'd like some beef.	**Jag ska be att få oxkött.**	yar(g) skar bay aht foa **ooks**khurt
a beef steak	**en biff**	ahn bif
some roast beef	**rostbiff**	**rost**bif
a veal cutlet	**en kalvkotlett**	ahn **kahlv**kotleht
lamb	**lammkött**	**lahm**khurt
a pork chop	**en fläskkotlett**	ahn **flehsk**kotleht
roast pork	**grisstek**	**greess**stayk
hare	**hare**	**harrer**
chicken	**kyckling**	**khewk**ling
roast chicken	**stekt kyckling**	staykt **khewk**ling
duck	**anka**	**ahng**kah
How do you like your meat?	**Hur vill Ni ha köttet tillagat?**	hewr vil nee har **khurt**ert til**arg**aht
rare	**blodig**	**bloo**dig
medium	**lagom**	**larg**om
well done	**genomstekt**	**yay**nomstaykt

Vegetables

What vegetables have you got?	**Vad för grönsaker finns det?**	vard furr **grurn**sarkerr finss day
I'd like some...	**Jag ska be att få ...**	yar(g) ska bay aht foa
I'd like some asparagus.	**Jag ska be att få sparris.**	yar(g) ska bay aht foa **spah**riss
green beans	**haricots verts**	hahreekoa**væær**
mushrooms	**svamp**	svahmp
carrots	**morötter**	moo**rurt**err
onions	**lök**	lurk
red cabbage	**rödkål**	**rurd**koal
lettuce	**grönsallad**	**grurn**sahlahd
spinach	**spenat**	spay**nart**
rice	**ris**	reess
peas	**ärtor**	**ært**oor
tomatoes	**tomater**	too**mart**err
green salad	**grönsallad**	**grurn**sahlahd
potatoes	**potatis**	poot**art**iss

Desserts

Nothing more, thanks.	**Ingenting mer, tack.**	**ing**ernting mayr tahk
Just a small portion, please.	**Bara en liten portion, tack.**	**barr**ah ehn **lee**tern por**choon** tahk

Have you any ice-cream?	**Har Ni glass?**	har nee glahss
fruit salad	**fruktsallad**	frewktsahlahd
fresh fruit	**färsk frukt**	færshk frewkt
cheese	**ost**	oost

Drink

What would you like to drink?	**Vad vill Ni ha att dricka?**	vard vil nee har aht drikah
I'll have a beer, please.	**Jag tar en öl, tack.**	yar(g) tarr ehn url tahk
I'll have a whisky, please.	**Jag ska be att få en whisky, tack.**	yar(g) skar bay aht foa ehn wisskew tahk

Wine

I'd like a bottle of wine.	**Jag ska be att få en flaska vin.**	yar(g) skar bay aht foa ehn flahsskah veen
red wine	**rödvin**	rurdveen
rosé wine	**rosévin**	roasayveen
white wine	**vitt vin**	vit veen
Cheers!	**Skål!**	skoal

The bill (check)

May I have the bill (check) please?	**Får jag be om notan, tack?**	foar yar(g) bay om nootahn tahk
Is service included?	**Ingår servis?**	ingoar surrviss
Everything's included.	**Allt ingår.**	ahlt ingoar
Thank you, that was a very good meal.	**Tack, det var en mycket god måltid.**	tahk day varr ehn mewker(t) goo moalteed

Travelling

Where's the railway station, please?	**Var är järnvägs-stationen?**	varr ai yærnvehgsstah-shoonern
Where's the ticket office, please?	**Var är biljettluckan?**	varr ai bilyehtlewkahn
I'd like a ticket to …	**Jag ska be att få en biljett till …**	yar(g) skar bay aht foa ehn bilyeht til
First or second class?	**Första eller andra klass?**	furrshta ehlerr ahndrah klahss

First class, please.	**Första klass, tack.**	furrshtah klahss tahk
Single or return (one way or round-trip)?	**Enkel eller tur och retur?**	ehngkerl ehlerr tewr o(k) retewr
Do I have to change trains?	**Måste jag byta tåg?**	mosster yar bewtah toag
What platform does the train leave from?	**Från vilken perrong avgår tåget?**	froan vilkern pærong ahvgoar toagert
Where's the nearest underground (subway) station?	**Var ligger närmaste tunnelbanestation?**	varr ligger næærmahster tewnerlbarnerstahshoon
Where's the bus station, please?	**Var är buss-stationen?**	varr ai bewssstah-shoonern
When's the first bus to . . . ?	**När går första bus-sen till . . . ?**	næær goar furrshtah bewssern til
the last bus the next bus	**sista bussen/ nästa buss**	sisstah bewssern/ nehsstah bewss
Please let me off at the next stop.	**Var god och låt mig gå av vid nästa hållplats.**	varr goo o(k) loat may goa ahv veed nehsstah holplahts

Relaxing

What's on at the cinema (movies)?	**Vad går det på bio?**	vard goar day poa beeoo
What's on at the theatre?	**Vad ger man på teatern?**	vard yayr mahn poa tayarterrn
What time does the film begin?	**När börjar filmen?**	næær burryarr filmern
And the play?	**Och teaterföreställ-ningen?**	o tayarterrfurrerstehl-ningern
Are there any tickets for tonight?	**Finns det några biljetter till i kväll?**	finss day noagrah bilyehterr til ee kvehl
Where can we go dancing?	**Var kan vi gå och dansa?**	varr kahn vee goa o(k) dahnsah
Would you like to dance?	**Får jag lov?**	foar yar(g) loav

Introductions

How do you do?	**Goddag.**	goodar(g)
How are you?	**Hur står det till?**	hewr stoar day til
Very well, thank you. And you?	**Tack bara bra. Och Ni själv?**	tahk barrar brar. o(k) nee shehlv

SWEDISH

SWEDISH

May I introduce Miss Philips?	**Får jag presentera fröken Philips?**	foar yar(g) prayserntayrah frurkern Philips
My name is...	**Mitt namm är...**	mit nahmn æær
I'm very pleased to meet you.	**Roligt att lära känna Er.**	rooligt aht læærah khehnah ayr
How long have you been here?	**Hur länge har Ni varit här?**	hewr lehnger harr nee varrit hæær
It was nice meeting you.	**Det var trevligt att träffas.**	day varr trayvligt aht trehfahss

Dating

Would you like a cigarette?	**Vill Ni ha en cigarrett?**	vil nee har ehn sigahreht
May I get you a drink?	**Vill Ni ha något att dricka?**	vil nee har noagot aht drikar
Do you have a light, please?	**Har Ni möjligen eld?**	harr nee muryliggern ayld
Are you waiting for someone?	**Väntar Ni på någon?**	væntahr nee poa noagon
Are you free this evening?	**Är Ni ledig i kväll?**	ai nee laydig ee kvehl
Where shall we meet?	**Var ska vi träffas?**	varr skar vee trehfahss
What time shall I meet you?	**När ska vi träffas?**	næær skar vee trehfahss
May I take you home?	**Får jag följa Er hem?**	foar yar(g) furlyah ayr haym
Thank you, it's been a wonderful evening.	**Tack, det har varit en underbar kväll.**	tahk day har varrit ehn ewnderrbarr kvehl
What's your telephone number?	**Vad har Ni för telefonnummer?**	vard harr nee furr taylayfoannewmerr
Do you live alone?	**Bor Ni ensam?**	boor nee aynsahm
What time is your last train?	**När går sista tåget?**	næær goar sisstah toaget
Good-night...	**God natt...**	goo naht

Banks

| Where's the nearest bank, please? | **Var ligger närmaste bank?** | varr ligger næærmahster bahnk |

Where can I cash some traveller's cheques?	**Var kan jag växla in några resecheckar?**	varr kahn yar(g) **vehks**lah in **no**agrah **ray**sser-shehkahr
What time does the bank open/What time does it close?	**När öppnar banken/När stänger den?**	næær **urp**nahr **bahn**kern/næær **stehng**-err dehn
I'm expecting some money from home. Has it arrived?	**Jag väntar pengar hemifrån. Har de kommit?**	yar(g) **vehn**tahr **pehng**ahr **hay**mifron. harr day **komm**it
Can you give me some small change, please?	**Kan jag få litet växel, tack?**	kahn yar(g) foa **lee**ter(t) **vehks**erl tahk

Shops, stores and services

Where is the nearest chemist's (pharmacy)?	**Var finns närmaste apotek?**	varr finss **næær**mahster ahpoo**tayk**
the nearest hairdresser's	**närmaste hårfrisörska**	**næær**mahster **hoar**-frisurrshkah
the photo shop	**fotoaffär**	**foo**tooahfair
the jeweller's	**juvelerare**	yewver**lay**rahrer
the department store	**varuhus**	**var**rewhewssert
the police station	**polisstation**	**poo**leessstahshoon
the garage	**garage**	gah**rar**sher
How do I get there?	**Hur kommer jag dit?**	hewr **komm**err yar(g) deet
Is it within walking distance?	**Kan man gå dit?**	kahn mahn **goa** deet

Service

Can you help me, please?	**Kan Ni vara snäll och hjälpa mig?**	kahn nee **varr**ah snehl o(k) **yehl**pah may
Can you show me this? And that, too.	**Kan Ni visa mig den här? Och den där också.**	kahn nee **vee**sah may dehn hæær? o(k) dehn dæær ok**soa**
It's too expensive/too big/too small.	**Den är för dyr/för stor/för liten.**	dehn ai furr dewr/furr stoor/furr **lee**tern
Can you show me some more?	**Kan Ni visa mig något mer?**	kahn nee **vee**sah may **no**agot mayr
something better	**någonting bättre**	**no**agonting **beh**trer
something cheaper	**någonting billigare**	**no**agonting **bil**igahrer
How much is this? And that?	**Hur mycket kostar den här? Och den där?**	hewr **mew**ker(t) **koss**tar dehn hæær? o(k) dehn dæær

| It's not quite what I want. | **Det är inte precis vad jag tänkt mig.** | day ai inter **prayss**eess vard yar(g) tehnkt may |
| I like it. | **Jag tycker om den.** | yar(g) **tew**kerr om dehn |

Chemist's (Pharmacy)

| I'd like something for a cold/for a cough/for travel sickness. | **Jag skulle vilja ha någonting mot förkylning/mot hosta/mot ressjuka.** | yar(g) **skew**ler **vil**yah har **noa**gonting moot furr-**khew**lning/moot **hoo**stah/moot **rayss**shewkah |
| Can you recommend something for hay-fever/for sunburn? | **Kan Ni rekommen-dera någonting mot hösnuva/mot solsveda?** | kahn nee raykomehn-**day**rah **noa**gonting moot **hur**snewvah/moot **sool**svaydah |

Toiletry

May I have some razor blades?	**Kan jag få några rakblad?**	kahn yar(g) foa **noa**grah **rark**blahd
some shaving cream some toothpaste	**rakkräm tandkräm**	**rark**krehm **tahnd**krehm
I'd like some soap.	**Jag ska be att få en tvål.**	yar(g) skar bay aht foa ayn tvoal
some suntan oil	**sololja**	**sool**olyah

At the barber's

I'd like a haircut, please.	**Jag skulle vilja ha håret klippt.**	yar(g) **skew**ler **vil**yah har **hoa**rert klipt
Short/Leave it long.	**Kort/Låt det vara långt.**	kort/loat day **var**rah longt
A razor cut, please.	**Klippning med rak-blad, tack.**	**klip**ning mayd **rark**blahd tahk

At the hairdresser's

I'd like a shampoo and set, please.	**Jag ska be att få håret tvättat och lagt.**	yar(g) skar bay aht foa **hoa**rert **tveh**taht o(k) lahgt
I'd like a bleach.	**Jag skulle vilja ha det blekt.**	yar(g) **skew**ler **vil**yah har day blaykt
a permanent a colour rinse a blow dry	**permanentat tonat fönat**	pærmah**nehn**taht **too**naht **fur**naht

Photography

I'd like a film for this camera.	**Jag ska be att få en film till den här kameran.**	yar(g) skar bay aht foa ayn film til dehn hæær **kar**mayrahn
This camera doesn't work.	**Den här kameran fungerar inte.**	dehn hæær **kar**mayrahn fewng**gay**rahr **int**er

At the post office

Where's the nearest post office, please?	**Var ligger närmaste postkontor?**	var **lig**gerr **næær**mahster **posst**kontoor
I'd like to send this by express (special delivery)/by air mail.	**Jag skulle vilja skicka det här express/med flygpost.**	yar(g) **skew**ler **vil**yah **shik**ar day hæær ehk**sprehss**/mayd **flewg**posst

Service stations

Where is the nearest service station, please?	**Kan Ni säga mig var närmaste bensinstation ligger?**	kahn nee **sai**gah may varr **næær**mahster behn-**seen**stahshoon **lig**gerr
Fill her up, please.	**Full tank, tack.**	fewl tahnk tahk
Check the oil, please.	**Kontrollera oljan, tack.**	kontro**lay**rah **ol**yahn tahk
Would you check the tyres?	**Skulle Ni vilja kontrollera däcken?**	**skew**ler nee **vil**yah kontro**lay**rah **dehk**ern

Street directions

Can you show me on the map where I am?	**Kan Ni visa mig på kartan var jag är?**	kahn nee **vee**sah may poa **kahr**tahn varr yar(g) ai
You're on the wrong road.	**Ni är på fel väg.**	nee ai poa fayl vaig
Go back to...	**Kör tillbaka till...**	khurr til**bar**kah til
Go straight ahead.	**Kör rakt fram.**	khurr rahkt frahm
It's on the left/on the right.	**Det är till vänster/till höger.**	day ai til **vehn**sterr/til **hur**gerr

Accidents

May I use your telephone?	**Kan jag få låna Er telefon?**	kahn yar(g) foa **loa**nah ayr tay**lay**foan

SWEDISH

SWEDISH

Call a doctor quickly.	**Ring genast efter en läkare.**	ring yaynahst ehfterr ayn laikahrer
Call an ambulance.	**Ring på ambulansen.**	ring poa ahmbewlahnsern
Please call the police.	**Var snäll och ring polisen.**	varr snehl o(k) ring pooleessern

Numbers

zero	**noll**	nol
one	**en, ett**	ayn/eht
two	**två**	tvoa
three	**tre**	tray
four	**fyra**	fewrah
five	**fem**	fehm
six	**sex**	sehks
seven	**sju**	shew
eight	**åtta**	otah
nine	**nio**	neeoo
ten	**tio**	teeoo
eleven	**elva**	ehlvah
twelve	**tolv**	tolv
thirteen	**tretton**	trehton
fourteen	**fjorton**	fyoorton
fifteen	**femton**	fehmton
sixteen	**sexton**	sehkston
seventeen	**sjutton**	shewton
eighteen	**arton**	arrton
nineteen	**nitton**	nitton
twenty	**tjugo**	khewgoo
twenty-one	**tjugoett**	khewgooeht
thirty	**trettio**	trehtioo
forty	**fyrtio**	fewrtioo
fifty	**femtio**	fehmtioo
sixty	**sextio**	sehkstioo
seventy	**sjuttio**	shewtioo
eighty	**åttio**	otioo
ninety	**nittio**	nittioo
one hundred	**hundra**	hewndrah
one thousand	**tusen**	tewsern
ten thousand	**tio tusen**	teeoo tewssern

Days

It's Sunday.	**Det är söndag.**	day ai surndar(g)
Monday	**måndag**	moandar(g)
Tuesday	**tisdag**	tissdar(g)
Wednesday	**onsdag**	oonssdar(g)

Thursday	**torsdag**	**toorsh**dar(g)
Friday	**fredag**	**fray**dar(g)
Saturday	**lördag**	**lurr**dar(g)
yesterday	**i går**	ee goar
today	**i dag**	ee dar(g)
tomorrow	**i morgon**	ee **mor**on
morning/afternoon	**förmiddag/efter-middag**	**furr**middar(g)/**ehf**ter-middar(g)
evening/night	**kväll/natt**	kvehl/naht

Months

January	**januari**	yahne**warri**
February	**februari**	faybre**warri**
March	**mars**	mahrsh
April	**april**	ah**preel**
May	**maj**	migh
June	**juni**	**yew**ni
July	**juli**	**yew**li
August	**augusti**	ahew**gew**sti
September	**september**	sehp**tehm**berr
October	**oktober**	ok**too**berr
November	**november**	no**vehm**berr
December	**december**	day**sehm**berr
Merry Christmas!	**God Jul! Gott Nytt**	goo(d) yewl! got newt oar
Happy New Year!	**År!**	

Reference section

Weight conversion

The figure in the middle stands for both kilograms and pounds, e.g., 1 kilogram = 2.205 lb. and 1 pound = 0.45 kilograms.

Kilograms (kg.)		Avoirdupois pounds
0.45	1	2.205
0.90	2	4.405
1.35	3	6.614
1.80	4	8.818
2.25	5	11.023
2.70	6	13.227
3.15	7	15.432
3.60	8	17.636
4.05	9	19.840
4.50	10	22.045
6.75	15	33.068
9.00	20	44.889
11.25	25	55.113
22.50	50	110.225
33.75	75	165.338
45.00	100	220.450

REFERENCE SECTION

1 kilogram or kilo (kg) = 1000 grams (g)

100 g = 3.5 oz.	½ kg = 1.1 lb.
200 g = 7.0 oz.	1 kg = 2.2 lb.

1 oz. = 28.35 g
1 lb. = 453.60 g

Metres and feet

The figure in the middle stands for both metres and feet, e.g.,
1 metre = 3.281 ft. and 1 foot = 0.30 m.

Metres		Feet
0.30	1	3.281
0.61	2	6.563
0.91	3	9.843
1.22	4	13.124
1.52	5	16.403
1.83	6	19.686
2.13	7	22.967
2.44	8	26.248
2.74	9	29.529
3.05	10	32.810
3.35	11	36.091
3.66	12	39.372
3.96	13	42.635
4.27	14	45.934
4.57	15	49.215
4.88	16	52.496
5.18	17	55.777
5.49	18	59.058
5.79	19	62.339
6.10	20	65.620
7.62	25	82.023
15.24	50	164.046
22.86	75	246.069
30.48	100	328.092

314

Centimetres and inches

To change centimetres into inches, multiply by .39.

To change inches into centimetres, multiply by 2.54.

	in.	feet	yards
1 mm	0,039	0,003	0,001
1 cm	0,39	0,03	0,01
1 dm	3,94	0,32	0,10
1 m	39,40	3,28	1,09

	mm	cm	m
1 in.	25,4	2,54	0,025
1 ft.	304,8	30,48	0,304
1 yd.	914,4	91,44	0,914

(32 metres = 35 yards)

Temperature

To convert Centigrade into degrees Fahrenheit, multiply Centigrade by 1.8 and add 32.

To convert degrees Fahrenheit into Centigrade, subtract 32 from Fahrenheit and divide by 1.8.

The car

Miles into kilometres									
1 mile=1.609 kilometres (km)									
miles	10	20	30	40	50	60	70	80	90	100
km	16	32	48	64	80	97	113	129	145	161

Kilometres into miles												
1 kilometre (km)=0.62 miles												
km	10	20	30	40	50	60	70	80	90	100	110	120	130
miles	6	12	19	25	31	37	44	50	56	62	68	75	81

Tire pressure			
lb./sq. in.	kg/cm^2	lb./sq. in.	kg/cm^2
10	0.7	26	1.8
12	0.8	27	1.9
15	1.1	28	2.0
18	1.3	30	2.1
20	1.4	33	2.3
21	1.5	36	2.5
23	1.6	38	2.7
24	1.7	40	2.8

Fluid measures					
litres	imp. gal.	U.S. gal.	litres.	imp. gal.	U.S. gal.
5	1.1	1.3	30	6.6	7.8
10	2.2	2.6	35	7.7	9.1
15	3.3	3.9	40	8.8	10.4
20	4.4	5.2	45	9.9	11.7
25	5.5	6.5	50	11.0	13.0

1 litre (l) = 0.88 imp. quarts = 1.06 U.S. quarts

1 imp. quart = 1.14 l   1 U.S. quart = 0.95 l
1 imp. gallon = 4.55 l   1 U.S. gallon = 3.81 l

This is your size

Ladies

Dresses/suits						
American	10	12	14	16	18	20
British	32	34	36	38	40	42
Continental	38	40	42	44	46	48

Stockings							Shoes			
American ⎱ British	8	8½	9	9½	10	10½	6	7	8	9
Continental	0	1	2	3	4	5	36	38	38½	40

Gentlemen

Suits/overcoats							Shirts					
American ⎱ British	36	38	40	42	44	46	14	15	15½	16	16½	17
Continental	46	48	50	52	54	56	36	38	39	41	42	43

Shoes						
American ⎱ British	5	6	7	8	9	10	11
Continental	38	39	41	42	43	44	45

In Europe sizes vary somewhat from country to country, so the above must be taken as an approximate guide.

| 1 a.m. | 2 a.m. | 3 a.m. | 4 a.m. | 5 a.m. | 6 a.m. | 7 a.m. | 8 a.m. | 9 a.m. | 10 a.m. | 11 a.m. | noon | 1 p.m. | 2 p.m. | 3 p.m. | 4 p.m. | 5 p.m. | 6 p.m. | 7 p.m. | 8 p.m. | 9 p.m. | 10 p.m. | 11 p.m. | mid-night |

Date Line

Eastern European Time

Central European Time

Western European Time (G.M.T.)

Atlantic Time

Eastern Time

Central Time

Mountain Time

Pacific Time

Alaska Time

REFERENCE SECTION

Countries which have adopted a time differing from that in the corresponding time zone. Note that also in the USSR, official time is one hour ahead of the time in each corresponding time zone. In summer, numerous countries advance time one hour ahead of standard time.

Currency converter

In a world of fluctuating currencies, we can offer no more than this handy do-it-yourself chart. You can get information about exchange rates from banks, travel agents and tourist offices. Why not fill in this chart too, for handy reference?

	£ 1	$ 1
Austria (shillings)		
Belgium (francs)		
Denmark (crowns)		
Finland (marks)		
France (francs)		
Germany (marks)		
Greece (drachmas)		
Italy (lire)		
Netherlands (guilders)		
Norway (crowns)		
Poland (zlotys)		
Portugal (escudos)		
Spain (pesetas)		
Sweden (crowns)		
Switzerland (francs)		
USSR (rubles)		
Yugoslavia (dinars)		

BERLITZ DICTIONARIES

Berlitz two-way dictionaries featuring 12,500 concepts in each language with pronunciation shown throughout. Also include basic expressions and special section on how to read a foreign menu. An essential and practical aid for all travellers.

Danish	Italian
Dutch	Norwegian
Finnish	Portuguese
French	Spanish
German	Swedish

Ask your bookseller.

BERLITZ PHRASE BOOKS

World's bestselling phrase books feature not only expressions and vocabulary you'll need, but also travel tips, useful facts and pronunciation throughout. The handiest and most readable conversation aid available.

Arabic	French	Polish
Chinese	German	Portuguese
Danish	Greek	Russian
Dutch	Hebrew	Serbo-Croatian
European (14 languages)	Hungarian	Spanish
	Italian	Lat.-Am. Spanish
European Menu Reader	Japanese	Swahili
	Korean	Swedish
Finnish	Norwegian	Turkish

BERLITZ CASSETTEPAKS

The above-mentioned titles are also available combined with a cassette to help you improve your accent. A helpful miniscript is included containing the complete text of the dual language hi-fi recording.